STO 09/12

F

GU01085504

7 5 ... 2019

GESTAPO

2 5 NOV 2019

Essex County Council

3013020263920 8

For my son William,
without whom this book would have been
written much more quickly

JAPAN'S GESTAPO

Murder, Mayhem and Torture in Wartime Asia

by

Mark Felton

Pen & Sword
MILITARY

First published in Great Britain in 2009
and reprinted in this format in 2012 by
PEN & SWORD MILITARY
An imprint of
Pen & Sword Books Ltd
47 Church Street
Barnsley
South Yorkshire
S70 2AS

Copyright © Mark Felton 2009, 2012

ISBN 978 1 84884 680 7

The right of Mark Felton to be identified as Author
of this work has been asserted by him in accordance with the
Copyright, Designs and Patents Act 1988.

A CIP catalogue record for this book is
available from the British Library

All rights reserved. No part of this book may be reproduced or transmitted in
any form or by any means, electronic or mechanical including photocopying,
recording or by any information storage and retrieval system,
without permission from the Publisher in writing.

Typeset in 11/13pt Sabon by
Concept, Huddersfield, West Yorkshire

Printed and bound in England
By CPI Group (UK) Ltd, Croydon, CR0 4YY

Pen & Sword Books Ltd incorporates the Imprints of Pen & Sword Aviation,
Pen & Sword Family History, Pen & Sword Maritime, Pen & Sword Military,
Pen & Sword Discovery, Wharncliffe Local History, Wharncliffe True Crime,
Wharncliffe Transport, Pen & Sword Select, Pen & Sword Military Classics,
Leo Cooper, The Praetorian Press, Remember When,
Seaforth Publishing and Frontline Publishing

For a complete list of Pen & Sword titles please contact
PEN & SWORD BOOKS LIMITED
47 Church Street, Barnsley, South Yorkshire, S70 2AS, England
E-mail: enquiries@pen-and-sword.co.uk
Website: www.pen-and-sword.co.uk

Contents

Acknowledgements

A great debt of thanks to the great team at Pen and Sword Books, particularly to Brigadier Henry Wilson, my editor Bobby Gainher, my copy editor George Chamier and to Jonathan Wright and Jon Wilkinson for all of their hard work. My thanks to Jill Durney, of the Macmillan Brown Library, University of Canterbury in New Zealand for the hours spent rooting through the dusty archives and disintegrating records of the International Military Tribunal for the Far East. Thanks to David Parker, OBE, Director of Information and Secretariat at the Commonwealth War Graves Commission regarding information on civilian internees in Shanghai. A great many thanks to Ron Taylor and the wonderful members of the Far East Prisoners of War Association (FEPOW) who have been such an important source of information. I should also like to extend my thanks to 'Hap' Halloran for relating his experiences of being shot down over Japan and held prisoner by the Kempeitai, and to Shirley Felton for her bibliographical research. Many thanks to the Photograph Archive at the Imperial War Museum in London, and the staff at the National Archives (Public Record Office) at Kew, and at the Australian War Memorial, Canberra. Finally, I thank my wife Fang Fang for her support and encouragement of my writing, and her love.

Introduction

This book is not for the fainthearted or easily disgusted. What follows through these pages is a glimpse into the dark heart of humanity. It is a catalogue of Man at his very worst. Recounted in these chapters are examples of hair-raising brutality that raised the bar of depravity at a time when the whole world seemed to have gone mad, when nations clashed and the little person counted for very little. Blood almost drips from the pages, and the screams of the long dead echo down the decades to us now in the security and comfort of the twenty-first century.

The villains at the centre of this book are Japan's wartime military police, a vast and nefarious organization called the Kempeitai, or 'Corps of Law Soldiers'. This book is by no means the definitive story of this depraved and hateful organization, but rather provides a glimpse of the myriad activities that the Kempeitai was intimately involved in all over occupied Asia. The crimes of the Kempeitai rival those of Germany's Gestapo in their breadth and savagery, and in many cases the Kempeitai went much further down the path of pure evil.

I live in a city where the Kempeitai once ruled with a will of iron. In Shanghai today there are many buildings still in existence that once were important parts of the Kempeitai empire. There are no plaques recording this dark history as one might expect in Berlin or Singapore, but nonetheless these rather nondescript and down-at-heel buildings that now huddle together with other old structures as the city around them rises into the sky in the form of glittering glass skyscrapers still have the aura of hate about them. North of the Bund, the famous 'Million Dollar Skyline' of 1930s Shanghai, is Suzhou Creek, and across the famous Garden Bridge is an area of buildings that in its heyday was a very upmarket area of the city but today is rather forlorn. Close to the river stands a large white 1930s apartment building called Bridge House. This was the main torture centre for the Kempeitai during the Second World War, where, as you will see as you read on, terrible things were done to Chinese and Western nationals inside its basements and converted apartments. In its courtyard the crackle of rifle fire was often heard reverberating off the walls as firing squads daily dispatched the broken and bleeding victims of Japan's mad experiment with empire.

If any building is full of restless spirits in Shanghai today it should be Bridge House, a true house of the dead. Today families live inside this place of sadism and murder, ignorant of the building's bloody past. No one lives in the Lubjanka in Moscow or at Gestapo headquarters at Prinz Albrecht Strasse in Berlin today, but in Shanghai history has a way of slipping into obscurity, and the sins of the past are easily expunged from the present. Bridge House is in many ways a fitting memorial to the Kempeitai, because like Bridge House most of these murderers escaped retribution after the war was over and most managed to metamorphose into something harmless and low-key in the post-war world.

The Kempeitai was the product of Japan's hysterical hatred, mistrust and fear of the West. It was also a reflection of the vast inferiority complex many Japanese retained about the Western Powers and their intentions towards Japan. The Kempeitai was the culmination of all these complicated feelings and political theories, and an expression of Japan's belief in the innate superiority of the Sacred Islands and the ideologies that propped up Japan's imperial ambitions. Millions died at the hands of the Kempeitai, but who in the world has ever heard of this organization? Like the war in Asia itself, the Kempeitai have become just a footnote to history, known only to academics and historians. Even the Japanese know little of its crimes, or the extent of its brutality. Read on and be disgusted, because that is how we should feel. And until Japan apologizes for her wartime record, we should keep reminding them of how disgusted we still are.

Shanghai
November 2008

Chapter One

Big Brother

The Emperor is a Revealed God among men, a Manifest Deity for us.

State Shinto belief, Japan

A man sat in a wooden chair with his head resting on his chest. Blood dripped from his mouth and chin. His hair was long and dirty and hung across his eyes like a veil. He was stripped to the waist, his torso oily with sweat. The man groaned and slowly raised his head to look at his inquisitors. There were two of them. One sat before the man on a chair, wearing an army shirt, breeches and riding boots, his sleeves rolled up, a cigarette in his right hand. The second, dressed similarly to the seated man, stood in the shadows, for the room was small and airless, holding a thick wooden club in his hands. The man tied to the chair moaned again and muttered something in English. The seated inquisitor leaned forward and cocked his ear towards the Englishman's lips, listening intently. Suddenly he jumped up and yelled, 'Liar! You lie to me again? You think that we do not already know the truth?' His accent was heavy, and he turned to his comrade and grunted an order in Japanese. The man with the club stepped forward and with a sharp intake of breath he brought the club down on to the Englishman's exposed back again and again, the blows raining down with rhythmic regularity, the strokes well-practised many times over in this dark, dank room. The Englishman screamed as the wood bit into his flesh, and he twisted and fought like a trapped animal, but his bindings were strong and held him firmly pinned to the chair which was itself bolted securely

9

into the grimy floor. Twenty blows later it stopped. The Englishman moaned and groaned while his Japanese torturer leaned forward to ask the same questions over and over again, as he had asked for several preceding days to obtain the confession he searched for. When the answers failed to satisfy, the Japanese pushed his lit cigarette into the Englishman's face, mashing the hot ash into the skin until the pungent smell of burned flesh filled the room. Then the beating began again. This was a vignette of horror repeated tens of thousands of times throughout the Occupied Territories of Asia during the Second World War, committed by an organization so unscrupulous, savage and obedient to Japan's war aims that torture and abuse were its stock in trade.

The merest mention of the name 'Kempeitai' struck fear and terror into the hearts of countless Allied prisoners of war and civilian internees during the Second World War. The name had the same effect upon the millions of subjugated peoples in the former European colonies and states overrun and occupied by the Japanese forces; and the name even began to strike fear into the Japanese themselves, both soldiers and civilians, as the war began to turn against their empire. The men of the Kempeitai bestrode the stage of the Far Eastern war like childhood bogeymen, slavish adherents to Japanese ultra-nationalist militarism and obedient torturers for the Japanese police state they helped to create. Their cruelty was renowned, their tortures rightly feared, and their position of power in the wartime Japanese empire seemingly unassailable.

The Kempeitai has been likened in character to Germany's dreaded Gestapo, the *Geheime Staatspolizei* or Secret State Police, and there were some similarities. But the remit of the Kempeitai was much broader in its duties and responsibilities than the Gestapo, having its fingers stuck deep into many more metaphorical pies than Heinrich Himmler's organ of terror ever managed. To take the analogy further, the Kempeitai featured elements of not only the Gestapo, but Nazi Germany's other police branches, such as the *Sicherheitsdienst* (SD), Germany's primary intelligence service, and the Wehrmacht's *Feldgendarmarie* or Military Police. Integrated into the Kempeitai were espionage sections comparable with Germany's other military intelligence organization, the Wehrmacht's *Abwehr*.

The Kempeitai was responsible for running Japan's prisoner of war and civilian internment camp system, and under its control the camps were as harsh and depraved as Himmler's concentration camps or Josef Stalin's Gulag. The Kempeitai was also a tool of propaganda, and contained sections that aped Dr. Josef Goebbels' ministry in Berlin. Other more sinister secret sections of the Kempeitai conducted biological and chemical warfare experiments at a series of specially constructed facilities throughout Asia that rivalled the amoral human experiments conducted by Dr. Josef Mengele and other SS doctors at Auschwitz. The Kempeitai was also a fighting organization, with its own specially trained commandos very similar to Otto Skorzeny's famous SS commandos, who successfully rescued the deposed Italian dictator Benito Mussolini in Italy in 1943 and infiltrated Allied lines in Belgium dressed as American military police during the Ardennes Offensive in 1944. It was a Kempeitai commando unit that made the first successful enemy landing in Australia.

The tentacles of Kempeitai power stretched into every unit of the Japanese army, every prison camp, every conquered city, every battlefield and every atrocity committed by the Japanese in the name of their divine Emperor. The cruelty of the Kempeitai was legendary, and its reputation as one of history's most blood-soaked organizations is richly deserved. Extreme barbarity and sadism was virtually the organization's creed, and its operators happy proponents of these tenets on innumerable occasions.

The Kempeitai was an old organization, much older than any comparable Nazi or Soviet force. It had been formed in 1881, at a time when Japan was rushing headlong towards modernity and the Westernization of its institutions and economy. Only thirteen years before, in 1868, the ancient Shogunate system of military dictators drawn from the samurai class had been ended by a bloody revolution, and the Emperor Mitsuhito restored to the position of constitutional monarch. The so-called Meiji Restoration, after the emperor's posthumous name, ushered in a massive and ambitious programme of modernization of all aspects of Japanese society. For over 200 years Japan had been closed to the outside world on the orders of the Shoguns and the nation had been bypassed by the Industrial Revolution, leaving her armed forces obsolete and the nation vulnerable to conquest by any number of European colonial powers vying for control in Asia.

The Japanese had only to glance across the ocean to China to see what potential fate was in store for their own nation if they did not act, and act quickly. The large, hungry and aggressive European dog was pushing at the gates trying to get in, and the Japanese understood that the threat to their culture and their independence was very real. The hungry dog had already begun to devour China in large, meaty chunks. Trade had turned into economic warfare waged by the most ruthless of means. 'In the eighteenth century British traders brought back [to Britain] porcelain and tea to a homeland besotted with chinoiserie and hooked on the green leaf (the Treasury was soon hooked on tea duties). The acquisition of bases in India opened the way for further British expansion eastwards, having given them access on the subcontinent to the one commodity which above all other found a welcome if illegal market in China: opium.'[1] China in the nineteenth century was feudal, corrupt, inefficient, and industrially backward. It was ruled by the same Manchurian dynasty (considered a foreign imposition by most Han Chinese) that had seized power from the Ming emperors in the early seventeenth century. The ruling house was weak and plagued by internal feuds and power struggles and despised by most of those it governed. When a show of unified strength was most needed to counter the threat the barbarians posed to the Celestial Empire the Chinese government was found to be lacking. The Emperor Hsien Feng's favourite concubine Tzu Hsi had proclaimed herself regent in 1864 when her son, the new emperor, had suddenly died after only three years on the throne. Only four years earlier in November 1860, Czarist Russia had forced the Chinese to cede to them the whole of east coast Manchuria from the Amur River to the Yalu River bordering Korea. Manchuria would later become a focus of Japan's expansion into Asia, and a favourite playground of the fledgling Kempeitai.

The Empress Dowager, as Tzu Hsi had become known, assumed the powers of regent to her infant nephew Emperor Kuang Hsu with the backing of the Household troops. This wily woman was the effective ruler of China from 1864 until her death in 1908, an Oriental Queen Victoria ruling without parliament or democracy. When Kuang Hsu came of age in 1889 and tried to introduce far-reaching reforms in the Chinese economy and the armed forces, Tsu Hsi had him placed under house arrest and continued her disastrous reign in traditional ignorance of the Foreigner. Her mismanagement would end the Qing Dynasty's claim on power. China's armed forces were badly organized, indifferently armed and led and utterly incapable of dealing with the modern industrial-military war machines of Europe, the United States and later Japan. 'Soldiering was regarded as a despised profession, so it was hardly surprising that the junior commissioned ranks were lazy, incompetent, more interested in their privileges than their duties, and as corrupt as the system that produced them ... The men themselves, ill-disciplined and uninterested, simply reflected the manner in which they were led and their conditions of service.'[2] Since 1839 China had been prey to the imperial designs primarily of Britain, who had engineered the Opium Wars, forced 'Unequal Treaties' upon the Imperial court in Beijing in 1842 and 1860 and gained five treaty ports along the China coast to use as gateways into the huge and untapped Chinese market, including the most significant market place of them all – Shanghai. China had been forced to cede the barren island of Hong Kong to the British in 1842 and made further land concessions by ceding Kowloon in 1860 and leasing the New Territories to Britain for ninety-nine years in 1898.

The Chinese government watched as its economy fell piece by piece into Western hands, and watched as every effort they made to reassert their authority was met by gunboat diplomacy as the Westerners protected their huge trade profits. Except Hong Kong, Weihai and Macau, the treaty ports remained a part of China but they were firmly under Western control, and from these ports missionaries and traders had fanned out into the interior preaching alien religious concepts and interfering with traditional Chinese culture as well as spreading the evils of drug addiction throughout the empire.

The steady expansion of Hong Kong was a further insult to the Qing court in the Forbidden City, and the whites who lived and worked in China were exempt from Chinese laws and punishments through the principle of extraterritoriality. Foreigners could only be punished by their own consuls and courts. The Japanese saw immediately that unless they modernized quickly and developed a modern and strong indigenous economy they would quickly be subordinated to Western trade interests and reduced to virtual vassal status.

The new, democratic Japanese government poured money into the creation of new so-called *keiretsu* companies such as Mitsui and Mitsubishi to compete with Western companies and prevent them from gaining a toe-hold in Japan. They also reorganized their armed forces into mirror images of their Western counterparts. An Imperial Army and Navy was created using Western military advisors from France, the United States and Britain, and new military ideologies and technologies were speedily absorbed to form efficient and strong divisions and fleets capable of deterring any Western designs on the nation. The Kempeitai was one such organization created at this time, modelled not on an English-style service police but instead copied from a French-style gendarmerie.

Institutionally, the new Kempeitai was part of the Imperial Japanese Army (IJA), functioning as a military police under the auspices of the Minister of War. It also functioned as executive police under the direction of the Interior Minister, and as judicial police under the Justice Minister, so the reach and influence of the Kempeitai was extensive from the very beginnings of its existence. In the early days the primary task of the Kempeitai was tracking down and capturing young peasant men who were intent on avoiding conscription into the IJA. Before 1868 national defence had not existed in Japan, and instead the country had been divided up into feudal fiefs each under the control of a regional warlord known as a *daimyo*. Each *daimyo* maintained a personal army of samurai warriors for his protection, and *daimyo* formed grand alliances from time to time during the interminable civil wars that wracked Japan. The most powerful *daimyo* became Shogun. After 1600, the Tokugawa clan dominated the shogunate and united the nation, and the post became hereditary until the system was overthrown in 1868 during the Meiji Restoration. However, the old animosities and jealousies had not disappeared with the introduction of a constitutional monarchy and parliamentary system of government, and some samurai had been excluded from the new government and opportunities because of their former loyalties to the Tokugawa family and the shogunate.

The new IJA had faced down several revolts by disenchanted samurai in Japan, the last serious outbreak occurring in 1877 when the Satsuma clan had led an army against the legitimate government. Japan needed to maintain a strong, modern, Western-trained and organized army not only to crush internal rebellion against the new regime's reforms, but also to act as a block on the Western Powers and their wish to plunder Japan like they were plundering China. Forcing young men to serve in the new army was difficult, as in the past peasants had been prohibited from owning weapons under pain of death from their samurai overlords. No military tradition existed among the rural poor. Parents resisted having their sons taken away from them because their labour was needed on the land, so the Kempeitai's job was difficult but necessary to the security of the new state.

During the late nineteenth century the Kempeitai remained a small organization numbering less than 400 men. A general affairs branch was in change of Kempeitai policy, personnel management, internal discipline and liaison with the various ministries. An operations branch was charged with distributing Kempeitai military police units to the various parts of the IJA, as well as performing general public security and intelligence-gathering duties. Intelligence gathering and maintaining public security became increasingly important as Japan's influence in Asia increased in the early twentieth century. The Kempeitai first served overseas when Japan flexed her military muscles in Korea in 1907 following her extraordinary victory over Czarist Russia in the Russo-Japanese War of 1904–5. Japan already had the beginnings of an overseas empire before defeating Russia in 1905. In 1894–5 the new and modern IJA and Imperial Navy had roundly defeated the Chinese during a short war, at the conclusion of which Japan had been awarded a naval base in northern China named Port Arthur (now Lushun), as well as the island of Taiwan and the Pescadores Islands. The world sat up in 1905 and took notice of this small island nation that had already defeated the enfeebled Chinese and had now achieved a stunning victory over modern Russian forces. Japan was the first Asian nation in history to defeat a Western country, and her victory had sent shockwaves through the halls of power in London, Paris, St. Petersburg and Washington DC. In 1910 Japan had formally annexed the Korean peninsula, and the Kempeitai came to prominence in maintaining a brutal Japanese occupation.

Japanese interest in Korea had begun in 1895 during the war with China. The Japanese wanted Korean ports opened to Japanese trade before the United States intervened. To aid this process the

Kempeitai assisted in the ruthless and despicable murder of the Korean emperor's influential wife, Empress Myeongseong (also known as Queen Min), who had sought the assistance of the Russians in preventing the Japanese from occupying Korea after the nation had emerged from Chinese control in 1895. The Japanese identified Empress Myeongseong as an obstacle against further overseas expansion and determined to remove her from power. Rebellions and uprisings were formented by the Japanese in league with collaborationist Korean royals and officials, but this only led Myeongseong to take a yet harsher and more vocal stand against the Japanese.

Miura Goro, Japan's Minister to Korea and a former IJA lieutenant general, decided to act. He organized a large group of Japanese soldiers into an assassination team led by a Major Niiro, and enacted Operation 'Fox Hunt'. Early on the morning of 8 October 1895 Niiro and his several dozen assassins broke into the Royal Palace at Kyungbok, killed the Korean household guards and burst into the king's chambers. King Gojong was thrown to the ground, and when his son tried to intervene he was beaten with a sheathed sword. Other assassins forced their way into Myeongseong's chambers and shot dead Palace Minister Lee Gyung-sik when he tried to protect the empress. A Russian military adviser working at the palace, Aleksey Seredin-Sabatin witnessed some of the assault. 'The court-yard where the queen's wing was located was filled with Japanese, perhaps as many as 20 or 25 men. They were dressed in peculiar gowns and were armed with sabres, some of which were openly visible.' Seredin-Sabatin recalled that while 'some Japanese troops were rummaging around in every corner of the palace and in the various annexes, others burst into the queen's wing and threw themselves upon the women they found there'. Seredin-Sabatin witnessed several assaults on women, recalling: 'Two Japanese grabbed one of the court ladies, pulled her out of the house, and ran down the stairs dragging her along behind them. Moreover, one of the Japanese repeatedly asked me in English, "Where is the queen? Point the queen out to us!"'[3] One of the Japanese assassins, Isujuka Eijoh, later wrote an account of what happened next. When they identified the 43-year-old Empress Myeongseong 'we stabbed her several times and stripped her stark naked. We examined her genitals ...' and then she was raped. Finally, the assassins 'poured oil on her body and set her on fire.'[4]

The Empress was burned alive. Her gruesome death and the preceding rapes were suppressed from the Japanese and Korean public for decades and they did not become widely known until the beginning of the twenty-first century. Many Japanese histories today still deny that the assassins behaved in this manner. Major Niiro and his men successfully escaped from the palace and were spirited out of Korea to Japan. Before he left, Niiro cabled the IJA's Chief of Staff in Tokyo: 'Queen dead and King safe.' There was widespread international outrage at the behaviour of the Japanese in assassinating a crowned monarch, but a ludicrous show trial of General Miura and his men staged at Hiroshima broke down through lack of 'clear-cut evidence' and no one was ever punished. Thereafter, Japanese influence over the Korean Court was virtually absolute until the Korean monarchy was abolished when Japan finally annexed the peninsula in 1910.

After 1910 the Kempeitai was charged with the maintenance of public order within Japan under the direction of the Interior Minister, and with the same task in Korea under the War Minister. Intelligence gathering, and specifically the rooting out of potential opponents of the Japanese regime, became an important Kempeitai mission. The Kempeitai organized a secret police unit called the *Tokubetsu Koto Kempeitai* (Special Higher Law Soldiers), known as the *Tokko*. There was, confusingly, already a similar civilian organization in Japan also called the *Tokko*, so by the early twentieth century the Japanese operated two separate secret police forces.

The Kempeitai *Tokko* was an all-powerful organization dedicated to hunting down anyone deemed a threat to national security, including communists, liberals, foreign spies, and those opposed to Japanese aggression in Asia. The *Tokko* had the power to arrest anyone it suspected of behaviour contrary to 'good' public order, and the *Tokko* did not require warrants when making arrests. By the 1930s the use of torture to extract information and confessions had become standard Kempeitai working practice, indeed the organization's *modus operandi*.

The Wall Street Crash of 1929 and the subsequent worldwide recession hurt the Japanese economy very badly. Japan was a famous textile manufacturer, and with American demand curtailed this primary industry was deeply affected. Unemployment increased, farmers went bankrupt, and families starved. The population of Japan had grown to sixty-five million people by 1930, and with their limited agricultural lands the Japanese had become increasingly reliant upon imported food. The textile industry had once paid for all of this, but by the early 1930s no longer could. Perhaps it was only natural that the Japanese, in such dire economic straits, should look abroad to discover the cure for all of their national ills. They cast covetous eyes upon northern China, particularly the province of Manchuria (now roughly Heilongjiang, Jilin and Liaoning) with its vast and under-exploited agricultural lands and huge mineral resources.

Asia was dominated by the European colonial nations and the United States, and surely it was only fair, thought many Japanese, that their country, as a civilized and well-developed nation herself, should also be admitted to the colonial club and permitted to build an empire. The Japanese already had control of Korea, Taiwan, Port Arthur and a sizeable chunk of the International Settlement in Shanghai. During the First World War Japan had been an ally of Britain, France and the United States, and backing the victorious powers had brought the nation further territories in China and the Pacific. The former German colony of Tsingdao (now Qingdao) in China and the Marshall, Caroline and Mariana Islands were now controlled by Japan and were busily being developed into significant naval and military bases.

By the mid-1930s Japan was in the throes of a nationalist revolution, with democracy slowly being pushed out of mainstream politics as reactionary elements in military and philosophical circles expounded the inequalities of British and American 'imperialistic' attitudes towards Japan. The Kempeitai and the rest of the IJA followed an ultra-nationalist, fascist political doctrine known as *Kodaha* (Imperial Way Faction) that had its genesis in the 1920s as a disparate alliance of nationalist groups formed among army officers and eventually, by the early 1930s, coalesced into one group.

Imperial Way was dedicated to establishing the army as the real political power in Japan, either by winning democratic elections or by more direct methods. Either way, the aim was the establishment of a military dictatorship and an expansion of the empire. The

Imperial Japanese Navy (IJN), though equally nationalist, followed a different course and made emperor worship its creed. There was considerable tension and distrust between the IJA and the IJN in the follow up to war and throughout the conflict. The Imperial Navy had its own version of the Kempeitai, and it was later deployed to root out resistance to naval rule in the occupied territories, whether the threats were real or invented. Called the *Tokei-Tai*, it had originally been formed as a low-key police and intelligence group to prevent the army from meddling in the navy's affairs. The *Tokei-Tai* was as brutal an organization as the army Kempeitai, and it was especially active in the areas of the South Pacific under IJN control. In common with the army Kempeitai, naval *Tokei-Tai* investigators used extreme tortures to obtain intelligence and confessions, often resulting in death or permanent disabilities for the victims.

The IJA wanted to use the Imperial Way Faction to create in effect a modern military shogunate, and this was later largely achieved when General Hideki Tojo became Prime Minister. Tojo was one of the Imperial Way leaders and a former commander of the Kempeitai in Manchuria, where the Japanese had engineered 'incidents' with local Chinese troops as an excuse to invade and occupy most of Manchuria, which they renamed Manchukuo in February 1932. The Great Depression coupled with early confrontations in China stirred the ultra-nationalists to take the lead in Japanese foreign policy. Those who stood in the way of the ultra-nationalists' goals often paid a high price. In 1930 Prime Minister Osachi Hamaguchi successfully challenged the military radicals in the army and navy and got the London Naval Conference treaty ratified by the Japanese parliament. The treaty limited the size of Japan's rapidly expanding fleet, and maintained the power balance in the Far East, with the Royal Navy and United States Navy remaining bigger than the IJN but in parity with each other.[5] Many ultra-nationalists saw the treaty as an insult to Japan, and a reflection of racist Western attitudes towards the Japanese people. In November 1930 Hamaguchi was wounded by a would-be assassin who shot the Prime Minister.

In 1931 a military coup was planned in Tokyo, but it was abandoned at the last minute. The following year IJN officers assassinated new Prime Minister Tsuyoshi Inukai in the hope of forcing the government to declare martial law, a move that would have placed the military in effective control of the nation, but their plot failed. Also, in Shanghai the IJN attempted to expand the Japanese settlement there by force of arms, threatening the Nationalist Chinese government and ignoring the admonitions of the other members of the Shanghai Municipal Council. When Japanese Naval Landing Troops launched an assault on the Chinese district of Chapei (now Zhabei) they met unexpectedly strong resistance from the Chinese 19th Route Army around the North Railway Station. The battle for Chapei lasted for five weeks, and only ended when Chiang Kai-shek, the Chinese leader, refused to support General Tsai Ting-kai with ammunition and supplies, preferring to keep his forces intact to deal with the Communist threat in the north-west. During the battle 'Japan introduced the world to checkerboard bombing, the same large-scale, indiscriminate bombing of a civilian population that would be seen a few years later in Guernica, Coventry, and Dresden.'[6] The IJN was ruthless in the application of modern weapons to a crowded city. 'From the landing decks of their cruisers off Hongkew, Japanese seaplanes daily skimmed across Chapei, releasing their deadly black cylinders over its buildings from a height of three hundred feet. Under continuous shelling, nearly 85 per cent of Chapei's buildings were destroyed ... Some ten thousand civilians would die in the conflict.'[7] Admiral Shiozawa, the Japanese naval commander, when brought to task over the high civilian death toll by a foreign journalist after the conflict merely replied, 'I used only thirty-pound bombs, and if I had chosen to do so I might have used the five-hundred-pound variety.'[8] Japan had won eventually, but her international reputation was in a shambles after film and photographs of dead or burnt Chinese babies were broadcast around the world. Japan looked like a bully and a nation with few scruples regarding how and where it waged aggressive war.

In 1936 a group of young Japanese army officers, all adherents of the Imperial Way Faction, launched another coup attempt in Tokyo, killing several prominent politicians in the process; but they also failed to bring the military to full power and they were arrested and later executed. But the idea remained of challenging the Western imperialist nations by forging a Japanese Asian empire. Sea power was going to play a central role in any future race for empire, as Japan depended almost entirely on imported resources, from iron ore to oil and wheat. The Japanese government soon felt secure and strong enough to ignore the naval restrictions imposed on her in London in 1930 at the instigation of the British and Americans, who were wary of a challenger to their regional hegemony. The United States and British governments drew in a collective breath, and wondered what they should do, as Japan embarked on a massive rearmament programme, shortly to be followed by German rearmament in Europe. Lured back to the conference table in 1935, Japan's diplomats quickly snubbed the negotiations, accusing the British and Americans of harbouring racist opinions of their country, and withdrew the next year.

The Kempeitai was the organization charged with making sure that soldiers in the IJA followed the ideology of the Imperial Way. The Kempeitai promoted the racial superiority of the Japanese and racialist theories concerning the other peoples of Asia, in particular promulgating drastic anti-Chinese ideas. The Kempeitai became a tool of the Imperial Way, to be used to destroy resistance to its rise to power. The Great Depression had caused serious labour and social unrest in Japan, and the Kempeitai was active in suppressing union activity and street demonstrations, labelling most agitators as 'communists' and anti-Imperialists. The wide range of powers of the Kempeitai, including the ability to arrest anyone without evidence or a warrant, meant that the leaders of the Imperial Way often used the Kempeitai to remove its political opponents and break the power of the unions over the economy. And when the designs of the Imperial Way were stymied at home by the remaining resistance of democratically elected politicians in parliament they decided to use the Kempeitai to engineer Japanese foreign policy from outside the nation. They turned to Manchuria, home to widespread Japanese business interests and projects, but still formally part of China, as the key to achieving their aims.

The story of how the Japanese conquered Manchuria shows how vital the Kempeitai had become in assuring a future Japanese empire. Manchuria was important to Japan primarily because of the huge deposits of raw materials it contained, which the Japanese extracted to fuel their economy and their growing military machine. Since 1906 Japanese troops had been garrisoned in the province in the Kwantung Leased Territory behind their base at Port Arthur. They guarded the Japanese-owned South Manchurian Railway which was vital for the economic development of the region. Renamed the

Kwantung Army in 1919, this force was the largest single unit of the IJA and its leaders were all Imperial Way hardliners.

By the early 1930s the Kwantung Army was behaving as though it was entirely autonomous of the democratic government in Tokyo, allowing it to engineer a crisis that would necessitate a strong Japanese response and allow Japan to seize the entire province and turn it into a colony. There had been debates as to whether Japan should attempt to conquer China and establish colonies on the mainland or strengthen economic ties with China and thereby minimize conflict between the two nations. China had been in political turmoil since the overthrow of the Qing Dynasty in 1912 and the establishment of a republic. Warlords and their private armies controlled the different provinces and there had been an almost continuous civil war until Chiang Kai-shek had launched an expedition to defeat the other warlords and unite the country under his personal authority. By 1930 Chiang had prevailed, and a national capital had been established at Nanking (now Nanjing). Chiang's foreign policy remained one of nonresistance, as he was preoccupied with dealing with Mao Zedong's Communists who still threatened the new regime. The Japanese could see the opportunity Chiang's policy offered them.

Many IJA officers, particularly those at Kwantung Army head-quarters, favoured invading and occupying Manchuria and replacing the government with either a colonial administration or a local puppet regime. They decided to act in 1931 by sabotaging a section of the South Manchurian Railway near Liutiao Lake and then blaming local Chinese troops. The Kwantung Army could then occupy the rest of the province, claiming that they were protect-ing Japanese economic interests. The plotters were led by Colonel Seishiro Itagaki, who was Chief of the Kempeitai Intelligence Section of the Kwantung Army. It was a classic 'false flag' intelligence operation of the sort the Kempeitai was well trained to conduct, and it worked perfectly. On 18 September a small bomb exploded beside the South Manchurian Railway, causing only superficial damage. The next morning Japanese troops attacked the local Chinese garrison, who were under strict orders not to resist, and put them to flight. By that evening Japanese troops had captured the most important city in the region, Mukden (now Shenyang) at the cost of only two Japanese soldiers killed. Five hundred Chinese troops had been killed in the attack. Chiang continued to order no resistance to the Japanese, but because of the poor state of communications some Chinese commanders did order their troops into action. Either way, within five months of the so-called 'Mukden Incident' all of Manchuria was under Japanese occupation.

The Kwantung Army installed a puppet regime in Manchuria led by the former Emperor of China, Pu Yi, who had been forced to abdicate in 1912 and evicted by a warlord from the Forbidden City in 1924. He became the Emperor of Manchukuo, as the Japanese renamed the province. International protests were ignored and relations with Britain and the United States sank to all-time lows. The Japanese felt more isolated then ever, and railed against their 'unfair' treatment by the Western Powers, who had themselves often resorted to similar displays of military force when carving out their own empires. The Japanese militarists viewed the international outcry as evidence of double standards and racism against a rising Asian power. At home, many ordinary Japanese began to agree with them, and a general feeling that Japan was being unfairly ostracized by the international community found widespread support. This sense of isolationism would find its perfect outlet in the thirst for conquest and dominion beyond the shores of the Sacred Islands. The Imperial Way and its Kempeitai friends had triumphed, but in so doing they would drag their nation to the very point of complete destruction.

Notes

1. Robert Bickers, *Empire Made Me: An Englishman Adrift in Shanghai* (London, Penguin Books, 2004), pp. 5–6.
2. Bryan Perrett, *Against All Odds! More Dramatic 'Last Stand' Actions* (London, Brockhampton Press, 1999), p. 122.
3. http://www.koreaweb.ws/ks/ksr/queenmin.txt, accessed 27 March 2008.
4. 'Eijoh Report', cited in Kim Ung Yong, *Japan's Annexation of Korea from Diplomatic Accounts* (1996).
5. The treaties signed in London and Washington in 1930 also meant that Britain's Royal Navy would no longer be the largest in the world, and in order to achieve parity of numbers with the

United States Navy the Admiralty actually had to scrap some British ships. America became an equal partner with Britain in ruling Asia and the Pacific.

6. Stella Dong, *Shanghai: The Rise and Fall of a Decadent City* (New York, Perennial, 2001), p. 215.
7. Ibid: p. 215.
8. Ibid: p. 217.

Chapter Two

Organ of Terror

The interviewer produced a small piece of wood like a meat skewer, pushed that into my left ear, and tapped it in with a small hammer. I think I fainted some time after it went through the drum.

Lieutenant Rod Wells, Australian Army

'Speak out!' roared Sergeant Yoshimura, 'Speak out and tell us the names!' More blows rained down on the helpless woman tied to a post as Yoshimura swung the heavy bamboo cane like a man possessed, spittle flying from his lips as he yelled into the woman's face. 'Speak out, you resistance bitch!' cried Yoshimura once again, and he brought the cane down on the woman's body once more with a heavy grunt. A girl was crying close by, her mother's anguished eyes fixed on the little girl strung up by ropes above a roaring fire. Yoshimura meant to burn the girl to death if the mother would not speak. The flames began to grow stronger and higher, but the brave little girl yelled out to her mother not to speak. 'Be very brave Mummy,' she sobbed, 'do not tell, we will both die and Jesus will wait for us in Heaven above.'[1] The woman, Mrs. Kathigasu, stared at her daughter, tears rolling down her cheeks but a fierce refusal to give in written across her anguished face. Yoshimura, the Kempeitai interrogator who had done terrible things to this woman for three and a half months roared with insane anger. 'Speak out or I will cut the rope and burn your daughter alive!' Kathigasu shouted 'No!' with her remaining strength, perhaps knowing that either way Yoshimura intended to kill them both. The mother and the daughter both knew that to speak would condemn dozens of their comrades in the Malayan resistance movement to certain death. The cane struck hard again, and with a final bellow Yoshimura brought the bamboo down with such force across Kathigasu's body that it broke with a loud crack. At that moment a car approached and Yoshimura paused, uncertain of his next move.

Kathigasu had been betrayed over three months before by a fellow Malayan resistance member in August 1943. She had been incarcerated at the Central Police Station in Ipoh, the capital of Perak in western Malaya, now used by the Kempeitai as a torture centre. Sergeant Yoshimura had been assigned to break Kathigasu. The Japanese wanted the names of the other resistance members hiding out in the Cameron Highlands on the borders of Perak and Piang states. Yoshimura and his men had degraded Kathigasu in just about every way imaginable. The tortures had been terrible. First she had been subjected to the water treatment, and this had been followed with red hot irons that seared the flesh on her back and legs. Kathigasu had been remorselessly beaten with bamboo canes and sometimes hung upside down by one leg for hours at a time. Metal slivers had been hammered beneath her finger nails. But Kathigasu had somehow not broken down under this appalling treatment. Whatever Yoshimura had tried Kathigasu had stayed silent, and her silence had saved many lives.

In mid-November Kathigasu had been taken to Kempeitai Head-quarters at Gopang Road in Ipoh and formally charged with having listened to the radio news, the possession of private radios being expressly forbidden under Japanese occupation rules. After being charged the questioning began again regarding the 'anti-Japanese campaign' that had become a Kempeitai obsession in Malaya. Hanging Kathigasu's young daughter above an open fire was Yoshimura's last gambit to get her to talk, but it failed. The car that Kathigasu and the Japanese heard approaching contained a Japanese army officer. He ordered his driver to stop and he marched imperiously up to the sweating Yoshimura, who immediately assumed the fawning submission of a Japanese soldier in the presence of his superior. With much attendant bowing Yoshimura explained what he was trying to achieve by his medieval display of brutality, but the officer evidently had some humanity and ordered Yoshimura to take the young girl down and send her home. Kathigasu was taken back to her cell at the police station where Yoshimura tortured her further, but in the end even he admitted defeat when she resolutely refused to talk. A month later, at a staged 'trial', Kathigasu was sentenced to death, but this was later commuted to penal servitude for life. She survived the war to be reunited with her daughter and to have the satisfaction of giving evidence against Yoshimura at a British war crimes trial in February 1946.

The Kempeitai acquired an infamous reputation for torturing suspects, and the organization equalled and often outperformed the horrors dreamed up by the Gestapo and Stalin's NKVD. The Japanese wartime military maintained an almost casual approach to the application of torture and physical violence against its opponents. Violence was an integral part of the Japanese regime's military ethos, and recruits had already been subjected to a very harsh regime during training, during which they were often assaulted for minor infractions of military discipline.

The Kempeitai, although Japan's expert torturers, did officially recognize that the use of violence was not always desirable and could be counter-productive when trying to extract information from suspects, an official interrogation handbook commenting: 'Care must be exercised when making use of rebukes, invectives or torture as it will result in his telling falsehoods and making a fool of you.'[2] Kempeitai interrogators were further warned against regarding torture as normal, for 'this method is only to be used when everything else has failed as it is the most clumsy.'[3] An American officer reviewing this material commented on the use of torture: 'It is interesting as representing an official view. Its application by individual commanders is quite another matter.' As we will see throughout this book there was a certain level of uniformity in the methods of torture used by the Japanese to extract confessions, but the degree of its use was determined by commanders in the field, and little regulation was applied to Kempeitai officers in the pursuit of 'truth'. The invention of novel forms of torture and punishment was permitted, and in particular Kempeitai offices around the Occupied Territories appear to have specialized in particular techniques. Deaths in custody and the subsequent torture of other prisoners were also quite unregulated, and decided by local Kempeitai commanders. The wholesale butchery of civilians and/or prisoners was perfectly acceptable when protecting the Empire from its enemies, within and without, real or imaginary.

Torture was very extensively practised throughout the Occupied Territories and even inside Japan, and very often Kempeitai inter-rogators turned immediately to its application with alacrity before trying other methods. The threat of torture loosened most tongues, and giving a suspect a beating before beginning interrogation usually so intimidated the victim that further violence was not necessary, although that did in part depend upon the sadism and/or thoroughness of the individual Kempeitai investigator.

The merest fact that someone had been arrested signalled guilt to the Kempeitai, the Japanese legal system of the period placing no stock in the concept 'innocent until proven guilty' or other Western liberal traditions. If the Kempeitai was interested in a person, so ran the official logic, it must be because that person had done something wrong to warrant such close scrutiny and suspicion in the first place. Therefore, the quickest way to loosen a suspect's tongue was often to dangle the possibility of physical pain in front of the person, or actually administer a quick dose before any questions were even asked. Kempeitai interrogations generally began with a severe thrashing of the suspect before any questioning so as to establish a climate of fear and helplessness among the prisoners. 'Many people talked for fear,'[4] wrote Willem Wijting, a Dutch underground operative who was arrested and tortured by the Japanese in Java. Some, of course, bravely tried to withstand 'questioning', but almost all eventually broke or took their secrets to the grave as the Kempeitai kept up the pressure until the prisoner was literally tortured to death.

The uniformity in methods of torture practised by the Kempeitai throughout the vast Japanese occupation zone suggested a definite policy adopted by the armed forces at the direct instigation of the government in Tokyo. Often, Kempeitai investigators cared little whether confessions were made voluntarily or made under duress, so torture served a useful and normally quick role in confirm-ing Kempeitai suspicions. Essentially, if you were arrested by the Kempeitai your fate was usually already sealed. Such an attitude on the part of the Kempeitai was a reflection of the Japanese justice system, which had always presumed the guilt of those arrested until they proved themselves to be innocent, the opposite of the English system of presumed innocence until proven otherwise. The Kempeitai were also largely able to dispose of the legal nicety of criminal trials as the war progressed, removing the last chance for an accused person to prove their innocence by challenging the Kempeitai's case against them before judgment was passed.

Torture was the Kempeitai's strongest trump card, and the threat of physical assault preceded the organization like a foul odour. Prisoners expected to suffer cruel and unusual punishments in Kempeitai hands, and the history of the war in Asia aptly demonstrates on countless occasions that institutional cruelty was not limited to the Kempeitai, but was widely practised throughout the Japanese army and navy. Japanese military violence was so widespread as to become the rule rather than the exception, and it was clear very early on in the war that no one was safe from the attentions of military police inquisitors. Genuine innocence could often only be proved after extensive physical abuse in Kempeitai torture centres that had sprung up like evil mushrooms in all of the cities and towns that had been trampled beneath the cloven hoof of Japanese imperialism. Many innocents died as a result of such abuse, the Kempeitai caring little whether they had indeed caught the 'right' people. An important function of the Kempeitai was as a state-sponsored organ of terror every bit as feared as the Gestapo or NKVD. The mere presence of Kempeitai troops instilled great fear among the local population – as was the intention.

The Japanese military employed extreme, sadistic and usually disproportionate violence against those suspected of challenging its rule, and even petty offences committed by prisoners of war or civilians carried hellish and terrifying punishments. Torture was such a part of official Kempeitai policy that the methods used were carefully outlined for officers in a useful little handbook. A copy of the Kempeitai handbook *Japanese Instructions on How to Interrogate* was captured by the Americans in August 1944 and it corroborated many of the stories of severe ill treatment of prisoners of war, civilian internees and local populations that had been emerging in a steady stream since the Allies began to advance on Japan. The booklet advised that threatening prisoners could be just as effective as torturing them. 'Hints of future physical discomforts, for example, torture, murder, starvation, solitary confinement, deprivation of sleep,' were all recommended. 'Hints of future mental discomforts, for example, not to be allowed to send letters, not to be given the same treatment as other prisoners of war, to be kept back in the event of an exchange of prisoners,' were also advised.[5] By and large, however, subtlety was not a weapon wielded with particular skill by members of the Kempeitai, and they usually opted immediately for some form of physical abuse in order to create the desired environment of fear, often because they enjoyed inflicting pain on fellow humans.

The methods used by the Kempeitai to torture its victims were not particularly sophisticated and most could be traced to the samurai period in Japanese history, earlier Chinese tortures or even medieval European ones. Some methods did employ modern technology in breaking prisoners. Most prisoners were given the water treatment as a standard opening gambit by the Kempeitai. This involved a water pipe being jammed into the prisoner's mouth and water pumped down the throat until the prisoner lost consciousness. The water was then evacuated when the Japanese guards would jump onto the prisoner's abdomen, and the process repeated several more times. Many people died during this violent and repellent procedure. At Woosung prison camp in Shanghai in early 1942 the Japanese army interpreter who worked for the Kempeitai was notorious for using the water treatment on American and British prisoners. Isamu Ishihara was known as 'The Beast of the East', and his version of the water treatment involved the following: 'Prop a ladder on a slope, tie the prisoner to it, feet higher than head, pound something into his nostrils to break the bones so he had to breathe through his mouth, pour water into his mouth till he filled up and choked, and then it was talk or suffocate.'[6] Ishihara's other favourite torture was called the 'Finger Wire'. This involved using a contraption that bent a prisoner's finger back until it broke or was dislocated.[7]

Heat was viewed as an efficient method to loosen tongues, particularly the application of heat to the very sensitive parts of the body. Hot irons were often used, as the case of Malayan resistance supporter Mrs. Kathigasu, and other forms of intense heat, such as lit cigarettes or pokers, were pressed against feet, groin, and (in the case of women) breasts. Pokers and cigarettes could also be inserted inside the victim's nostrils, resulting in excruciating pain. Two American airmen shot down over China in 1945 were paraded through the streets by the Kempeitai, beaten up and then doused with petrol and burned alive as an example to the local populace.

Japanese tortures were not usually administered individually; normally a victim would be softened up with a beating and/or the water treatment, followed by more medieval procedures if a confession was not forthcoming. Like the Gestapo, the Kempeitai had early on discovered the usefulness of electric current as a torture device. Electric shocks could be applied to many of the same areas as heat, particularly the genitals, and the pain dosage more carefully controlled than by mashing a lit cigarette into someone's nipple or inner ear.

On occasion unusual objects were used to inflict excruciating pain and permanent damage to victims. Women often had sharp objects thrust into their vaginas. Lieutenant Rod Wells, a 23-year-old Australian prisoner of war, was discovered with illegal radio parts and sent to Outram Road Jail in Singapore from a prison camp at Sandakan in North Borneo in 1943. His experiences at the hands of the Kempeitai left him disabled for life. 'The interviewer produced a small piece of wood like a meat skewer,' recalled Wells of his torture, 'pushed that into my left ear, and tapped it in with a small hammer. I think I fainted some time after it went through the drum. I remember the last excruciating sort of pain, and I must have gone out for some time because I was revived with a bucket of water. Eventually it healed but of course I couldn't hear with it. I have never been able to hear since.'[8]

Some of the tortures practised by the Kempeitai were similar to those used by the Spanish Inquisition and throughout Europe hundreds of years ago. The Japanese adopted the old Chinese technique of hammering slivers of bamboo beneath a victim's fingernails, which had also been practised in Europe using small pieces of iron. Another similar torture was the ripping off of finger or toenails with a pair of pliers. A common Japanese torture was known as the 'knee spread'. The victim, as Lord Russell of Liverpool notes in his *Knights of Bushido*, had his hands tied behind his back. He was 'forced to kneel with a pole, sometimes as much as three inches in diameter, inserted behind both knee joints so as to spread them as pressure was applied to his thighs, sometimes by jumping on them.'[9] This torture caused the separation of the knee joints, incredible pain and often permanent disability for the victim. The knees also formed the focus of another Japanese torture where victims were forced to kneel on sharp objects for lengthy periods of time. Usually the edges of square wooden blocks were used, and victims were forced to kneel on these for hours at a time. If they tried to move they were beaten with heavy sticks or flogged back into position with whips.

Burying was another unusual but widely practised Japanese torture or execution method. During the infamous Rape of Nanking in 1937–38, when marauding Japanese troops under the nominal command of Major General Iwane Matsui (but in reality commanded by Emperor Hirohito's uncle General Prince Asaka) raped, abused and killed over 300,000 Chinese civilians and prisoners of war in an orgy of unbelievable cruelty, many of the victims were actually buried alive. The Kempeitai practised burial as a non-lethal torture device as well. A Malay-Indian magistrate at Kuala Trengganu was picked up by the Kempeitai and charged with being a spy. Although the charges were ludicrous, the magistrate was nonetheless extensively tortured to extract a false confession. After spending a night tied to a table leg, the next morning Kempeitai soldiers kicked him almost to death before dragging the terrified man outside. There they 'buried me in the ground leaving just my head above ground. I was then made to close my eyes. When I did so one of the Kempei Tai men put his sword against my throat as if to cut it, and kept it there for some minutes. After that I was unburied and left out in the sun for the rest of the day.'[10] A variation on the theme of water torture was then tried the next morning on the unfortunate magistrate. The Kempeitai 'put me in a benzine [sic] drum with forty gallons of oily water. They placed the lid on top of the drum and when I could not breathe any longer I tried to escape from the water. Using my full strength I managed to jerk the lid and it fell to the ground.'[11]

Suspension was a commonly applied torture used by the Kempeitai, and it was often accompanied by flogging. The victim was tied in such a way that when lifted off the ground he was slowly strangled. The process could be repeated many times as the victim swam in and out of consciousness. Beatings with a wooden bat were very commonly applied by the Japanese throughout the prison camp system and by the Kempeitai during interrogations. The ferocity of such assaults over often very minor infractions of Japanese rules was severe and remorseless. The Kempeitai ran the prison camp system, and brutality was an important component of their regime of terror.

At Macassar Camp in the occupied Netherlands East Indies (now Indonesia) the British and Dutch prisoners, as elsewhere through the occupied territories, were denied furniture, bedding or new issues of clothing. They were overworked, underfed and exposed to every tropical disease known to science. Dysentery and malaria were the most common, but deficiency diseases also killed many. No Red Cross parcels were distributed. The Japanese illegally kept them for themselves to pilfer at their leisure. There were no recreation facilities and even singing was forbidden. Lastly, the prisoners received no mail from home, nor were they permitted to send any. What the prisoners did receive plenty of, apart from heavy labour, was punishment. The camp commandant, Captain Yoshida, enjoyed personally beating his prisoners for the tiniest infractions of the rules. One punishment involved prisoners being forced to climb a tree full of stinging red ants and remain aloft for hours at a time.

Yoshida and his cronies often deliberately beat prisoners unconscious. Examples of Yoshida's sadism are numerous and were repeated thousands of times throughout the entire Japanese prison camp system. A Dutch sergeant named Smit sprang to attention next to a Japanese guard a little too quickly, startling the Japanese. The guard accused Smit of trying to threaten him because at the time the prisoner was holding a shovel as he was on a work detail. The guard proceeded to beat the unfortunate Dutch soldier thirty times across the back with a pick axe handle as punishment. When Yoshida heard about the incident he in turn gave Smit fifty blows himself. On 4 August 1944 one British prisoner was personally beaten *seventy* times by Yoshida because he had failed to give a satisfactory 'eyes right' when his working party had marched past the commandant. On 5 August Stoker Wilkinson of the Royal Navy was punished for having allowed a working party to leave the camp one man short – Yoshida beat him over *200* times with a pick axe handle and then forced the grievously injured Wilkinson to stand to attention for two hours afterwards.

Even the Kempeitai's medics were violent and sadistic. In February 1945 a Japanese army doctor was inspecting Macassar Camp hospital when he spotted some food remnants inside a dustbin. The senior Dutch medical officer and his two assistants were made to stand for a long time with their heads over the dustbin while all the other doctors and orderlies were fallen in at the hospital gate and severely beaten by a pack of guards. They were then each given the water treatment. The appalling regime at Macassar Camp was not in any way unique. It was, once again, the rule rather than the exception.

The use of animals, particularly ants, to torture prisoners was very popular throughout the prison camp system. At Soengi Geru Camp on the island of Sumatra in the Netherlands East Indies British, Dutch and Malay prisoners of war were regularly abused by their Japanese captors. Because the Kempeitai administered the entire POW camp system the regime was deliberately sadistic and cruel at the behest of Prime Minister Tojo himself, and the officers and men running the camps were encouraged to beat, humiliate and work European prisoners to death. Flogging was the most common form of punishment for even the tiniest infraction of camp rules or the most polite and careful complaint regarding the insanitary conditions existing inside the camp at Soengi Geru.

As we shall see, the methods of torture outlined in this chapter were just some of the horrendous acts of sadism we shall encounter. The Kempeitai was endlessly inventive when it came to the infliction of pain and were masters of inquisition. Their disregard for the Rules of War and the agreements concerning the rights and treatment of prisoners of war were breathtaking, and their determination to enforce General Tojo's desire to see prisoners labour for the Empire meant that their methods were endorsed and encouraged at the very highest level of the Japanese government.

Notes

1. Lord Russell of Liverpool, *The Knights of Bushido: A Short History of Japanese War Crimes* (London, Greenhill Books, 2002), p. 280.
2. Ibid: p. 275.
3. Ibid: p. 275.
4. The National Archives (TNA): Public Record Office (PRO) WO 325/151, Statement No. 1504: *Statement of Mr. B.F. Witing*, 13 October 1945.

5. Box 252, Exhibit 1462, Allied Translation and Interpreter Section South West Pacific Area, Document No. 552, Research Report No. 65 (Suppl No. 1), 29 March 1945, MacMillan Brown Library, University of Canterbury, Christchurch, New Zealand.

6. Gavan Daws, *Prisoners of the Japanese: POWs of the Second World War* (London, Pocket Books, 1994), p. 150.

7. Chester M. Briggs, Jr., *Behind the Barbed Wire: Memoirs of a World War II US Marine Captured in North China in 1941 and Imprisoned by the Japanese until 1945* (McFarland & Company, 1994).

8. 'Rod Wells', *Stolen Years: Australian Prisoners of War*, Australian War Memorial, http://www.awm.gov.au/stolenyears/ww2/japan/sandakan/story3.asp, accessed 17 March 2008.

9. Lord Russell of Liverpool, *The Knights of Bushido: A Short History of Japanese War Crimes* (London, Greenhill Books, 2002), p. 276.

10. Ibid: p. 278.

11. Ibid: p. 278.

12. Ibid: p. 184.

Chapter Three

Slaves for the Emperor

Remember your status as prisoners of war. You have no rights. International Law and the Geneva Convention are dead.

Commandant's Address to Prisoners
Tan Toey Camp, Ambon Island, 1942

The treatment of Allied prisoners of war earned Japan the condemnation of the world in 1945. The Kempeitai was intimately involved in creating a terror gulag as reprehensible as Hitler's concentration camps or Stalin's salt mines. The Japanese operated a total of 676 slave labour camps throughout the Home Islands and Occupied Territories. 140,000 White Caucasian prisoners were held in these camps, the entire system coming under the control of the Kempeitai. Although the camps were actually under the command of Japanese army officers, it was the Kempeitai, operating out of regional offices, that was in charge of investigating 'crimes' committed by inmates, rooting out escape plots or anti-Japanese elements, and even in deciding the types of punishments that were used on the prisoners.

General Hideki Tojo, the Japanese Prime Minister, was formerly commander of Kempeitai forces in occupied Manchuria, and it was his harsh regulations concerning the treatment of POWs that were strictly adhered to by camp commandants and local Kempeitai. It was not unusual for a prisoner to be first punished by the camp commandant, who would then call in the Kempeitai to 'investigate' the offence, and for the Kempeitai to punish the prisoner again separately. For example, at River Valley Road Camp 17 near Omuta in Japan, the commandant was informed that an American prisoner named Hubbard had been caught with a scrap of a Japanese newspaper on his person. The Japanese, and especially the Kempeitai, were obsessed with preventing news of the disastrous progress of the war from falling into prisoners' hands, and they went to extraordinary lengths of barbarity to root out radio receivers and news sheets in the camps. Hubbard was beaten up by a group of camp guards and then thrown into the guard house. The commandant informed the local Kempeitai, 'Next day three Kempeitai corporals came to the camp. They beat Hubbard ... with their rifle butts. Four days Hubbard's screams echoed across the subdued camp – until merciful death claimed him at last.'[1]

Examples of Kempeitai cruelty to prisoners are legion and their rendition would require a library of books to do justice to. Here we can only gain a glimpse of the reprehensible treatment dished out to surrendered Allied soldiers. In April 1942, one month after the Allies had surrendered Java in the Netherlands East Indies to the Japanese, 2,600 British, Australian and American prisoners were marched to Bandoeng to a former Dutch barracks complex for Indonesian colonial troops. The camp was soon known as Bicycle Camp, as the original troops it had been built to house had been military cyclists. The soldier POWs were soon joined by the bedraggled Australian and American survivors from the cruisers HMAS *Perth* and USS *Houston*, numbering around 500 officers and ratings in an appalling condition of neglect. The naval prisoners marched slowly and painfully into Bicycle Camp, covered by Japanese guards toting their long rifles and fixed bayonets, as the military POWs silently watched the tragic procession. Most of the shipwrecked POWs had lost most of their clothing, and many could only walk with the assistance of their comrades. Since being taken prisoner by the Kempeitai the seamen had been denied any medical attention, with the result that over eighty per cent of the POWs shuffling painfully into Bicycle Camp were ridden with either malaria or dysentery, some with both.

The unfortunate Australian and American sailors had been herded by army guards into the town of Serang when they had first been captured, accompanied by Australian troops who had surrendered on Java, some Australian and British soldiers who had managed to escape from Singapore before the end, and many Dutch civilians with children in tow. The Japanese had placed them all inside a cinema, and their guards had refused all medical aid to those who were injured. 'At night they had to lie on top of each other in the stink of festering wounds. The latrine was an open pit outside, with flies rising off it in huge clouds, making a blaring noise like a brass band.'[2] The senior officers among the prisoners were taken away, and then the rest of them were herded into the town jail, packed tightly into cells by the Kempeitai. The sailors were again denied medical care, systemically starved and given little water until in April they were transported as pitiable, diseased wrecks to Bicycle Camp.

One of the greatest crimes overseen by the Kempeitai was the shipment of Allied prisoners around the vast Japanese labour camp system. It was Tojo himself, the former Kempeitai general, who had exhorted camp commandants not to allow prisoners to lie idle, but to use their labour and their skills for the Japanese war effort, in direct violation of the 1907 Hague Convention (ratified by Japan) and the 1929 Geneva Convention (which the Japanese government had signed but not ratified). As the war turned inexorably against Japan after the Imperial Navy's defeat at the Battle of Midway in June 1942, prisoner labour became ever more important to the Japanese economy. Japanese soldiers in the occupied territories feared being cut off from the sacred Home Islands, and all Japanese knew that those Home Islands were particularly vulnerable to a naval blockade. Keeping the empire's defensive perimeter intact was every Japanese soldier's duty. General Douglas MacArthur's strategy was aimed at effecting amphibious landings in the Philippines as soon as possible. The Japanese defence was based upon the Imperial Navy's Combined Fleet based at Truk, a central position from which it could move to plug any gaps in the front line. Three enormous air bases, at Rabaul, Saipan and Taiwan, protected the east, south and west from penetration. A ring of islands had been heavily fortified and garrisoned to provide the Japanese with a thick defensive barrier and protect these vital bases.

By June 1943 MacArthur, supported by Admiral 'Bull' Halsey's Third Fleet, 1,800 aircraft and seven divisions of troops, advanced on Rabaul. Admiral Chester W. Nimitz, commanding the huge Pacific Fleet, fanned out across the Central Pacific towards Saipan and Taiwan. The Americans and Australians overcame fierce Japanese resistance at some of the outlying defensive positions protecting the inner empire. But many of these heavily defended islands were simply bypassed by the Americans, keen to preserve their fighting men for the bigger prize of the Philippines, and eventually Japan. The bypassed islands were left to 'wither on the vine', in the words of Nimitz. The Japanese, because of the extremely effective American submarine blockade of the Home Islands, could no longer supply their troops once the Americans had leapfrogged past the first line of defence, and so these islands were effectively neutralized. Once certain key areas of the Philippines had been recaptured, American strategy was divided on either attacking Taiwan or Okinawa, both operations bringing America one step closer to launching a full-scale invasion of southern Japan and ending the war. The British, meeting stiff resistance on the Burmese border, were isolated from the main theatre of operations and they were unable to really influence American strategic planning or choice of goals. This meant that for tens of thousands of British POWs slaving for the Japanese in Thailand, Malaya, NEI and Borneo there would be no military conquest by Allied forces to liberate them, and their eventual freedom was entirely dependent upon the successful defeat of Japan by the United States.

When MacArthur waded ashore from a landing craft on the island of Leyte in the Philippines on 20 October 1944 and declared, 'I have returned', the Japanese empire was effectively cut in half, with the government in Tokyo only exercising real control over those territories north of the Philippines, such as occupied China, Burma, Korea, Manchuria, Hong Kong and the Home Islands. The American naval blockade and position of American forces in the Philippines meant that the massive Japanese forces in the NEI, Malaya, Borneo and French Indochina were no longer being supplied or reinforced from the motherland. They remained in control of cowed civilian populations but were bypassed by events closer to Japan. The bulk of British POWs remained in these locations.

As the Americans struck ever closer to the Home Islands, the Japanese responded by gathering up their white slaves and transporting them further north. If evacuation was not an option the Japanese often killed all of their remaining prisoners to prevent their liberation by Allied forces, as we will see later at Sandakan in Borneo. The Japanese moved prisoners around their vast empire on rusting merchant ships, crammed like slaves on the Middle Passage in fetid, dark and often airless holds or left on deck through extremes of weather and temperature. The upshot of taking men whose health had already been broken by back-breaking labour and starvation on land out to sea was a gigantic humanitarian disaster. Over 50,000 Allied prisoners were transported in this way.

The real killer was not the Japanese but the American submarine blockade of Japan. The Japanese refused to mark ships that were carrying prisoners, and so submarine skippers could not tell the difference between a rusty tramp steamer loaded with ammunition and a rusty tramp steamer loaded with Allied servicemen. When these ships were torpedoed and sank the Japanese often deliberately kept Allied prisoners locked in the holds to drown them, or if they managed to get into the ocean Japanese sailors would machine gun floating prisoners or simply refuse to rescue them. Examples of the horrific body count when 'Hellships' were sunk are many: the *Montevideo Maru* sailed from Rabaul in July 1942 loaded with over 1,000 Australian POWs and civilian internees crammed like sardines into her holds. The ship was torpedoed and sunk by an American submarine off Luzon in the Philippines. None of the prisoners survived.

In the occupied British colony of Hong Kong, which had fallen to the Japanese on Christmas Day 1941, 1,816 British and Commonwealth POWs were loaded aboard the *Lisbon Maru* for transportation as slaves to Japan. Packed into the ship's three holds, insufficient room was left for all of the men to lie down at the same time, so each unit worked out a rota to allow the men to rest during the journey. In No. 1 hold below the forecastle was a contingent of Royal Navy prisoners from the destroyer HMS *Thracian* and assorted gunboats that had helped defend Hong Kong and elements of the Royal Scots and the Middlesex Regiment.[3] Hold No. 2 contained some small units and was located just aft of the bridge, while hold No. 3 held officers and men of the Royal Artillery. The voyage began with reasonable conditions. There was plenty of water and the men were allowed on to the deck to queue for the latrines, but there were no washing facilities. Also embarked aboard the ship were 2,000 Japanese soldiers travelling back home. A junior officer, Lieutenant Wado, was nominally in charge of the guards, but real power was exercised by 'Shat in Pants' Nimori, senior translator in

Hong Kong appointed by the Kempeitai. Nimori was 'at all times brutal and callous' according to a witness.[4]

The ship was struck by an American torpedo at 7am on 1 October, the weapon exploding in a coal bunker. The *Lisbon Maru*'s engines stopped immediately and all the lights went out. The few POWs who were on deck waiting to use the latrines were ordered below, and extra sentries were posted on the hatches to prevent any POWs coming topside. Nimori ordered that the hatches be battened down. Tarpaulins were placed over the hatch covers and secured with rope. The intention was to trap all 1,800 POWs in the holds when the ship went down, drowning them. Lieutenant-Colonel Henry Stewart, the senior British officer present and commanding officer of the Middlesex Regiment, appealed several times to Nimori to at least leave some part of the hatches open. Stewart shouted that men were dying of suffocation and the water supply was exhausted. Nimori ignored his requests until 4am the next morning when, for the sick amusement of himself and the guards, he had a bucket full of urine passed down into Stewart's hatch. Nimori also shouted down into the hold, 'You have nothing to worry about, you are bred like rats, and so can stay like rats.'[5]

Inside the holds many of the men were ill with dysentery and diarrhoea; repeated requests to visit the latrines were refused and no alternative toilet facilities were provided so the holds soon became even more hellish chambers of torture. No. 3 hold was also flooding, and the POWs were required to man the pumps in appalling heat, which also led to several deaths. During the night most of the Japanese troops were taken off the *Lisbon Maru* to safety, and the foundering vessel taken in tow. Colonel Stewart and some of the other officers and men were preparing to break out of their hold when the ship suddenly stopped dead. Lieutenants Howell and Potter, together with the POW interpreter and several others, made a small opening in the hatch and climbed onto the deck. 'As they were walking towards the bridge to request an interview with the ship's captain they were fired upon by the Japanese guards. Howell was hit and subsequently died of his wounds.'[6] Japanese guards ran to the small opening and fired several shots into the hold, wounding two more British officers. The ship then gave a sudden lurch and began to settle rapidly by the stern, water pouring into No. 2 hold through the hatch. Lieutenant G.C. Hamilton, Royal Scots, recalled of those terrifying moments: 'As soon as the ship settled the men stationed at the hatch cut the ropes and the canvas tarpaulin, and forced away the baulks of timber, and the prisoners from my hold formed into queues and climbed out in perfect order.'[7] As soon as the POWs appeared on deck the Japanese opened fire on them, forcing the prisoners to dive over the ship's rail into the sea. The Japanese continued to fire at the men swimming in the water. 'About three miles away I could see some islands and a swift current was running in their direction,' recalled Hamilton. 'Four Japanese ships were standing by, but they appeared to be as inhospitable as the rocky islands for they showed no signs of wanting to pick up any of us.'[8] When desperate POWs attempted to climb ropes dangling from these vessels' sides, they were 'kicked back into the sea.'

Eventually the Japanese changed their minds about leaving the POWs to perish by drowning or to be eaten by sharks, and the ships began to pick them up. Some managed to make it alone to the islands Hamilton had seen in the distance, where six of them, with the help of local Chinese, managed to escape from the clutches of the Japanese. The rest, although cared for by the locals, were later rounded up by Japanese Naval Landing Parties. On 4 October the survivors were assembled at the docks in Shanghai. A total of 970 men were present, 840 had died when ample time had existed to have saved all of them. Six were free. None of this gave 'Shat in Pants' any pleasure, and he made sure that the survivors were severely punished for having the audacity still to be alive. Addressing the assembled prisoners, Nimori told them: 'You should have gone with the others.'[9] The POWs, many sick and all exhausted, were ordered to remain standing from noon on 4 October until 8am on the 5th. Anyone who sat down or fell down was beaten, 'Shat in Pants' taking the lead by beating prisoners with his sheathed sword, and encouraging the guards to go in with rifle butts and boots. On 5 October the prisoners were ordered to embark on another transport, the *Shinsei Maru*, to continue their nightmare journey to Japan. As a final indignity 'Shat in Pants' ordered that they would travel naked, and the POWs were told to remove their uniforms. One Regimental Sergeant-Major who refused was savagely kicked in the testicles.

According to conservative Japanese figures nearly 11,000 Allied prisoners perished at sea. One transport which sank loaded with

Americans claimed more prisoners' lives than all those murdered on the Bataan Death March in 1942. As the war progressed conditions on these 'Hell Ships' continued to deteriorate, the Japanese seemingly undecided between preserving the prisoners for their labour and deliberately killing as many as possible for sport.

In the occupied NEI dozens of prison camps existed, packed with Dutch, British and Australian soldiers. When Allied aircraft raided the island of Ambon in September 1944, severely damaging the main settlement, the Japanese panicked, fearing an invasion, and decided to ship most of their prisoners out to Java. For the previous fifteen months British and Dutch prisoners had laboured in hellish conditions on Ambon and most were diseased, suffering from malnutrition and near the end of their endurance when Lieutenant-Colonel Anami, commanding the local gulag system, ordered 500 aboard a small steamer named the *Maros Maru* on 17 September. On the morning of the move the 500 men, most barely clothed and barefoot, struggled through a tropical rainstorm that turned the dusty road to thick mud, and trudged dejectedly towards barges prepared to ferry them across to a small, rusting ship. The senior officer present, Flight Lieutenant W.M. Blackwood of the Royal Air Force, recalled the journey. 'With guards harassing us to hurry, the beri-beri crippled being pushed and bullied, and the stretcher bearers being goaded into a shambling trot, we made the jetty in about half an hour.'[10]

The Japanese left the prisoners, including the sick, sitting in the mud under the cold rain for three hours until they were ferried across to the *Maros Maru*. 'When we drew alongside I could scarcely believe that all five hundred of us were expected to get aboard,' recalled Blackwood. 'When I realized that the holds were full and battened down, and we were to travel as deck passengers, I was staggered.'[11] The overcrowding reminded Blackwood of a London tube train at rush hour. The sick suffered the worst as there was no place for them to lie down. 'Picture a small ferry boat, with a maximum beam of not more than thirty feet, and a space of about forty-five feet from the after bulkhead of the forecastle to just abaft amidships, available for our whole party.'[12] Once out to sea rough weather that night sent waves breaking across the decks, killing one man. Worse was to follow. 'Day after day, men who were grievously ill lay on the hatch cover fully exposed to the pitiless sun,'[13] wrote Blackwood. The young officer made repeated requests to the Japanese for an awning to be erected to protect the sickest from the effects of the blinding sun, but the Japanese only relented after thirty men had died. Drinking water was strictly rationed at about half a pint per man per day, but the prisoners were forced to watch while their Korean guards washed in the drinking water, laughing heartily at the terrible looks of despair in the prisoners' eyes. One day one of the prisoners fell overboard while trying to use one of the two wooden boxes that had been hung over the ship's sides as rudimentary latrines. The *Maros Maru* put about and rescued the man but the Japanese guard commander, Lieutenant Kurishima, ordered all Dutch and British officers to parade before him and had them lashed with a rope for not keeping control of their men. On 21 September the *Maros Maru* arrived at Raka Moena on the Celebes Island. A Japanese junk puttered along beside them crammed with another 150 mostly naked and sick British and Dutch prisoners led by Captain van der Loot, and amid much shouting and blows from rifle butts the fresh slaves were herded onto the already overcrowded ferry.

Once more the *Maros Maru* headed back to sea and the suffering of the prisoners increased. 'All the men lay spread out on the uneven bundles of firewood blistering horribly in the tropical sun,' recalled Blackwood. 'Tongues began to blacken, raw shirtless shoulders to bleed, and all vestiges of sanity deserted many.'[14] Blackwood recalled that one young British soldier, 'delirious with sunstroke, shouted the thoughts of his disordered mind for thirty hours before he became too weak to utter another word. Just before he died he grabbed a full tin, that was being used as a bed-pan, and drank the contents greedily, thinking it was water'[15] The death rate averaged eight each day. When the old ship's engines broke down the Japanese ordered a Royal Navy petty officer and two other men to take charge below. They reached Macassar, where the remaining fit prisoners were used to unload some of the ship's cargo. Then the *Maros Maru* rode at anchor for forty days, the prisoners remaining aboard her. A total of 159 perished while the ship remained stationary. Then the vessel steamed a short distance and lay off a small island near Macassar for another forty days, the total number of deaths reaching 250 by the time the *Maros Maru* slowly moved off towards Surabaya in Java. There had been 630 prisoners loaded aboard her in total, but by the time the ship arrived at Java only 325 were still alive, and 'most of them were mere ghosts of their former selves, half starved, half demented wrecks of humanity, diseased, dirty and crawling with vermin.'[16] The voyage of the *Maros Maru* was by no means unique, but fairly representative of the conditions the Japanese created aboard their slave ships.

On land the situation was just as dire. When the *Maros Maru* called at the island of Macassar in the Netherlands East Indies there was a prison camp located inland that was grossly overcrowded with British and Dutch soldiers. Although the war was clearly winding down by late 1944, the regime of terrorization and labour continued to be strictly enforced throughout the Japanese gulag.

On the big island of Sumatra south-west of Singapore the Japanese decided during the last year of the war to construct a railway line to transport coal and troops. In a replay of the infamous Burma-Thailand 'Railway of Death' but on a smaller scale, the Japanese shipped in thousands of prisoners, most of whom died when their transport ships were sunk by American submarines. Utilizing the remaining prisoner labour available on Sumatra, 5,000 British and Dutch servicemen were pressed into service alongside 30,000 coolies to construct the railway. The death rate among the white soldiers was 12 per cent, while that of the coolie labour was a staggering 80 per cent. The railway was finished, but never used.

In the end it became a numbers game for Allied prisoners – calorific intake and quantity of rations versus the remaining months of the war. All too often a mountain of corpses was the result. In North Borneo the Japanese had shipped in 1,496 Australian soldiers taken prisoner in Singapore in February 1942. They had been housed at Eight Mile Camp and brutally treated. Any prisoner who disobeyed the rules was severely punished, and some were transported to Outram Road Jail in Singapore where they were extensively tortured by the Kempeitai. As related in Chapter 2, Lieutenant Rod Wells, a 23-year-old Australian prisoner, was discovered with radio parts and sent to Outram Road from Sandakan in 1943. This was where his experiences at the hands of the Kempeitai left him disabled after a Japanese hammered a meat skewer through his ear drum.

The prisoners at Eight Mile Camp were needed to construct an airfield for the Japanese. Conditions at the camp steadily deteriorated throughout 1943 and 1944. By the beginning of 1945 the daily ration for each prisoner had been reduced to a small quantity of tapioca and sweet potatoes, a few greens and four ounces of rice. Incredibly, the Japanese demand for working parties had increased as soon as the Allied fight-back had begun to make progress.

Notes

1. Raymond Lamont-Brown, *Kempeitai: Japan's Dreaded Military Police* (Stroud, Sutton Publishing, 1998), p. 125.
2. Gavan Daws, *Prisoners of the Japanese: POWs of the Second World War* (London, Pocket Books, 1994), p. 59.
3. Commodore Alfred Collinson had few naval assets remaining in Hong Kong when the Japanese invasion began. There was one destroyer, HMS *Thracian* that was later run aground and recovered by the Japanese, five former Yangtze River gunboats (HMS *Tern, Robin, Cicala, Moth*, and *Redstart*) and eight Motor Torpedo Boats (MTBs). Most were sunk or scuttled during the battle, where they acted as anti-aircraft platforms.
4. Lord Russell of Liverpool, *The Knights of Bushido: A Short History of Japanese War Crimes* (London, Greenhill Books, 2002), p. 122.
5. Ibid: p. 126.
6. Ibid: p. 123.
7. Ibid: p. 124.
8. Ibid: p. 124.
9. Ibid: p. 125.
10. Ibid: p. 130.
11. Ibid: p. 130.
12. Ibid: p. 130.
13. Ibid: p. 131.
14. Ibid: p. 132.
15. Ibid: p. 133.
16. Ibid: p. 134.

Chapter Four

Bridge House

Who would be next on the Kempetai [sic] list? The honeymoon period was over. The Japanese were showing their teeth and, from their record of cruelty in China, we knew that many of us were going to suffer indescribable ill-treatment.

British journalist Ralph Shaw, Shanghai 1942

Screams loud enough to curdle the blood could be heard emanating from the floor above. Grimy white faces stared horror-struck at the ceiling as they squatted in their own filth inside an overcrowded and poorly lit cell. The sounds of violence and raised voices above went on and on for hour after hour, testing the nerves and the courage of the white people shivering inside their ragged cotton uniforms. Occasionally, hard footfalls could be heard along the corridor outside their cell, followed by the jangling of keys in a lock and a stream of guttural Japanese orders. The sounds of hard slaps and pitiful pleas for mercy from exhausted prisoners were followed by the noise of someone being dragged along the corridor between two grunting soldiers, whimpering gently in resignation of what was to follow. Another unfortunate had been taken from their cell for torture.

The Japanese had only been in complete control of Shanghai for less than two months, but already their Kempeitai detention centres were crammed with those they considered threats to their total rule. Journalists, businessmen, former policemen and the old taipans of pre-war Shanghai filled the cells. Among these unfortunates was

Britain's fledgling sabotage and intelligence-gathering organization in Shanghai, whose members now huddled together in stark terror at what awaited them at the hands of Kempeitai interrogators.

Pre-war Shanghai had been a hotbed of espionage activity involving many different European and Asian nations, and the Japanese had for some months been monitoring British and American intelligence operatives within the city, at least those they had identified or suspected. When Winston Churchill had ordered the formation of a new sabotage organization with orders to 'Set Europe ablaze!' after the Dunkirk evacuations in 1940, Special Operations Executive (SOE) had been born. The group's task was straightforward – to link up with resistance organizations inside Europe and carry out acts of subversion and sabotage against the Germans. SOE was placed under the auspices of the Minister for Economic Warfare, Hugh Dalton, and it was quite separate from Britain's existing pre-war intelligence departments. These were the Security Service or MI5 and the Secret Intelligence Service or MI6. The 'MI' stands for 'Military Intelligence', and today MI5 is tasked with dealing with intelligence threats inside the United Kingdom, whereas MI6 operates abroad. SOE was something new and untested, designed specifically for the war, and viewed with great suspicion by the established intelligence organizations and their leaders.

As the clouds of war began to gather in the Far East in late 1940 Dalton was asked to create an SOE section for the Orient. SOE had experienced great difficulties in establishing operations in German-controlled France and decided to act quickly in creating a similar organization on the ground in the Far East *before* an expected Japanese takeover became a reality. The SOE branch in the Far East was named the Oriental Mission (OM), and A.E. Jones was dispatched to Singapore in January 1941 and charged with establishing a headquarters and a regional organization. Jones was ordered to appoint a 'No. 1' in Shanghai who would be responsible for all of northern China, an area of great economic importance to Britain at the time. Unfortunately, OM was to prove an extremely amateurish organization that completely underestimated the abilities of the Kempeitai, which was already operating throughout the city since the Japanese had occupied all of Shanghai except the International Settlement and French Concession following the Japanese invasion of China in 1937. Even within the International Settlement, dominated by the British and Americans, the Kempeitai was running an efficient intelligence-gathering network on its potential enemies, operating from the Japanese concession located across Suzhou Creek in Hongkou.

In May 1941 a permanent head of OM was appointed and Jones became the organization's second-in-command. SOE chose as head a man well known among the international business community in Shanghai, a former vice-chairman of Imperial Chemical Industries (ICI) and a former member of the exclusive Shanghai Municipal Council, Valentine Killery. Killery assumed the codename 'O.100' and set up his office in Singapore. He was commissioned a lieutenant colonel in the army and he created Special Training School (STS) 101, although perhaps its former name sums up its real purpose – the School of Demolitions.[1] The two star instructors in unorthodox warfare at the school were pre-war adventurer and mountaineer Major Freddy Spencer-Chapman and Royal Marine Colonel Alan 'Cocky' Warren. They worked hard to create stay-behind parties of demolition and ambush specialists in Malaya, should the Japanese succeed in capturing the peninsula.

Killery faced several challenges in making OM work, not the least of which was his complete lack of experience in espionage work and his inability to make straightforward decisions. MI6 operated its own agents throughout Asia, and along with the British diplomatic community remained very wary of Killery's collection of amateur spies, adventurers and saboteurs. Despite these problems Killery organized a skeleton OM organization in Shanghai, and his knowledge of the local expatriate business community led him to recruit his agents from among his old contemporaries at the Shanghai Club and other social institutions of the British merchant elite. These men were very different from the young, tough and energetic soldiers being put through STS 101 in Singapore. W.J. Gande, a wholesale liquor merchant, was appointed 'No. 1' in Shanghai, assuming the codename 'O.5000'. The 55-year-old Gande in turn recruited four other middle-aged British expats as agents from the business and social world of the International Settlement who would create an espionage and sabotage network ahead of an expected Japanese takeover of the settlement in the near future. The agents were Joseph Brister, a 56-year-old manager at Ilbert & Co.; George Jack, manager of the Confederation Life Insurance Company, aged 55; John Brand, a local businessman aged 52, and Sydney Riggs, a surveyor aged 49. Two other prominent Britons became OM associates; 41-year-old stockbroker Edward Elias and 65-year-old former deputy commissioner of the Shanghai Municipal Police and president of the Shanghai St. Patrick's Society, W.G. Clarke.

All seven OM operatives in Shanghai were completely loyal to the Crown and undeniably brave, but none of them were trained espionage agents, and their lack of tradecraft proved their undoing. The amateur nature of the organization was further demonstrated by the fact that all of these men would attract the attention of the Kempeitai as soon as the Japanese captured the International Settlement, as all were prominent enemy personages, and would undoubtedly be swiftly interned as the Kempeitai relieved them of their business assets and liberty to move about the city. How useful these men would have proved to SOE stuck inside an internment camp was anyone's guess.

For the time being Japan was a threat, but not a real enemy. Inside Shanghai were considerable numbers of German and Italian business, military and naval assets, and SOE intended to use the middle-aged gentlemen of OM to strike a blow for Britain against the Axis Powers. OM Shanghai had been issued with four main objectives by Killery in Singapore, the second of which read: 'Organize sabotage of enemy interests, such as shipping, enemy goods, wireless broadcast propaganda etc.'[2] Gande was determined to conduct sabotage attacks against German and Italian military targets in Shanghai, but his plans were frustrated by interference from MI6. The Foreign Office pointed out that the International Settlement was neutral territory, after Whitehall had been tipped off by MI6's agent in Shanghai of OM's intentions. The British government was still actively appeasing the Japanese while its full attention was on stopping Hitler and Mussolini in Europe and North Africa, and Britain, as the largest and most influential 'treaty power' in the port city of Shanghai since it was first forced open to international trade after the Opium War in 1842, stood to lose a lot if she broke that neutrality.

One particular OM scheme caused MI6 and the Foreign Office to stymie OM plans. The Royal Italian Navy had four vessels moored on the Huangpu River in Shanghai in 1941, the gunboats *Carlotto* and *Lepanto*, the liner *Conte Verde* and the subject of OM's interest, the colonial sloop *Eritrea* that had recently arrived from Kobe after the Japanese had refused to allow her captain to begin intercepting Allied convoys in the North Pacific.[3] The Foreign Office thought that if OM Shanghai somehow managed to damage or sink the *Eritrea*, which was under Japanese protection, this would have provided the Japanese with the excuse they desired to complete their takeover of the International Settlement. 'We have very large interests there and no means of protecting them,' wrote the Foreign Office to OM headquarters in Singapore in reference to Shanghai. '[It] would therefore be rash for us to disturb the virtual truce now existing in the International Settlement, which though Chinese soil, has always enjoyed a quasi-neutral status.'[4] The *Eritrea* remained, along with the other Italian vessels, safely moored on the Huangpu River until the Italian armistice in September 1943, when Italy changed sides. The *Eritrea* dashed successfully to Colombo in Sri Lanka and surrendered to the British, while the captains of the other Italian vessels scuttled their ships in mid-channel and went into Japanese prisoner-of-war camps in Shanghai for the duration. Neutrality did not necessarily hinder the British effort against the Axis later in the war. Perhaps the most famous example of a raid instigated by British Intelligence and utilizing middle-aged amateurs was an attack on interned German merchant ships in Goa harbour in Portuguese India in March 1943. Retired officers of the Calcutta Light Horse club in India purloined an old tramp steamer, which they sailed around the subcontinent to Bombay, before launching a daring raid into Mormugao harbour in Goa, boarding the German merchantman *Erhrenfels* and then sinking her with scuttling charges. The destruction of the *Erhrenfels* encouraged three other German skippers to scuttle their vessels, fearing that a full-scale British commando attack was underway. The Germans had been transmitting Allied ship movements to U-boats operating in the Indian Ocean, and the British had been forced to engage middle-aged 'volunteers' to conduct the raid so that the government would not be charged with violating Portuguese neutrality. Before the raid U-boats had sunk twelve Allied ships in the Indian Ocean during March 1943. After the raid only one ship was lost for the rest of the month. It was an event later immortalized in the 1980 movie *The Sea Wolves*.

No such successes would be achieved by OM Shanghai. It was realized by SOE that Gande and his men did not know the first thing about sabotage, and when the Japanese took over the International Settlement and joined the Axis, issues of neutrality would be history. With this in mind in August 1941 John Brand travelled to Singapore to receive explosives and sabotage training at STS 101, and Gande was given £5,000 sterling as a working budget for OM Shanghai. Incredibly, the money was remitted through the Hong Kong & Shanghai Bank on the Bund, and when the Japanese came to liquidate HSBC after their takeover of the city the entry was discovered in a book and the Kempeitai duly informed. It was an astounding blunder and indicative of the well-meaning but amateur nature of Allied intelligence operations in the city.

For several weeks prior to the Japanese takeover the Kempeitai had gained information about OM Shanghai. The Kempeitai knew it was an intelligence organization linked to the British Ministry for Economic Warfare, and this information had come to them through another elementary mistake made by an OM member. Gande kept certain secret files relating to his organization in his safe in his work office, and other employees also had access to that safe. One, a Romanian national, stole several of these files after recognizing their value and sold them to the Kempeitai. The Kempeitai then covertly organized the tapping of Gande's telephone and recorded all of his conversations with his superiors and his agents.

The war came to Shanghai in the early hours of 8 December 1941, about the time Japanese carrier planes were heading in towards the slumbering US Pacific Fleet at Pearl Harbor across the International Date Line in Hawaii. Thousands of Japanese troops had long since been massed throughout the Chinese sectors of the city under their control since 1937, and the International Settlement was militarily indefensible. The only military resource the Allied nations had available in Shanghai that cold winter's morning was the Shanghai Volunteer Corps (SVC), a part-time army unit that had first been created in 1854 and was composed of many different nationalities but modelled on the British Army and commanded by a seconded British colonel. The SVC wisely chose not to fully mobilize and later its members stacked their arms and returned to their homes.

On the Huangpu River the might of the Royal Navy was represented by a single British gunboat, HMS *Peterel*. Moored close by was an American gunboat, the USS *Wake*. Both vessels' main guns had been immobilized and the crews reduced to a skeleton. Together they represented the only remaining Allied military forces in China apart from the US North China Marines who were scattered as guards at the various American diplomatic missions up-country.

The *Wake* was swiftly boarded and taken by Japanese troops without a shot being fired, but the British provided the Japanese with the only resistance in an otherwise bloodless occupation of the Settlement. The British Consulate at the north end of the Bund telephoned the *Peterel*'s skipper and informed him that a state of war now existed between His Majesty's Government and Japan. The young commanding officer, a plucky New Zealander serving in the Royal Naval Reserve, Lieutenant Commander Stephen Polkinghorn, ordered his two dozen remaining sailors to 'action stations'. Machine guns were manned before a launch arrived containing several Japanese military officers. The Japanese came aboard and informed Polkinghorn that he must surrender his vessel immediately or face being blown out of the water. Across the river the old Japanese cruiser *Idzumo* and a gunboat had menacingly levelled their main armament directly at the small British vessel. Polkinghorn looked the Japanese squarely in the face and bellowed, 'Get off my bloody ship!' The astonished Japanese did leave, but within minutes a furious barrage of high explosive shells slammed into the waters around the little British gunboat as desperate ratings triggered long streams of bullets impotently from their puny machine guns at the great grey Japanese warship. Within a few minutes the *Peterel* had been struck several times and some of the crew were dead or wounded. Polkinghorn, naval honour having been served by his brief stand, gave the order to abandon ship as the burning gunboat began to list dramatically. The men leapt clear of the hull as the *Peterel* rolled over in the river and they began swimming furiously towards Chinese sampans and junks nearby whose crews had watched the one-sided battle with open mouths. Some of the British sailors made it to the safety of a nearby Norwegian merchant ship, but within the hour Japanese sailors had rounded up all those who were still alive at bayonet point and herded them towards imprisonment. One member of the crew of the *Peterel* managed to avoid capture. A petty officer radio operator, he had been ashore at the time of the assault and he immediately went underground, working with the Chinese resistance in the city throughout the rest of the war under the alias 'Mr. Trees'. The Kempeitai hunted him for years but they never came close to snatching him from his hiding places.

The relatively bloodless takeover by the Japanese of the International Settlement appeared to bode well for the white population of the city. Most remained at their businesses and living in their houses, for the time being. However, the Japanese ordered a census of the 'foreign' population to be taken within days of the occupation so that the Kempeitai would have a clear picture of the numbers of foreigners now under their control, and more importantly, recorded their names, addresses and nationalities. Similar censuses were also conducted in the Chinese Municipality and by the collaborationist Vichy authorities in the French Concession. The censuses revealed that the largest non-Chinese group in Shanghai was the Japanese, followed by stateless White Russian immigrants and European Jews who had fled the Nazis. There were over 6,000 British citizens in Shanghai and about 1,300 Americans.

The census enabled the Kempeitai to begin arresting members of OM Shanghai, beginning with 65-year-old W.G. Clarke, the former senior policeman and the oldest and most physically vulnerable of the group. Clarke was dragged from his bed in the early hours of 17 December by plainclothes Kempeitai soldiers and bundled into a car. Driven over Suzhou Creek to Bridge House, used by the Kempeitai as their main interrogation centre in Shanghai, Clarke was thoroughly worked over at the instigation of Lieutenant Yamamoto who was investigating the OM case. Bridge House was an eight-storey white apartment one block north of Garden Bridge (now Waibaidu Bridge) that spanned Suzhou Creek. 'Once arrested, a prisoner was issued a cotton gown and trousers and put into a windowless cell with as many as thirty other prisoners,' writes Stella Dong in *Shanghai: The Rise and Fall of a Decadent City.* 'Men and women, foreigners and Chinese, were indiscriminately crowded into a space so confined that everyone had to sit with knees drawn up on the filthy concrete floor.'[5] The Kempeitai made sure that conditions inside Bridge House were as unpleasant as possible for inmates. Aside from fearsome interrogations, 'rats and disease-infested lice were everywhere, and no one was allowed to bathe or shower, so diseases from dysentery to typhus to leprosy ran rampant.'[6]

It has been assumed that OM Shanghai operative Clarke quickly broke under Kempeitai torture and filled in the blanks for the Japanese regarding the rest of the British organization. He was thrown into a bare cell with American journalist John B. Powell, who had also been extensively tortured, and the former Shanghai policeman was in a bad way. According to Powell, Clarke was pushed 'into the corner alongside me, and I saw he was in severe pain. He was suffering from several boils on his neck; they had become so infected and swollen, because of lack of medical attention, that his head was pressed over against his shoulder.'[7] Powell was one of many foreign journalists who had been living and working in Shanghai for years. Almost all were trenchantly opposed to Japanese foreign policy, and they had on many occasions published articles highlighting Japanese atrocities, particularly since the invasion of China in 1937. This made them obvious targets for Japanese retribution, and the Kempeitai took a special delight in destroying the lives of these brave men. According to the *North China Daily News* reporter Ralph Shaw the 'Kempetai [sic] torturers wreaked their vengeance on the brave American [Powell] and subjected him to atrocious assaults, beating him unmercifully.' These beatings included 'kicking, usually in the genital region, beating – anything connected with physical suffering.'[8]

Powell was the editor of the *China Weekly Review* and he was imprisoned and tortured alongside fellow countryman Victor Keen of the *New York Herald Tribune*. 'When the questioning began, they [the prisoners] had to remove all their clothing and kneel before their captors. When their answers failed to satisfy their interrogators, the victims were beaten on the back and legs with four-foot bamboo sticks until blood flowed.'[9] If beating proved ineffective, other more invasive tortures were used, such as the water treatment, electric shocks or suspension.

Another British journalist named Healey who ran the XMHA radio station, was subjected 'to treatment which plumbed the depths of human depravity,' according to his friend Ralph Shaw. 'He went insane and died bloodied and crippled in his rat-hole of a cell in the Bridge House.'[10] The greatest prize for the Kempeitai was a British writer and journalist named H.G.W. Woodhead, editor of

Oriental Affairs and weekly columnist in the *Shanghai Evening Post and Mercury* who had spent years denouncing Japanese militarism in China. Woodhead had also widely broadcast twice weekly a strong anti-Japanese message on Shanghai's XMHC and XCDN radio stations at the direct behest of the British government. On 5 December 1941 the nervous British Consulate had advised Woodhead to leave Shanghai as quickly as possible, and the harried journalist had booked passage on a Panamanian ship scheduled to sail four days later. This delay meant that Woodhead was still in Shanghai the day the Japanese walked in. He took refuge in a friend's house in the French Concession, but eventually emerged and registered as an enemy alien, as all British, American, Free French, Dutch, Norwegian, Greek and other nationals were required to do by the Japanese. For the time being the Kempeitai left Woodhead alone, but that was about to change.

Yamamoto now had sufficient information to pick up OM Shanghai's Gande, Brister and Jack on 27 December 1941, and these men were also tortured extensively at Bridge House. Information forthcoming from these interrogations led to the arrests of Brand and Elias on 13 January 1942 and Riggs on 5 February. In the meantime, Powell had managed to get the broken Clarke sent to the Municipal Hospital where he was properly treated and his life saved. The interrogations were brutal. Riggs recalled that they 'were carried out under hideous conditions' inside the rat-infested Bridge House, and that 'such a thing as a bath or a shave was unheard of and when dragged from cells and bombarded with questions hour after hour with a very lowered condition of health due to under-nourishment and squalid living conditions is an ordeal which to me to-day seems but a bad nightmare.'[11]

For weeks on end prisoners at Bridge House were systematically starved, physically and mentally abused and denied the right to wash or receive medical treatment. Most emerged covered from head to foot in lice and infected rat bites, wearing torn and filthy clothes, and with long dirty hair and beards. American journalist John Powell, who was extensively tortured at Bridge House alongside the OM agents, was crippled. He was 'a permanent invalid, [and] was later shipped home to the United States aboard a repatriation vessel ... Gangrene set in and Powell had part of a leg amputated. He never recovered and died shortly later.'[12] Women suspects were treated as badly as the men who were tortured. One Russian woman 'suffered degrading indignities which included the insertion of sharp objects in her vagina, violent electric shocks applied through her nipples, the pulling out of her finger- and toe-nails and blows which had broken her jaw.'[13]

British Consular staff were not immune from abuse at the hands of the Kempeitai, even though in time of war diplomatic niceties meant that consular staff were repatriated at the earliest opportunity. In Tokyo, the British ambassador, Sir Robert Craigie, and his twenty staff had been subject to close Kempeitai surveillance since the late 1930s. In the ramp-up to war a wave of anti-British propaganda had appeared throughout the city that tried to show that all British living and working in Japan were spies. Posters appeared showing a foreigner dressed in Sherlock Holmes costume, with a pipe and deerstalker hat.

The Kempeitai had first murdered a British subject in 1940. It was a messy affair that had done much to sour British-Japan relations and demonstrated to Craigie and other foreigners living in Japan that the rule of law no longer applied. Melville 'Jimmy' Cox was a 40-year-old Reuters News correspondent in Tokyo. He and his wife had adopted two Japanese orphans, and Cox was a popular member of the city's foreign press corps. On 27 July 1940 the Kempeitai arrested Cox and charged him with espionage. Cox had been singled out by the Kempeitai as harbouring anti-Japanese sentiments after he had repeatedly asked awkward questions at Japanese government press conferences. Someone powerful within the Japanese government decided to silence Cox permanently. He was taken to the Tokyo Kempeitai headquarters located beside the Imperial Palace moat and subjected to extensive 'questioning'.

Two days after his arrest, Cox was seen to fall from an open window onto the concrete courtyard at Kempeitai HQ. He was pronounced dead at the scene, and the Kempeitai called a press conference to explain what had happened to the journalist. According to the Japanese, Cox had been well treated after his arrest, but he had committed suicide by jumping from the window after the Kempeitai had produced evidence showing that he was a British agent. Cox had left a note to his wife, in which he wrote that, 'I have been quite well treated. But there is no doubt how matters are going.' None of the foreign diplomats and journalists who attended the briefing were convinced that the Kempeitai was telling the truth. Rumours abounded that Cox had been so badly beaten during his interrogation that a problem had arisen for the Kempeitai. They could not simply have Cox 'disappear', as Sir Robert Craigie and Reuters would ask too many questions. They wanted Cox dead, and they wanted to explain away his injuries, so the Kempeitai threw him out of a high window and forged the note to his wife. The case was closed, and the Kempeitai had sent a powerful warning to other foreign journalists in Japan to stop asking awkward questions of the government. Mrs Cox was later sent to Canada, and her adopted children vanished in Japan. By the time the war actually began in Asia, the Kempeitai was keen to get its hands on many Western journalists who had been creating trouble for the Japanese in the ramp-up to war.

It was not just Western journalists who felt the full force of the Kempeitai early in the war, but also diplomats. At the British Embassy in Tokyo the head of the information department fell under Japanese suspicion soon after war was declared. Herbert Vere Redman had also published an anti-Nazi news sheet, and this time pressure from the Germans led to Redman's arrest and torture. When the Kempeitai came to arrest him, Redman had already left for work at the embassy, so they arrested his French wife and held her hostage to ensure his surrender. Diplomatic pressure succeeded in obtaining the release of Mrs Redman, and she took shelter in the embassy with her husband. Sixty Kempeitai arrived at the British Embassy one morning to take Redman into custody. Sir Robert Craigie refused to give him up, pointing out that the embassy was the sovereign territory of another country, and that Redman and his family had diplomatic protection. None of this influenced the Kempeitai in the slightest; they broke into the embassy and literally dragged poor Redman out of the front door while embassy staff tried to prevent his seizure. One Japanese officer struck the British ambassador in the face during the fracas.

Redman was subjected to an incredible *800* hours of beatings and interrogation, but eventually even the thorough Kempeitai had to admit that he was innocent. He was tried and acquitted and returned to the embassy compound. In London, the Foreign Secretary had ordered the arrest of a member of the Japanese Embassy staff on being informed by Craigie about events in Tokyo. Kaoru Matsumoto was held by the Metropolitan Police to ensure Redman's eventual release – and it might be added, treated with respect and dignity as befitted his diplomatic status.

Repatriation was possible for some Allied nationals during the early months of the war, but few of the large numbers of Westerners living in Asia were able to escape the Japanese occupation. In June 1942 the Italian liner *Conte Verde* sailed to the Portuguese colony of Mozambique from Shanghai carrying 639 Americans, Canadians and assorted South American passport holders, many of whom, such as John B. Powell, had been recently released by the Kempeitai. They were exchanged for Japanese nationals. Two months later 224 British and other Allied nationals and 100 Indians boarded a ship bound for Liverpool. Later, in August, 906 British diplomats and Free French officials along with Dutch, Belgian and Norwegian citizens managed to get out of the city with Japanese permission. But for most whites, repatriation was out of the question, and they would be forced to see out the rest of the war as prisoners of the Japanese, living in increasingly harsh conditions as the war turned against Japan.

The Kempeitai began stoking anti-Western flames in Shanghai with backing of the Anti-Anglo-American Association's propaganda effort that served primarily to show local Chinese that the Japanese had finally vanquished the hated colonialists and liberated the oppressed Chinese masses into the bargain. Certainly there was plenty of collaboration between local Chinese and the Japanese occupation forces, and the Japanese eventually set up a puppet Chinese government in the city under top collaborator Wang Ching-wei, who had formed a new Chinese government in occupied Nanjing.

In October 1942 Allied nationals were required to purchase red armbands from the Japanese. Upon each armband was printed a letter denoting the wearer's nationality ('B' for British, 'A' for American, 'N' for Dutch etc) and an individual identification number. Local Germans, allies of the Japanese, took to wearing Nazi swastika armbands so that they would not be arrested by the nervous Japanese. At the same time that Allied civilians were being forced to buy armbands, the Kempeitai also issued new rules concerning the behaviour of Westerners. Until this time whites had been pretty much left alone to continue running Shanghai for their new masters. The Shanghai Municipal Police officer corps was still primarily British and American, the public utilities were still run by foreign engineers, and the banking houses and great businesses of Shanghai like Jardine Matheson and British-American Tobacco continued to function under their pre-war managers. This situation remained largely unchanged into 1942, but the Japanese did decide to undermine the social life of the Allied expatriate community. They ordered that Allied nationals were forbidden to enter theatres, cinemas, dance halls, nightclubs, the Canidrome in the French Concession or the Race Course (which now forms People's Square in modern Shanghai). In addition, all Allied nationals were ordered to surrender their radios, cameras and telescopes.

These measures heightened a climate of fear that gripped the foreign population in occupied Shanghai. 'Who would be next on the Kempetai [sic] list?' wrote *North-China Daily News* reporter Ralph Shaw. 'The honeymoon period was over. The Japanese were showing their teeth and, from their record of cruelty on China, we knew that many of us were going to suffer indescribable ill-treatment.'[14]

The Kempeitai continued to hunt for enemies among the white civilians, both real and imaginary. 'Every day, the news spread of more arrests ... All we could do was wait, tense, racked daily by terrible fear, sleepless in our beds as the sound of footsteps anywhere sent us into cold sweats and heart-pounding terror.'[15] In the early hours of 5 November the Kempeitai launched a series of coordinated raids across the International Settlement and French Concession that netted 243 Britons (including Shaw), sixty-five Americans, twenty Dutchmen and an assortment of Greeks, Canadians and other Allied nationals, totalling in all 350 men. Labelled 'Prominent Citizens' by the Japanese, they were bundled into army trucks and driven to a rudimentary internment camp set up at Haiphong Road. After being fingerprinted by the Shanghai Municipal Police, the prisoners were herded into thirty-two rooms that were virtually devoid of fixtures and fittings, where they tried to make themselves as comfortable as possible.

In the meantime, another wave of arrests was made by the Kempeitai, and Bridge House was kept fully occupied with more unfortunate victims. The British journalist H.G.W. Woodhead, scourge of the Japanese with his newspaper editorials and radio broadcasts, was picked up at 2.45am on 5 March. Sir Frederick

Maze, former inspector-general of Chinese Customs was arrested and sent to Bridge House, joining three other senior British customs officials, along with an American and two Chinese. The Kempeitai tortured all of them for four weeks before releasing them without charges. Ellis Hayim, one of Shanghai's fabulously wealthy Iraqi-British Jews who had stayed on in the city after occupation was also arrested. Formerly president of the Shanghai Stock Exchange, Hayim was arrested because he had hosted several pre-war garden parties at his large garden villa dedicated to the Allied nations, and these events had been broadcast on the radio in Shanghai.

Moves were swiftly made by the Japanese against the amateur British spies of SOE's Oriental Mission (OM) that they had arrested earlier. The Kempeitai confiscated leader W.J. Gande's OM budget and used the cash to finance their operations in Shanghai. Under constant torture and awful sanitary conditions Gande developed infected toenails, among other things. A Kempeitai medical officer had the unfortunate prisoner held down and then tore Gande's toenails off with a pair of pliers without first administering any anaesthetic. After several weeks of this kind of treatment the broken men of OM Shanghai were suddenly transferred to 15th Army Headquarters located ten miles outside the city at Kiangnan. There they were each placed in solitary confinement, but their wives were permitted to send them food parcels which the Kempeitai guards first carefully pilfered.

On 28 April 1942 all of the OM agents, except former Shanghai policeman W.G. Clarke who remained in hospital, were placed before a military court and speedily sentenced to prison terms. Perhaps even the Japanese recognized how irrelevant an organization OM Shanghai really was, and that it had achieved exactly nothing for the Allied war effort before being broken up by the Kempeitai. The heaviest sentence was given to the leader, Gande – fours years' imprisonment. They were to serve their sentences at Ward Road Jail in Shanghai, which was fortunately still under the control of the Shanghai Municipal Police, and where to their astonishment they discovered many of the warders were British who had been ordered to remain for the time being at their posts by the Japanese. The prison was crowded with Chinese, and many other British and American military and civilian prisoners who had been through the hell of Bridge House.

Gande spend the remainder of the war inside Ward Road Jail. His accomplices, Riggs, Brister, Jack and Brand were exchanged for Japanese prisoners held by the British at the neutral port of Lourenço Marques in Portuguese Mozambique in the autumn of 1942. Edward Elias was released in October 1943, and it was suspected by MI6 that the OM man was now working for the Japanese. Clarke made a full recovery from his Bridge House experience and was released from prison at the end of 1942. The former senior policeman elected to stay on in Shanghai when he was offered repatriation to Britain. Several reasons for this decision have been suggested, including that his wife was of Indian birth, or that he had cracked under interrogation and feared possible repercussions if he had returned home, or that he was an MI6 agent all along.

The Kempeitai had very efficiently and ruthlessly exposed Britain's weaknesses in trying to run an intelligence-gathering and sabotage organization inside Shanghai, but SOE learned from its mistakes and did begin again with its Oriental Mission in the city. The key to success, and the key to avoiding the attentions of the Kempeitai, was to recruit indigenous personnel and send them in as spies. Many Chinese were recruited and they were able to blend into the city in a way that no middle-aged white businessman could ever have done. But the first outing for OM Shanghai had proved a terrible failure, and one that was to leave its mark permanently upon those brave patriots but inept spies who had ended up in the Bridge House.

Even as OM Shanghai was being taken apart by the Japanese, the final internment of an estimated 7,600 Allied men, women and children was being put into effect by the Kempeitai. Between January and July 1943 these thousands of civilians were rounded up and told that they could bring into the camps whatever they could carry. Force-marched through downtown Shanghai, the Japanese tried to make an example of the whites by parading them before huge crowds of Chinese onlookers. Single men were sent over the Huangpu River to Pudong and interned in a dilapidated old three-storey godown belonging to British-American Tobacco, while the rest went into six other camps in the city or at Longhua (immortalized in the novel and movie *Empire of the Sun*). Fortunately for the internees, only the Haiphong Road Camp was run by the Japanese army, and the other seven camps came under the jurisdiction of the Japanese consul-general and his consular police. Food was always short, there was severe congestion, minimal washing facilities and occasional bouts of Japanese brutality, but by and large disease claimed a greater number of lives than beatings and firing squads.

British journalist Ralph Shaw was imprisoned at Haiphong Road and described the 'camp' as two large courtyards around which were arranged over twenty Chinese halls. The property, surrounded by a high brick wall, was once a traditional, but huge, Chinese court-yard house, many of the halls previously being the homes of the former master's many concubines. Before the war the whole estate had been used as barracks for the 'North China Marines', a large detachment of US Marines sent to Shanghai to protect American lives and property during the Japanese invasion of China in 1937. Haiphong Road was therefore well equipped with showers, modern toilets and a huge kitchen.

The Japanese commandant, Colonel Odera, was also an Anglo-phile, having attended a training course in Britain before the war. He had subsequently grown the sort of luxuriant moustache normally associated with RAF fighter pilots, and the prisoners immediately nicknamed him 'Old Handlebars'. Odera, speaking through his interpreter, Lieutenant Honda, told the prisoners that they 'were not to be afraid. We would be well treated. We should not try to escape for this would mean heavy punishment. So long as we behaved our-selves and obeyed orders all would be well.'[16] It was this paradoxical behaviour of the Japanese towards prisoners that mystified many captives. On the one hand, they treated many of the internees appallingly and authorized hell-holes like Bridge House to torture mostly innocent people with the utmost sadism. On the other hand, someone like Colonel Odera made sure that his prisoners were taken care of and protected. At the Woosung Prisoner of War Camp close to Shanghai, the Haiphong Road's former occupants, the US Marines, were abused, exposed to disease and generally neglected by their guards. Even though the Kempeitai was nominally in charge of all prison camps, there was no standardized treatment for prisoners, and the degree to which POWs suffered was usually attributable to the personality of the camp commandant. Gavan Daws makes the important point in *Prisoners of the Japanese*: 'The Japanese running the camps ranged from careful men to average men, to outright incompetents, slovens, drunks, sadists, and homicidal maniacs.'[17]

Conditions in the other Shanghai internment camps were generally good. People mucked in together, families lived together, and through the prisoners' organizational skills conditions in the camps gradually improved. 'The camp-dwellers were at least able to obtain basic levels of food and shelter and, with notable exceptions, were not subjected to the kind of barbaric cruelty routinely inflicted on Allied servicemen in Japanese prisoner-of-war camps.'[18] Death rates for civilian internees in Shanghai were low compared with the huge numbers of Allied prisoners of war who died in Japanese gulags. Figures from incomplete records listed twenty-six deaths in 1943, rising to thirty-nine in 1944 and forty-nine in 1945.[19] Most were due to disease or old age, but some bore the hallmarks of Japanese involvement, for example, the death of Joseph Ethrington, a 52-year-old Briton who passed away on 11 February 1943 at Kempeitai headquarters at Jessfield Road.

All along the China coast and in the interior ports British and other Allied nationals were interned in similar camps. They were business people and missionaries, language teachers and university professors, engineers and administrators, and many had lived in China for decades; some had even been born there. It was a terrible wrench for most of them to be plucked from jobs and professions that they loved and to be parted from their Chinese friends and colleagues. Perhaps the most famous of them to die was British missionary Eric Liddell of *Chariots of Fire* fame. He had been Olympic 400 metres gold medallist at the 1924 games. Liddell was born in China, where his father was a missionary, and after retiring from athletics he had returned to the land of his birth to assist with his father's mission in Shandong Province. Liddell and fellow Allied nationals were interned at Weihsien Camp in the city of Weifang, and he died there from a brain tumour in February 1945 at the age of only forty-three.

Another high-profile victim was Sir Elly Kadoorie, Shanghai multi-millionaire and philanthropist, and a prominent member of the rich Iraqi-British Jewish community in the city since the late nineteenth century. The powerful Kadoorie family owned banks, rubber plantations, electric power utilities and real estate, including the famous Peninsula Hotel in Hong Kong. When the Japanese occupied Shanghai they appropriated Kadoorie's vast house, Marble Hall,[20] which sports the largest ballroom in Asia, and then forced

Sir Elly and his grown-up sons into an internment camp where he died in 1944 aged seventy-seven. His sons survived the war and rebuilt the Kadoorie business empire in Hong Kong.

The Japanese occupation became the great leveller of pre-war white Shanghai society. All classes, from the richest multi-millionaire to the lowliest policeman found themselves locked up together and treated as criminals by the Japanese. It was one of the darkest episodes in the history of China's wealthiest and most cosmopolitan city.

Notes

1. Colin Smith, *Singapore Burning: Heroism and Surrender in World War II* (London, Penguin Books Ltd, 2005), p. 78.
2. Bernard Wasserstein, *Secret War in Shanghai: Treachery, Subversion and Collaboration in the Second World War* (London, Profile Books Ltd, 1998), p. 118.
3. Mark Felton, *Yanagi: The Secret Underwater Trade Between Germany and Japan 1942–1945* (Pen & Sword Books Limited, 2005), p. 71.
4. Bernard Wasserstein, *Secret War in Shanghai: Treachery, Subversion and Collaboration in the Second World War* (London, Profile Books Ltd, 1998), p. 121.
5. Stella Dong, *Shanghai: The Rise and Fall of a Decadent City* (New York, Perennial, 2001), p. 272.
6. Ibid: 272.
7. John B. Powell, *My Twenty-Five Years in China* (New York, 1945), p. 386.
8. Ralph Shaw, *Sin City* (London, Warner Books, 1997), p. 207.
9. Stella Dong, *Shanghai: The Rise and Fall of a Decadent City* (New York, Perennial, 2001), pp. 272–3.
10. Ralph Shaw, *Sin City* (London, Warner Books, 1997), p. 208.
11. Bernard Wasserstein, *Secret War in Shanghai: Treachery, Subversion and Collaboration in the Second World War* (London, Profile Books Ltd, 1998), p. 124.
12. Ralph Shaw, *Sin City* (London, Warner Books, 1997), p. 208.
13. Ibid: p. 208.
14. Ibid: p. 207.
15. Ibid: p. 207.

16. Ibid: p. 215.
17. Gavan Daws, *Prisoners of the Japanese: POWs of the Second World War* (London, Pocket Books, 1994), p. 99.
18. Bernard Wasserstein, *Secret War in Shanghai: Treachery, Subversion and Collaboration in the Second World War* (London, Profile Books Ltd, 1998), p. 140.
19. Courtesy of David Parker, OBE, Director of Information and Secretariat, *Commonwealth War Graves Commission,* in a letter to the author, 14 March 2008.
20. Marble Hall still exists and can be visited by the paying public. It now belongs to the state and is a Children's Palace located on Nanjing Road West.

Chapter Five

Resistance is Futile

Three times in one day he was called out and so severely thrashed with different instruments ... that he was in no condition to stand or lie and was covered with bloodstains. The following day he was called again twice, thrashed, treated with electrical current and finally subjected to the water treatment.

Dr R. Flachs, Bandoeng

'Oh Jesus, I piss blood!' exclaimed Australian soldier John Douglas as he was led into the interrogation room. Douglas walked with obvious pain as he shuffled past fellow prisoner Willem Wijting inside Bandoeng's Kempeitai office on the Dutch island of Java. He looked tired, and there were bruises on his face. His body had grown thin after weeks of starvation and his beard was wild and crawling with lice. Once he was seated, a Kempeitai officer asked him, 'Are you sure that the war will be won by the Allies?' Douglas looked up defiantly and replied: 'I am sure that Japan will lose it.'[1] Douglas was one of dozens of people arrested by the Kempeitai on Java in mid-1942 who were believed to be associated with a Dutch resistance group called 'Underground Action' that had been set up shortly after the Japanese conquest of the island in March 1942.

Douglas's defiant stance had brought him only terrible consequences. He had been severely tortured in a variety of increasingly sadistic ways that had almost broken his body and nearly crushed his spirit. Eventually, a Japanese court martial had sentenced the young soldier to death – the method of execution to be beheading by sword. When his tormentors asked Douglas what he thought of being beheaded, the Australian replied, 'I know very well what I am doing and naturally I take the consequences.' The Japanese officer guffawed, 'Do you know that beheading is a very dishonourable death?' to which Douglas said stoically, 'To an Australian it means dying for his country.' The Japanese officer continued to taunt Douglas in the hope of getting him to confess his crime and name his accomplices. 'An Australian does not get an honourable death,' said the Japanese, adding that they would set him free should he confess. 'When I am set free by you people, I should be sentenced to death by the Australians,' said Douglas, 'and that would be a very dishonourable death really.'[2] Douglas had survived all of the abuse the Kempeitai had thrown at him, which was, as we shall discover, unbelievably painful and insulting. He had refused to divulge any information that the Japanese could use against his comrades. He had caused as much trouble as he could, annoying the Japanese by refusing to divulge his rank for example, claiming one day to be a sergeant, the next a major and then a private. He knew that he was never going to get out of Kempeitai custody alive, so he determined to fight them to the end.

The end for John Douglas came at 4pm on 10 April 1943 when he was sentenced to death alongside two of his Dutch compatriots, Captain de Lange and Mr. W. van der Vorst. It was surmised by other prisoners that John Douglas, a.k.a. Smith, was an agent with the British Secret Intelligence Service (MI6), but we will never know for sure. Even on the night before his execution Douglas kept up his non-cooperation with the Japanese. At roll call he refused to answer in Japanese and was badly beaten on the head with a sword scabbard. Forty-eight hours later, as he was being led along the filthy prison corridor to be beheaded, Douglas's stoicism was undiminished. As he passed Wijting's cell he smiled and said, 'William, keep fit, keep smiling!' Wijting said afterwards, 'I have never in my life seen a more brave soldier than John Douglas.'[3]

One of the primary missions of the Kempeitai was the discovery of plots against Japanese rule. These came in many different forms, from the activities of foreign intelligence agents, as with the British in Shanghai, to indigenous resistance encountered in Malaya and the Philippines, to organizations that grew within the ranks of the defeated and subjugated white colonists of Asia. There were also plots that owed more to the breadth of imagination of Kempeitai officers than to reality, but in all instances, whether real or phantom, the Kempeitai was frighteningly thorough not only in investigating individuals and groups, but also in the retribution it visited upon those brave or foolhardy enough to have risked antagonizing the Japanese occupation authorities. In all cases, many innocent people died, as the Kempeitai always threw its net very wide indeed when it scented insurrection in the air.

The conquered Netherlands East Indies (NEI), modern Indonesia, proved to be a busy hunting ground for the Kempeitai and its informants and spies. The Allied defence of the NEI had been very short-lived. Japan needed Dutch oil to fuel its expanding war machine, and the Dutch and other Allied forces defending the archipelago were inadequate and too widely dispersed to hold the Japanese off. Java was the administrative capital of the NEI, and the main Japanese invasion forces consisting of 35,000 troops under the command of Lieutenant General Hitoshi Iwamura began landing on 1 March 1942. Opposing them were 25,000 Dutch troops, mostly indigenous personnel, under the command of General Hein ter Poorten, as well as 3,500 British, 2,500 Australian and 1,000 American troops under the overall command of British Major General Hervey Sitwell. Although the Allied soldiers fought valiantly, they were soon over-whelmed and forced to surrender on 12 March. With Java invested by the Japanese, the rest of the far-flung NEI was rapidly occupied by the Japanese over the following weeks.

Anti-Japanese organizations existed among both the Dutch population and native peoples. Many had been formed shortly after the Japanese attack in March 1942 in the hopelessly ridiculous belief, reinforced by Dutch propaganda, that the Dutch would recapture the NEI within three months. Members of the Royal Netherlands Indies Army (KNIL), colonial officials and civilians made preparations for the happy day that did not materialize. They were intensely patriotic, and a number of schemes and groups flourished in those first months, many devoted to sabotage. The Japanese managed to identify three of the groups, whose names were 'Wernick', 'Depok' and 'Wetter'. One of the main groups based on the island of Java had been named by the Dutch 'Underground Action'. Even when the Dutch realized that it was likely to be years rather than months before Allied troops set foot in the NEI again, the organizations mostly remained in existence and their members managed to keep hidden from the Japanese. Some, however, were picked up by the Kempeitai and subjected to the most appallingly brutal treatment imaginable.

It was not only Dutch soldiers and civilians who formed resistance groups, but also British soldiers left on Java after the surrender who joined with surviving KNIL men. Armed, and with no way to escape, they went into the hills of east Java and tried to resist the Japanese for as long as possible. They numbered around 200 men, and were concentrated close to the town of Malang. The Kempeitai launched a coordinated campaign to enforce their capture or surrender within a month of gaining control of the island. The British and Dutch soldiers were dealt with in the most brutal manner. Labelled 'terrorists' by the Kempeitai, they would not be treated as other military prisoners-of-war. The men were forced into 3-foot long pig baskets that the locals used to transport swine. These baskets, with their screaming and desperate human cargo, were then loaded on to five trucks and driven to a railway siding in a temperature of 100 degrees Fahrenheit. The men were transported aboard open goods wagons to a waiting ship at a coastal port, stacked like any other cargo atop the railway trucks.

The atrocity that followed was witnessed by several Dutch civilians who recalled the terrible cries and screams of the Allied soldiers trapped in the tiny baskets, many of them pleading for water. A small coastal steamer took the prisoners and their Kempeitai guards out to sea off the coast of Surabaya. The Japanese then heaved all of the pig baskets containing the wretched prisoners over the ship's side; they drowned, and their bodies were consumed by hundreds of sharks that quickly gathered at the scene. A lack of evidence or any survivors able to give clear testimony meant that this crime was very hard to prosecute after the war, and most of those involved were never punished.

Dutchman Willem Wijting, a 24-year-old dental student, was an active member of Underground Action in 1942. The methods used by the Kempeitai to extract confessions from prisoners meant that many brave and loyal Dutch citizens cracked under such physical strain and unfortunately named other members of resistance organizations who were quickly picked up. Wijting's arrest on 8 August 1942 was the result of the confession of a fellow resistance member who had been 'tortured so much he could not keep his mouth shut anymore.'[4] Wijting was to be interrogated thirty-seven times by the Kempeitai before his eventual sentence of five years imprisonment.

Another unfortunate who survived Japanese incarceration to give a statement to Allied war crimes investigators was Major A. Zimmerman, who was an infantry officer in the Royal Netherlands Indies Army. He was arrested on 4 February 1943 at his home in Buitenzorg, near the Javanese capital of Batavia (now Jakarta). Zimmerman was directly connected with an underground organization in Buitenzorg, along with many other local Dutch officials and civilians. His name had come up during a separate Kempeitai investigation, along with the name of one of his helpers in Batavia, a young woman named T. Thierens. Zimmerman was warned of the imminent arrival of Kempeitai soldiers at his house and he and his wife managed to destroy 'practically all the evidence in my house, copies of telegrams and original reports of my informers'[5] The Kempeitai searched Zimmermann's home five times after his arrest, but they found nothing. If a suspect was not at home when the Kempeitai came calling, they sometimes arrested the person's family and neighbours instead, recalled Wijting, 'and these people were heard [interrogated] many times under a lot of torturing. These people were then held at the Kempetai [sic] until enough evidence was had or until the persons required came in.'[6]

On the afternoon of 4 February Zimmerman and Thierens were taken to a room inside the Kempeitai office at Koninsplein in Batavia. Sergeant-Major Yoshida 'then took a wooden club about three feet in length, at the "working-end" about three inches thick and tapering towards the handle.' Yoshida explained that Zimmerman was accused of being a spy and/or the leader of a 'spy gang', and that he knew the name and address of his 'best assistant', which the Kempeitai wanted. Yoshida then began to 'question' Zimmerman. 'Yoshida questioned me about my Chinese helper and each denial of knowing a Chinese spy whose name started with a T ... which fact was known to the Kempei-Tai [sic] when I was arrested, was followed by a blow with the wooden club at the back of the body near or approximately upon the kidneys.'[7] Zimmerman recalled being struck between twenty and thirty times by Yoshida, who, noted Zimmerman, beat him 'systematically, each new blow being placed close to the preceding one.'[8] Internal bleeding was the result of this physical abuse, along with 'big swellings and a blackish-blue discolouring of the skin which remained visible for at least two months.' Miss Thierens was beaten in the same way, also causing her kidney trouble. The two prisoners were then handcuffed and thrown into the cells for the night at the Buitenzorg Kempeitai office.

On 5 February, around dusk, Zimmerman was taken from his cell and placed before Yoshida again. 'I refused to admit that I was mixed up in espionage or that I know a Chinese spy, after which Yoshida took me to another room, telling me that he was going to "hang me".'[9] Suspension was one of the favoured torture methods used by the Kempeitai, and Zimmerman noted that 'the system is quite simple and very effective.'

> I was placed on a small wooden case, with the hands rope-bound behind my back and the ankles bound. After this thick rope was pulled under my armpits, led through a wooden beam over the door so that when the wooden case was kicked away I was hung with my full weight from my armpits. By the pull of the weight of my body, nerves and blood vessels were tied off, and gradually I felt my hands first, then my wrists and after that my arms 'die'. During the hanging ... the torturer was sitting behind me, whispering questions and trying to make me confess that I was a spy, which I denied.[10]

Zimmerman's arms were paralysed for a month after this session. Miss Thierens was also hung, but she did not suffer any paralysis, which led Zimmerman to conclude that the Kempeitai were experts in inflicting pain and paralysis when they chose, largely through the rope work used during a session. Zimmerman refused to divulge any information to Yoshida and so on 8 February he was given the water treatment. After twenty minutes he was taken to Yoshida's room again and there he found Thierens. 'Yoshida ... there confronted me with Miss Thierens, who under severe torture (hanging) ... had confessed that she had acted as a messenger and had taken telegrams, which I had composed, from Batavia to Buitenzorg, where she had handed them over to the Buitenzorg branch of the organisation, which arranged to transmit them from near Buitenzorg to Australia.'[11]

Zimmerman feigned anger and shouted at Thierens in Dutch. They spoke quickly, and Zimmerman established exactly what Thierens had told Yoshida. 'It was no use to deny any longer that I had been doing spy work and I confessed exactly the same things as Miss Thierens had confessed to have done,' related Zimmerman. 'Yoshida then took her from the room, gave me several blows on the right arm with a wooden leg of a chair ... and told me that now I had confessed that I was a spy I would understand that this was a crime which would be punished by death.'[12] On 21 February Zimmerman was given another dose of the water treatment, which he related after the war:

> I was bound tightly and in a horizontal position on a wooden bench. There was no rope used but electrical wire of rubber with a copper kernel, which the torturers seem to prefer because it does not stretch. The wire is bound around the body from the foot upwards to the shoulders in such a way that the victim is unable to move at all. Over the throat a thin wire is bound so that the victim cannot move his head without cutting his throat. After this was done a thick handerchief [sic] was used to strap the mouth and prevent me from closing it.'[13]

The Japanese wanted more information about the Chinese spy whose name began with the letter 'T'. Zimmerman refused to cooperate and was slapped several times in the face. A rubber hose was then forced into Zimmerman's mouth. 'Water was in this way poured into my mouth, causing me almost to suffocate. It may be that the word is not right: they tried to drown me. As soon as I was on the verge of getting unconscious they stopped the water but opened the tap again the moment I tried to breathe. Sometimes they gave me a few moments of relaxation by letting the water flow into the eyes, the nose or the ears.'[14] Zimmerman soon learned that a trick to get them to stop briefly was to shout, 'I want to speak'. Once they discovered that Zimmerman had nothing to say, the Japanese resumed the torture. The Kempeitai soldiers kept asking about the Chinese man, demanding his name and address, and at every refusal they opened the tap again. When the torturers showed him photographs of Chinese that they suspected, and Zimmerman denied knowing them, one of the Kempeitai men gave him a black eye.

Zimmerman withstood all that the Kempeitai could throw at him and he never divulged the identities of his co-conspirators. The Japanese had insufficient evidence to sentence him to death, but he was detained for a considerable time. Many other resistance members picked up by the Kempeitai at the same time were not so lucky. Dr Olaf Munck from Buitenzorg was hung by Yoshida 'until both arms were paralysed completely. They never recovered and when Dr Munck was executed (beheaded) [in] June 1943 his arms still were paralysed.'[15] Another Dutchman, surnamed De Rooy, received the same treatment as Zimmerman, but after the water treatment he was extensively burned with cigarettes and afterwards beheaded on 1 May 1943.

In April 1943, as the war situation in the south-west Pacific deteriorated for the Japanese after a determined American assault on Guadalcanal in the British Solomon Islands and New Georgia, the Dutch colonists and many local peoples took heart and believed that the time of liberation was drawing closer. Underground activity suddenly increased, naturally drawing the attention of the Kempeitai. Most of the organizations were based on Java or nearby Sumatra in the western NEI, home to the largest population of whites. The Japanese moved quickly, and through a network of spies and informers largely recruited from among Indonesians who hated the Dutch colonialists and wished to achieve independence by supporting the Japanese, the Kempeitai was able to identify many of the major players in several resistance groups. A large-scale Kempeitai operation on Java, and later extended to Sumatra, was codenamed 'JI' and was mounted between August 1943 and March 1944. Later, Operation 'KO' supported 'JI' and would result in hundreds of executions.

In charge of the operation was a Japanese Army staff officer and Chief of the Judicial Affairs Department named Masugi, assisted by Kempeitai Major Murase, Chief of Department Headquarters in Java. Two adjutants assisted the senior officers, Captain Nomura of the regular army and Lieutenant Onishi of the Kempeitai respectively. The operation was entirely under the control of Masugi and Murase, though they nominally reported to the local army headquarters. Musase was later replaced by Major Katsumura, who was extensively interrogated by the Dutch immediately after the Japanese surrender and who provided a detailed explanation of Kempeitai operations during Operations 'JI' and 'KO'.

Following Operations 'JI' and 'KO' the Kempeitai was even more paranoid than before – literally seeing spies and saboteurs everywhere in the NEI. No one was safe from investigation, and investigation always meant torture. Even citizens of neutral countries came under close Japanese scrutiny, and some were arrested and cruelly treated in direct violation of international law. One example was Dr. R. Flachs, a 40-year-old chemical engineer from Switzerland who was working for Royal Dutch Shell in the NEI in 1944 when he was arrested by the Kempeitai. It was not the first time that he had been hauled in for questioning; it was the third interrogation since the Japanese conquest. Flachs was married with two teenage children and living in Bandoeng (now Bandung), an industrial city established by the Dutch in 1810 in western Java, south-east of the capital Batavia. On 2 June 1944 the Kempeitai came knocking at Dr Flachs's front door. 'At about 4.30am, while still in bed a tremendous uproar arose in front of my house ... On opening the door I was immediately seized by two officers of the Kempei [sic] and two officers of the Bandoeng police and handcuffed,'[16] recalled Flachs. He was allowed to dress and was then manhandled aboard a Japanese army truck where he was eventually joined by five other unfortunates all bound for the Kempeitai office in Bandoeng. Japanese soldiers thoroughly searched Flachs's house, removing cameras, binoculars, children's school atlases and even photo albums. 'To crown it all the police wanted to arrest also my wife after the last search,' recalled Flachs. 'My wife suffers since years of nervous heart disease and owing to the shock of seeing me arrested she fainted. A friend of mine however managed to induce the police to abstain from arresting her.'[17]

At the Kempeitai office Flachs and the fellow prisoners were released from their handcuffs, but their wrists were immediately bound with ropes that 'lacerated the skin of the knuckles. Without asking a word I had to remain kneeling on the floor for about an hour, before, still bound, I was removed to a cell.'[18] The cell was over-crowded with fourteen people. 'More and more prisoners arrived,' recalled Flachs, indicating a large-scale Kempeitai operation in Bandoeng, 'the number amounting to 80, including also women with children of tender age and old men of about 70.'[19]

Each prisoner was assigned a number; Flachs from now on was known only as 'Prisoner No. 30'. Each morning the Japanese would call out the numbers of the people they wanted to question. It was a malevolent lottery designed to further weaken a prisoner's resolve to resist. The morning selection 'always caused trepidation amongst the prisoners, who thought their turn had come so that all lived in perpetual agitation, which was slowly but surely leading to a nervous breakdown.'[20] The Japanese deliberately kept prisoners waiting for their first interrogation session because 'in this waiting was a sort of system, as we could hear and see others being tortured and the intention was naturally to make us very much afraid for the questioning and with a view of making us talk immediately.'[21]

They were starved for weeks, Dr. Flachs recalling that the 'prisoners were so famished that they began to eat toothpaste and the skins of the bananas thrown away by the guards.'[22] The authorities eventually permitted relatives to send in small daily quantities of food so long as they paid the Japanese, and every Monday relatives were allowed to send in one fresh change of clothes and take away the dirty clothes for washing. Soap, toothbrushes and toothpaste were permitted. 'Most of the prisoners were Dutch of mixed blood with a sparse growth of hair,' wrote Flachs. 'The few fullblooded Europeans ... looked however after 2 months very much like St. Nikolas. There was no question of shaving or a haircut and soon the beards were swarming with inhabitants.'[23] Hygiene was very poor and the 'condition of the latrine was filthy beyond description and the stench unbearable, especially after an outbreak of dysentery.' One hundred people used one latrine and a single water tap.

Interrogation was a grisly business. When the prisoner was led into the cellar the Kempeitai officer asked: 'Why have you been arrested?' to which 'most of the prisoners replied, that they did not know. This was usually followed by a flogging, varying from 50–300 strokes.'[24] Flachs waited for ten days in his cell before his number was called out. After failing to give a satisfactory answer to the above question he was flogged and then asked again. 'I pointed out ... that I was a Swiss subject and not to be trifled with. I further commented on the shameful treatment of the prisoners.'[25] The Japanese officer told Flachs that they were not animals, and that they themselves had families, but in order not to lose face he ordered one of his men to thrash Flachs again. The Japanese had just finished abusing another prisoner, and they were ready to put aside their whips and use considerably more unpleasant methods on Flachs unless he talked, 'but I simulated a nervous breakdown, which was not difficult for me, as I really was near one.'[26]

Dr Flachs commented at length about the methods used by the Bandoeng Kempeitai to terrorize suspects into making a confession, and whipping was only the beginning. Each Kempeitai unit appears to have favoured particular methods of torture, or to have been more accomplished in their application than other units. Hanging or suspension, for example, does not seem to have been practised often at Bandoeng, whereas it was very common elsewhere. Flogging was instead extremely popular among interrogators. The weapons used to flog prisoners at Bandoeng included a stick, rattan canes of varying thicknesses, a flogging whip with leather thongs weighted with metal balls, and a variation of this instrument, 'the leather thongs of which, were provided with iron hooks, which simply tore the flesh to bits,'[27] recalled Flachs. Electrocution was a common form of torture, and the water treatment was used often, along with finger bandaging and burning the flesh with cigarettes. Two novel treatments included shaving the head of the prisoner and then cutting the scalp to induce painfully infected wounds, and the Japanese martial art of ju-jitsu. The local Japanese police chief and his assistant often practised their judo skills on the prisoners, as Flachs wrote;

A fellow prisoner, 50 years old, related how he was catapulted from one corner of the room to another, just like a ball and that only by the greatest dexterity and luck did he contrive to fall so that no damage was done to arms, legs and neck. For a whole year afterwards he still had pains in his chest and recalls with trepidation, what these two wellnourished [sic] creatures had done to a famished man, who was thrown about till he finally became unconscious.[28]

The treatment dished out to locals was generally as bad as that suffered by European prisoners, and in many cases it was far worse. 'No. 5, a Menadonese, was most severely illtreated [sic],' recalled Flachs, 'three times in one day he was called out and so severely thrashed with different instruments . . . that he was in no condition to stand or lie and was covered with bloodstains. The following day he was called again twice, thrashed, treated with electrical current and finally subjected to the water treatment.'[29] Small wonder then that huge numbers of people died under Kempeitai interrogation, long before they were ever formally charged with any crime.

Flachs was to get off lightly compared with some of the interrogations of white people performed by the Kempeitai in Surabaya on Java. Willem Wijting recalled two particularly unpleasant examples to post-war investigators. Kuypers van Steenbergen, a 32-year-old Dutchman, 'Had to sit on the floor with his head close to one of the edges of the table,' wrote Wijting. 'When he denied the questions asked he got a heavy blow on the back of his head and fell with his forehead against the edge of the table. This was done many times and in the end blood was dripping all over his face.'[30] Another man, F. van Hutten, was placed in a bathtub, the top of which was closed with a gauze cover, and then filled with water until van Hutten almost drowned. With his face pressed against the gauze as he desperately tried to gulp air, van Hutten was further abused by the Japanese guards who burned his eyelids with cigarettes.

Dr Flachs's initial complaint about the condition of his fellow prisoners evidently had some effect upon the Japanese, perhaps because Flachs was a Swiss citizen and Japan was sensitive about complaints from that quarter. He was allowed to send out for some drugs and he managed to cure various infections among his comrades and treat the worst dysentery cases. He also administered sedatives to calm down people who were literally living on their nerves twenty-four hours a day. 'Due to the undernourishment and the continual screaming day and night,' said Flachs, 'the prisoners became gradually extremely nervous, and more so, when the first cases of dysentery started to occur.'[31] The drugs Flachs ordered helped many of his fellow prisoners to survive their terrible ordeal, when otherwise they would have perished from abuse and disease. Flachs did not stop there, however. 'A second simulated nervous breakdown put me into the position to requisition through the same police officer some more medicines which enabled me to help also some lady-prisoners.'[32]

Flachs was finally charged eighteen days after his arrest with having given financial support to families in internment camps and having listened in to foreign radio stations and circulated enemy news. On the second charge, Flachs confessed. 'Only to avoid being discharged later from prison a confirmed invalid, I confessed having listened to the French Radio from Saigon in the belief that this was allowed, since Saigon was under Japanese control.'[33] After further examination Flachs signed a document written in Malay and then waited a further two and a half months before photos and fingerprints were taken and he was transferred with forty other prisoners to Bantjeuj Prison.

To describe Bantjeuj Prison as hell on earth would not be to do it justice. It was designed essentially to kill its inmates as slowly and painfully as possible, and Flachs only barely survived his ordeal within its walls. Thirty-five men were forced into cells designed for a maximum of thirteen. The prison was run by Indonesians under Kempeitai control, and they forced the prisoners to pay for virtually everything that they needed, even blankets. An elaborate system of couriers, known by the prisoners as 'submarines', smuggled food, medicines, letters and other essentials into the prison in return for high bribes. Trying to manage on the rations handed out by the Japanese was a shortcut to an early grave.

The prison was appallingly filthy, 'abominable and worse than at police headquarters. The drinking water was brownish and taken from a hole about 8 metres deep. At the same hole the dead from bacilliary dysentery were washed.'[34] The prisoners were expected to survive on only 750 calories a day, so they lost huge amounts of weight and could not recover from infections and disease contracted inside the prison. The first prisoners in Flachs's party died of dysentery only six days after arrival. Everyone contracted dysentery, and unless a prisoner could afford to smuggle drugs into the prison, it usually resulted in death. The prison doctor and prisoner-nurses, 'consisting mostly of convicted thieves and other scum, did what they liked. The dead were hardly cold, before their miserable rags were torn from their emaciated bodies,' recalled Flachs. One nurse collected gold teeth in a jar. The 'hospital' consisted of a 'small narrow hall with about 12 iron cots with straw mattresses ... such an abominable stench prevailed, that with the best of will it was impossible to stand it more than 5 minutes.' The patients were dumped into this room and left to die. 'It often happened that 2 patients lay in one bed suffering from dysentery, they often discharged involuntarily either into the bed or next to it on the floor. The place was swarming with flies.'[35]

The Kempeitai visited the prison often, and their arrival heralded more torture for selected inmates. The Indonesian guards also punished prisoners viciously for the slightest infraction of the rules. Some prisoners were hanged by the neck until they were almost dead, taken down and revived, and then hanged again. Flachs noted that one prisoner was hanged five times in succession, and then forced to drink the water from the latrines, after which he contracted dysentery. Other tortures were also used. 'In the floor of block "B" of the prison,' wrote Flachs, 'a wooden cross was cemented in, on which prisoners were strung up by the wrists and with the legs bound to the cross for 24 hours or more.'[36] The prisoners on the cross were flogged regularly.

Starvation, disease and abuse carried off plenty of prisoners, as the Japanese intended. Flachs contracted dysentery and soon was nearing death. 'I still remember lying in the corner of the cell while my fellow prisoners prayed for me,' wrote Flachs, 'and how the lice swarmed up my legs and a rat ran over my face.'[37] Flachs was saved by a small amount of medicine smuggled into the prison by a submarine. Eventually, after over a year in Kempeitai custody, and following pressure from the Swiss Embassy in Tokyo, Dr Flachs was released on 16 April 1945, a shambling, dirty, emaciated, diseased and terrified man, to go back to his wife.

The Netherlands Forces Intelligence Service (NEFIS) determined from captured Japanese documents that the total number of people swept up by the Kempeitai during their operations in Java in 1943–44 was 1,918. Of this number, 743 died in Kempeitai hands. Captain Charles Jongeneel, Head of the NEFIS War Crimes Section, broke down these figures. He discovered that those sentenced to death and executed consisted of '439 persons, viz. 113 Europeans, 296 Indonesians and 30 Chinese and other orientals.' A further '1175 persons, viz. 545 Europeans, 517 Indonesians, and 113 Chinese and other orientals,'[38] had been 'punished', with sentences ranging from one year to 'lifelong imprisonment.' Shockingly plain statistics of the numbers who died before sentence was even passed demonstrate the ferocity of Kempeitai interrogation methods and Japanese efforts to portray the deaths in custody as attributed to natural causes rather than official abuse. '304 person, viz. 92 Europeans,

117 Indonesians and 35 Chinese and other orientals,' are listed as dead before sentence. 'Random tests revealed that persons, who according to sworn statements were tortured to death, are listed as having died from illness,' wrote Captain Jongeneel, 'cause of death "heart failure".'[39]

The Kempeitai officer in charge of interrogating prisoners and organising prosecution of suspects, as well as having responsibility for executing prisoners, was Major Katsumura. He explained that the reasons why so many were killed were simple: it was a matter of time and numbers. 'At this time there were many suspects picked up and held by each unit of the Kempeitai; in view of the number of suspects and the place, they weren't sent up to Court-Martial because otherwise the latter would not have been able to cope with the work.'[40] Katsumura added that in light of the numbers arrested, established by Captain Jongeneel of NEFIS to have been in excess of 1,900 individuals, 'a speedy settlement was difficult.' Katsumura also pointed to the war situation as a factor in the large number of executions, as in the opinion of the Kempeitai on Java it 'was daily growing more unfavourable to us, and in view of the possibility of an Allied landing it was decided to deal with the criminals as quickly as possible.'[41] What this meant in practice was an arbitrary decision regarding the guilt or innocence of a victim being made at the local Kempeitai office, followed by a decision to kill or imprison that person and a speedy rubber stamping of the decision by local army headquarters. 'Consequently, where the crime was clearly proved,' said Katsumura, ignoring how a confession was extracted to 'prove' guilt, 'and the death sentence considered suitable, on the decision of Army the criminals were punished therever [wherever] they were.'[42] The rule of law had thus been abandoned by the Japanese in favour of bulk imprisonment, bulk torture and mass execution.

Notes

1. The National Archives (TNA): Public Record Office (PRO) WO 325/151, Statement No. 1504: *Statement of Mr. B.F. Witing,* 13 October 1945.
2. Ibid.
3. Ibid.
4. Ibid.

5. Box 258, Exhibit 1749A, Netherlands Forces Intelligence Service (NEFIS), Document No. 5748: *Report on Torture by the Japanese Military Police (Kempei Tai) drawn up by Major ZIMMERMAN R.N.I.A., No. OM/235/E*, 7 June 1946, MacMillan Brown Library, University of Canterbury, Christchurch, New Zealand.
6. The National Archives (TNA): Public Record Office (PRO) WO 325/151, Statement No. 1504: *Statement of Mr. B.F. Witing*, 13 October 1945.
7. Box 258, Exhibit 1749A, Netherlands Forces Intelligence Service (NEFIS), Document No. 5748: *Report on Torture by the Japanese Military Police (Kempei Tai) drawn up by Major ZIMMERMAN R.N.I.A., No. OM/235/E*, 7 June 1946, MacMillan Brown Library, University of Canterbury, Christchurch, New Zealand.
8. Ibid.
9. Ibid.
10. Ibid.
11. Ibid.
12. Ibid.
13. Ibid.
14. Ibid.
15. Ibid.
16. Netherlands Forces Intelligence Service (NEFIS), Box 258, Exhibit 1752, Document No. 5751: *Letter of Dr. R. Flachs, Bandoeng, Report No. 3: Concerning the third arrestation of Dr. R. FLACHS through the Kempei Dai Nippon and the police of Bandoeng*, 11 June 1946, MacMillan Brown Library, University of Canterbury, Christchurch, New Zealand.
17. Ibid.
18. Ibid.
19. Ibid.
20. Ibid.
21. The National Archives (TNA): Public Record Office (PRO) WO 325/151, Statement No. 1504: *Statement of Mr. B.F. Witing*, 13 October 1945.
22. Netherlands Forces Intelligence Service (NEFIS), Box 258, Exhibit 1752, Document No. 5751: *Letter of Dr. R. Flachs, Bandoeng, Report No. 3: Concerning the third arrestation of*

Dr. R. FLACHS through the Kempei Dai Nippon and the police of Bandoeng, 11 June 1946, MacMillan Brown Library, University of Canterbury, Christchurch, New Zealand.

23. Ibid.
24. Ibid.
25. Ibid.
26. Ibid.
27. Ibid.
28. Ibid.
29. Ibid.
30. The National Archives (TNA): Public Record Office (PRO) WO 325/151, Statement No. 1504: *Statement of Mr. B.F. Witing,* 13 October 1945.
31. Netherlands Forces Intelligence Service (NEFIS), Box 258, Exhibit 1752, Document No. 5751: *Letter of Dr. R. Flachs, Bandoeng, Report No. 3: Concerning the third arrestation of Dr. R. FLACHS through the Kempei Dai Nippon and the police of Bandoeng*, 11 June 1946, MacMillan Brown Library, University of Canterbury, Christchurch, New Zealand.
32. Ibid.
33. Ibid.
34. Ibid.
35. Ibid.
36. Ibid.
37. Ibid.
38. Netherlands Forces Intelligence Service (NEFIS), Box 258, Exhibit 1746, Document No. 5731: *Statement by Charles JONGENEEL, Capt., RNIA, head of War Crimes Section, NEFIS*, 8 July 1946, MacMillan Brown Library, University of Canterbury, Christchurch, New Zealand.
39. Ibid.
40. Netherlands Forces Intelligence Service (NEFIS), Box 258, Exhibit 1760, Document No. 5756: *Javint report 3106/3, Statement of Major Katsumura, Kempeitai,* 20 October 1945, MacMillan Brown Library, University of Canterbury, Christchurch, New Zealand.
41. Ibid.
42. Ibid.

Chapter Six

Double Tenth

To give an accurate description of the misdeeds of these men it will be necessary for me to describe actions which plumb the very depths of human depravity and degradation. The keynote of the whole of this case can be epitomized by two words – unspeakable horror.

Lieutenant-Colonel Colin Sleeman,
Chief Allied Prosecutor at the Double Tenth Trial

Six commandos in three black canoes, known as folding boats or 'Folboats' for short, paddled their craft close to Singapore Harbour. Each little boat was heavily laden with military hardware and stores, primarily magnetic limpet mines. Leading the attack was Captain Ivan Lyon of Force 136, part of Special Operation Executive's Far East operations. It was 26 September 1942, seven months since the British had surrendered Singapore to the Japanese; and if the raid went well it would be a little payback for that terrible humiliation to British arms.

Lyon and his men were identically dressed in two-piece black silk suits, their faces also blackened. Each man wore a belt with a holstered .38 revolver and ammunition, knife, compass and first-aid kit. They also carried a cyanide capsule in case of capture, as none relished becoming prisoners of the Kempeitai. The lights of Singapore burned brightly in the darkness, silhouetting the ships riding at anchor in the harbour. The Japanese felt secure; Singapore was deep behind their lines, and none suspected that a plucky group of British and Australian soldiers and sailors was going to make a play for the fat tankers and freighters at anchor in the Roads and tied up along the city's wharves.

Lyon, sitting low in his Folboat, divided his men into three attacking sections. He would mine ships at Examination Anchorage, while the other two boats would attack vessels in Keppel Harbour and along the Pulau Bukum wharves respectively. When the commandos assigned to Keppel Harbour reached their target they could find no ships so they paddled over to the Roads instead. The harbour was silent, just the sound of water slapping against the sides of the merchant ships as they swung at their anchor cables and the chimes of clock towers in the city ringing off the quarter hours. It took the commandos twenty minutes to deal with each ship, to paddle up, place their limpet, and make off. Lyon and his men mined seven ships and then made off for their rendezvous south.

The first explosion tore across the harbour at 5.15am, followed by six more as all hell broke loose. The booming detonations of the mines rattled windows in Singapore, and the rising sun revealed ships slowly sinking in the harbour, with huge columns of black smoke billowing into the sky and oil burning on the surface of the water. Ship's sirens wailed and Japanese patrol boats raced in and out of the wrecks looking for the perpetrators of this dastardly attack. Lyon and his men were long gone as the Kempeitai exploded from their offices in Singapore, a furious glint in the eyes of its officers as the hunt began for those responsible.

The Kempeitai special investigation branch in Singapore was headed by Lieutenant-Colonel Haruzo Sumida. He had been charged by his superiors with rooting out 'anti-Japanese elements' among the local population and the large number of interned British and Commonwealth citizens being held at Changi Jail. His main headquarters was inside the Art Deco YMCA building on Stamford Road. In overall command of the 2nd Field Kempeitai in Singapore was Lieutenant-Colonel Oishi. There were about 200 regular Kempeitai stationed in Singapore, supported by 1,000 auxiliaries seconded directly from the regular army. The main Kempeitai prison was Outram Road Jail, and there were other field offices on Smith Street in Chinatown and at the Central Police Station.

Chinese Communist guerrillas, armed and trained by SOE, had launched many acts of sabotage against the occupying Japanese forces throughout Malaya since the surrender in February 1942. In

Singapore, local resistance acts had included the cutting of telephone wires and setting fire to dock warehouses full of military supplies. The Kempeitai had dealt harshly with anyone even remotely suspected of harbouring anti-Japanese sentiments, and they had displayed the results on iron stakes erected outside the YMCA and the Cathay Building, home of the Japanese propaganda department. Atop the stakes were severed human heads, a powerful warning to the populace to tow the line. Rudy Mosbergen, a 12-year-old in 1942, recalled of the heads: 'Being somewhat curious and adventurous, I decided to see one for myself ... I could see the bloodied head of a male Chinese on show ... After a week's exposure, the heads eventually shrank and turned blue-black ... It was truly a disgusting sight.'[1]

Lieutenant-Colonel Sumida did not believe that the Chinese were acting alone, and his suspicions had already fallen upon several of the European internees being held at Changi Jail as the likely organizers of the resistance. The Japanese knew that some of the inmates maintained rudimentary communications with friends on the outside who were either working for the underground or were in contact with the resistance groups. Sumida had ordered the arrest and torture of several British inmates, but each time he had released them through a lack of evidence or confessions. It was the outside intervention of Allied forces, who had absolutely no communication with the poor souls under lock and key at Changi, that would allow Sumida to unleash the full horrific force of the Kempeitai in Singapore in a reign of terror and blood that cost many innocent lives.

Operation Jaywick, Ivan Lyon's daring attack on shipping in Singapore, was the catalyst for a terrible revenge wreaked upon the local population and Allied internees by the Kempeitai. The British had been very keen to be seen to be doing something in Asia after they had been kicked out of Malaya, Burma and Hong Kong. The war in the Pacific had devolved into a mostly American-dominated affair, led by the charismatic and vain General Douglas MacArthur from his headquarters in Australia. The British lacked the military resources to launch a comparable military campaign of reconquest, and Churchill had placed most of Britain's Far Eastern resources into the recapture of Burma. But some junior officers nonetheless believed that striking at other Japanese occupied territories throughout Southeast Asia was not only feasible, but necessary if Britain was to regain her colonies after the war was over. It would also go a little way to assuaging some of the complicated feelings caused by the humiliating defeat in Malaya and Singapore in 1942.

Pricking the bubble of Japanese invincibility and taking the war quite literally into the enemy's backyard was an attractive proposition, especially for the maverick officers of SOE's Far Eastern branch, Force 136. But striking at the Japanese, even on a very limited scale, was to engender terrible retribution from a humiliated enemy, and give the Kempeitai the excuse it had long been searching for in Singapore to remove what it perceived to be enemies among the civilian prisoner population.

The brainchild behind what would become Operation Jaywick was Lyon himself, an energetic young Scottish aristocrat from the Gordon Highlanders. Lyon was twenty-eight years old, and during the months before the Japanese invasion of Malaya he had already been involved with organizing 'stay behind' parties of indigenous personnel who would form the nucleus of a resistance movement to the Japanese. An unorthodox soldier, Lyon had been recruited by SOE and had escaped capture when Singapore fell. Within a few months he had proposed raising a small force of Australian and British commandos which he would lead in a daring seaborne attack on Japanese shipping in Singapore, a raid that would be as brilliant as that launched by the more famous Cockleshell Heroes in France. SOE considered launching such an attack from India to be impractical, and so Lyon was sent to Australia to launch his attack from the south-east, up through the Netherlands East Indies. The Americans were quite hostile to Lyon's plan, and MacArthur's team, known as the Bataan Gang after scrambling out of Corrigedor with their boss in 1942, actually tried to quash the operation; but as the funding was coming from London American assistance was not required.

Lyon reported directly to Major General H. Gordon Bennett, the soon-to-be disgraced former commander of the 8th Australian Division during the Battle of Malaya who had controversially managed to escape Singapore on the day that Lieutenant General Arthur Percival had surrendered the colony, 15 February 1942. Bennett had abandoned his men to Japanese imprisonment. Bennett sent Lyon to Melbourne to meet Lieutenant Colonel G.S. Mott, the chief of the Australian version of SOE, the Special Reconnaissance

Department (SRD) who would assume overall command of the proposed operation. On 17 July 1942 the Governor-General, Lord Gowrie, arranged for Lyon to meet with Commander R.B.M. Long, the director of the Australian Navy's intelligence-gathering outfit in Melbourne and the SOE contact in Australia. Long recommended Lyon's plan up the chain of command to Admiral Royle and the Australian Naval Board, who granted a reluctant approval to a scheme most officers thought near-suicidal.

Finding a suitable boat to get the Jaywick attack force in range of Singapore was the next challenge. Lyon had already planned to use collapsible two-man canoes, the Folboats, for the actual attack inside Keppel Harbour in Singapore, but one vessel was required to carry both the attackers and the support personnel and crew to the target through thousands of miles of enemy territory. A boat that attracted as little attention as possible was the obvious choice for this kind on infiltration and attack mission. Ivan Lyon's co-conspirator in dreaming up Jaywick was a 61-year-old Australian civilian named Bill Reynolds who by chance had carried many refugees to safety ahead of the advancing Japanese in a 70-foot requisitioned Japanese coastal fishing boat, the *Kofuku Maru*. Lyon had the vessel shipped to Australia where it was fitted with radio equipment and the hull and deck armoured. Lyon also renamed the vessel *Krait*, after a particularly deadly Asian snake. For the mission to sink shipping in Singapore, Z Force consisted of four British and eleven Australian personnel led by Lyon. On 13 August 1942 the *Krait* left Thursday Island in New South Wales with the commando team aboard and sailed to the US Navy base at Exmouth Gulf in northern Western Australia where the boat was refuelled and repairs were made.

Operation Jaywick got fully underway on 2 September when Lyon and his team, the *Krait* disguised as an Asian fishing boat, began the long journey to Singapore. The team members had dyed their skin dark brown to appear more convincingly Asian from a distance and were dressed in native clothing. Stowed aboard the *Krait* were limpet mines, the Folboats, Sten guns, revolvers and hand grenades. The team eventually arrived close to Singapore without incident on 24 September. That night the six men making the attack clambered aboard their black painted Folboats and began paddling the thirty miles towards Keppel Harbour and their targets. Each boat contained one officer and one enlisted man, the officers consisting of Lyon, Lieutenant Donald Davidson of the Royal Naval Reserve, and Australian Army Lieutenant Bob Page. The men established a forward operating base in a cave on a small island close to the harbour and on the night of 26 September they boldly paddled into Keppel Harbour in their Folboats.

The raid was a spectacular success, and it knocked the Japanese for six. They truly did not believe that the Allies were able to penetrate the defensive screen thrown up by the Imperial Japanese Navy that protected Singapore to the south and south-east. Lyon and his men sank or seriously damaged seven Japanese ships totalling 39,000 tons, and they all escaped alive. The Japanese went crazy as soon as the first explosions boomed out across the harbour, and Singapore resembled a disturbed ant's nest as Japanese soldiers and Kempeitai troops took to the streets and patrol boats raced around the harbour, searchlights stabbing the darkness that was lit only by the flames of the burning ships. American intelligence later confirmed two of the ships sunk by the Jaywick team, the *Kizan Maru* (5,007 tons) and the *Hakusan Maru* (2,197 tons). The Kempeitai was virtually apoplectic with rage at the destruction caused and by the audacity of the attack. However, the Kempeitai, and in particular their local commander, Lieutenant-Colonel Sumida, firmly believed that the Jaywick raid was the result of cooperation between Chinese guerrillas from mainland Malaya and imprisoned British civilians in Changi Jail. It never occurred to Sumida and his cronies that the attack was a well-planned and well-executed commando raid launched from outside Japanese territory.

Whilst the Japanese searched high and low for the 'guerillas' who had raided Keppel Harbour, Lyon and his team lay low on the small island close to Singapore. They waited until the commotion had subsided before moving. As for the crew of the *Krait*, they spent several nervous days cruising up and down through the islands trying to look like an innocent fishing boat going about its lawful business, and they miraculously managed to avoid the attentions of Japanese naval patrols. On 2 October Lyon and his team rendezvoused with the *Krait* and on 19 October they all arrived back at Exmouth Gulf unharmed and victorious.

For those whites interned in Singapore there was no celebration when news reached them of the Jaywick attack. 'After scouring the environs of Singapore Harbour and finding no trace of an Allied commando party, [the Japanese] concluded that the raid was the work of fifth columnists who had already perpetrated a series of far less spectacular acts of sabotage.'[2] Criticism has been levelled at Lyon and his superiors for allowing the raid to take place, and the question has been asked whether Jaywick was actually justified, especially considering its relatively limited strategic results and the subsequent Kempeitai campaign of retribution against innocent people. At the time, the Allies did not claim responsibility for Operation Jaywick because they did not want the Japanese to findout how the commandos had managed to penetrate Japanese defences. This meant that the Allies could use the same strategy again at a future date of their own choosing. But by not claiming responsibility they lent credence to Sumida's belief that the operation was a cooperative effort between Chinese 'bandits' and British internees. 'The attack on Singapore Harbour by the Jaywick team and the loss of shipping was an enormous blow to Japanese prestige and they reacted aggressively.'[3] The Japanese did not divert significant military resources to the stiffening of Singapore's defences, but instead allocated greater resources to the Kempeitai so that they could root out the supposed 'anti-Japanese elements' among the local population and internees and exact reprisals for the Japanese humiliation.

What was interesting was that thousands of miles to the west a similar raid had been launched in occupied France by Royal Marine Commandos. The targets of the 'Cockleshell Heroes' were Japanese and German merchant ships in Bordeaux harbour engaged in the secret *Yanagi* trade in weapons and raw materials between Europe and Japan. The Germans and the Japanese actively cooperated with each other throughout the war, and exchanged ideas on everything from machine guns to jet aircraft, submarines and atomic weapons, as well as doing a roaring trade in rubber and raw materials from the Far East to supply the Nazi war machine.[4] Operation Frankton was a British raid dreamt up by 28-year-old Major Herbert 'Blondie' Hasler of the Royal Marines, and it occurred a few months after Jaywick in December 1942. Twelve marines paddling six two-man Cockle Mk. II Canoes were launched from the submarine HMS *Tuna* on 7 December ten miles from the mouth of the Gironde Estuary. Only four men reached the target, the rest of the canoes being sunk in the extreme conditions the marines faced, and the men forced into an escape and evasion situation ashore or drowned. Those who were captured were turned over to the Gestapo and later shot, following Hitler's infamous Commando Order of October 1942 that demanded death sentences for captured enemy commandos. The four men who reached the harbour placed limpet mines on several ships, and they managed to flood four enemy cargo ships and damage a German minesweeper before they tried to escape to freedom overland with the help of the French Resistance. Only two men made it home: Major Hasler and his fellow canoeist Marine William Sparks, the other pair being betrayed to the Gestapo and later shot. Hasler was awarded a DSO and Sparks a Distinguished Conduct Medal for their bravery.

Colonel Sumida's suspicions fell fully upon the unfortunate inmates of Changi Jail. The Kempeitai operated under the directions of the Japanese criminal justice system, but the system was flawed. The system 'stipulated that a prisoner had to confess to a crime before he or she could be charged with it. Therefore, the interrogator was permitted to use any amount of force, intimidation or coercion to extract a confession.'[5] Regarding the Jaywick operation, the very methods used by the Kempeitai to extract 'confessions' would actually lead to the Japanese tying themselves up in knots as the pieces of the giant 'anti-Japanese' conspiracy puzzle refused to fit together, no matter how hard they beat and tortured the suspects. It became known as the 'Double Tenth Incident' in Singapore. In the end, even the dreaded Kempeitai had to admit defeat, though in finding out the 'truth' fifteen internees from Changi died under torture.

Two examples sum up the terrible suffering of those who Sumida and his henchmen insisted were involved in the attack on Keppel Harbour. On the morning of 10 October the Kempeitai had assembled all of the internees at Changi Jail, and a thorough search of their quarters had revealed several items of contraband. Included among the forbidden items were some radio parts. Under torture, several of the internees revealed that the parts had come from a hospital canteen operator named Choy Khun Heng who worked at Tan Tock Seng canteen. The Kempeitai arrested Choy on 29 October. A few days later the unfortunate man's wife, Elizabeth Choy, was asked by the Japanese to come to the YMCA building on Orchard

Road in Singapore where it was promised that she would be permitted to see her husband. On arrival Elizabeth was immediately arrested by the Kempeitai and thrown into a tiny windowless cell. The cell was only ten feet by twelve, but the Japanese crammed twenty other people, locals and foreigners, in with her, a mixture of civil servants, businessmen and doctors all suspected of involvement with the 'sabotage' in the harbour. 'Packed like sardines, we knelt from morning till night,' recalled Elizabeth. 'Some of us suffered serious sores on our knees.' Conditions in the cell were virtually intolerable and were all part of the regime of torture. 'I was the only female among [the prisoners]. Inside the cell was a tap and underneath it, a hole meant for toilet purposes. There was no privacy to speak of – our daily business was conducted there in full view of everyone.'[6] The terrified and terrorized inmates lived in abject filth and squalor inside the overcrowded cell, waiting with bated breath to be hauled off for another session of torture. 'The stench coming from our perspiration, human waste and stagnant water fouled up the small cell and was suffocating,'[7] recalled Elizabeth.

At the first interrogation session the Kempeitai officer told Elizabeth that some Japanese ships had been sunk in Keppel Harbour. They wanted to know the location of a large sum of money that must have been used to fund the attack. Of course, Elizabeth had absolutely no knowledge of any of this, and she told the Japanese the truth. Her punishment was 193 days of torture. She was severely beaten, spat at, whipped and kicked. Electric shock torture was used on her extensively. 'During the torture, it was impossible to show defiance and be brave,' recalled Elizabeth's biographer Zhou Mei, 'it was impossible to suppress the screams, or to stop the tears and mucus from streaming down her face.'[8] 'We had to crawl out through a small trap door at the side [of the cell] for interrogation. Our captors beat us up, subjected us to electric shocks and pumped us up with water as part of the interrogation routine,' said Elizabeth after the war. 'The feeling of having one's belly pumped full of water and then seeing the water gushing out of the body was hardly bearable.'[9]

Elizabeth's husband was also suffering terribly in Japanese hands, but perhaps the worst torture he faced was to be forced to watch his wife being abused by the grinning Japanese devils in front of him. 'When my interrogators could not get any information out of me, they dragged my husband from Outram Prison, tied him up and made him kneel beside me. Then, in his full view, they stripped me to the waist and applied electric currents to me.'[10] No-one was safe from Kempeitai suspicions. The Bishop of Singapore, the Rt. Rev. Leonard Wilson, who was interned along with other British nationals at Changi, was hauled off to the YMCA building and placed in a cell next to Elizabeth's. For three days the churchman was severely beaten by Japanese interrogators, but it became clear early on that the Bishop had no information to offer, and he was released shortly afterwards covered in cuts and bruises. Elizabeth was set free after nine months, by which time the Kempeitai had meticulously followed up every point in her story, cross-examining everything she said against the results of other interrogations. Half-starved, filthy and in considerable pain Elizabeth tasted freedom. 'Not having seen sunlight during my imprisonment, my eyes could hardly open as I stood directly under the sun. My mind was a complete blank. The clothes that I had been wearing for 200 days smelt foul. My body ached from my injuries,' recalled Elizabeth. 'For a long while, I felt I had just returned from death.'[11] Elizabeth's biographer records that the 32-year-old had shown incredible heroism and bravery during her terrible imprisonment. 'No matter how severe the tortures, she always managed to walk back to her cell with as much resolution as she could muster. Typically, she was far more concerned about the welfare of her cell-mates than her own suffering. Her compassion and selflessness, as well as the fact that she remained undefeated to the end won her the admiration of her fellow detainees.'[12]

Dozens of people were similarly abused for months by the Kempeitai, but no information of any value was forthcoming. 'As none of the suspects had even heard of Jaywick, let alone been part of it, any confessions they made were meaningless. This further enraged the Japanese.'[13] The man charged with finding the truth, Colonel Sumida, 'was mystified. Despite great suffering, not one of his victims had told him anything about the raid itself, how it had been organised or where the explosives had been obtained.'[14]

In 1946 Elizabeth was made an Officer of the Order of the British Empire (OBE) and she went on to become Singapore's first female legislator, as well as a fashion model and teacher. When asked whether she wanted the death penalty given to Colonel Sumida and his Kempeitai henchmen, Elizabeth replied firmly with a 'no'. 'If not for war, they would be just like me. They would be at home with their family, doing just ordinary things and peaceful work. Let us pray that there will be no more war.' Elizabeth Choy died of cancer in 2006 at the age of ninety-six.

Back in Australia following Operation Jaywick, Prime Minister John Curtin recommended Captain Ivan Lyon for the Victoria Cross. For complicated political reasons it was not to be, and Lyon was eventually given a DSO. Bob Page was also awarded a DSO and two of the enlisted men on the raid received Military Medals. Planning began soon after for another raid on Singapore utilizing new motorized semi-submersible canoes called 'Sleeping Beauties' that were seen as an improvement on the Folboats used in Jaywick. Folboats would also be taken along as a back-up. The new operation was named Rimau, the Malay word for 'tiger'.

Led by the newly-promoted Lieutenant-Colonel Lyon, in total twenty-two men of Z Force would mount the operation. They were dropped off by the submarine HMS *Porpoise* on 11 September 1944 close to Merapas Island and shortly after commandeered a Malay junk named the *Mustika*. After loading the Sleeping Beauties, Folboats, mines, weapons and stores aboard her, Lyon and his party set off for Singapore, hoping once again to pass unnoticed through enemy patrols by appearing to be a harmless local fishing boat. This time the ruse failed and the men of Z Force got into a short but bloody firefight with a Japanese patrol boat that came too close. Lyon ordered the *Mustika* scuttled along with the Sleeping Beauties, and ordered most of the men to withdraw to Merapas Island to await recovery by submarine. Lyon and a party of five men did not withdraw. Instead they loaded mines and firearms aboard three Folboats and paddled once again into Keppel Harbour. The limpets they placed managed to sink three Japanese ships. However, on the return journey the raiding party was cornered by Japanese troops on Soreh Island and in a bloody encounter on 16 October Colonel Lyon and another officer were killed by a hand grenade, and many of the others wounded. One of the commandos was captured, but the rest managed to make it to Tapai and Merapas Islands.

The Royal Navy submarine that was supposed to take the men off Merapas Island never materialized or answered increasingly urgent radio calls for assistance, and the men soon realized their situation was hopeless. During fierce battles involving the cornered commandos, including those who had withdrawn earlier to Merapas under Lyon's orders, thirteen were killed and the remaining ten were captured alive by the Japanese. In return, it is estimated that the Rimau commandos killed upwards of sixty Japanese soldiers. As expected, the Kempeitai showed the prisoners no mercy, and they were extensively tortured until all the details of the operation were given up. The Japanese also learned for the first time of the identity of the Jaywick commandos. After imprisonment at Outram Road Jail in Singapore, alongside many innocent civilians brought in for questioning by the Kempeitai during the Double Tenth Incident that had followed the Jaywick raid, the ten surviving commandos were placed before a military court and sentenced to death. The sentences were carried out on 7 July 1945, very close to the war's end, when all ten men were beheaded with swords.

Some degree of retribution and justice for those who were victims of the Double Tenth incident was the arrest of Colonel Sumida and twenty of his colleagues of the Singapore Branch of the Kempeitai by the British, who subsequently charged them with the commission of war crimes. On 3 September 1945 the cruiser HMS *Cleopatra* carrying the Commander-in-Chief East India Fleet, Admiral Sir Arthur Power, steamed into Keppel Harbor. The next day Rear Admiral C.S. Holland aboard the cruiser HMS *Sussex* and Rear Admiral J.A.V. Morse, flag officer designate Malaya aboard HMS *Kedah* arrived with 5th Indian Infantry Division and Headquarters XV Corps from Rangoon, Burma. That evening the Japanese army and navy commanders in Singapore were ushered aboard the *Sussex* where they signed the official instrument of surrender. Almost immediately the hunt commenced for Japanese war criminals among the more than 50,000 surrendered Japanese soldiers in Singapore and Johore, and Colonel Sumida and his men, who were trapped in Singapore, were quickly identified and arrested.

Sumida and the Singapore Kempeitai section were charged with contriving to arrest in particular fifty-seven civilians interned at Changi Jail, and thereafter ill-treating them, resulting in the deaths of fifteen.[15] The trial was conducted in the Supreme Court Building before a Military Court presided over by Lieutenant-Colonel S.C. Silken of the Royal Artillery, assisted by Major S.F. Hodgens of the Australian Army Legal Corps and Captain R.J. Topping of the 6/8th Punjab Regiment. The accused were given full access to Japanese defence counsel, and they were not abused or maltreated during their period in remand. The Japanese were given every opportunity to mount a defence. The prosecution team consisting of Lieutenant-Colonel S.C. Sleeman, 16th/5th Lancers, and Captain A.A. Hibbert, Royal West African Frontier Force, convinced the court of the guilt of many of the defendants, and damning evidence including that of witnesses proved conclusive. After a twenty-one day hearing the judgments were delivered on 15 April 1946. Colonel Sumida and seven of his cronies were sentenced to death by hanging. Three more received life sentences, one got fifteen years and two others eight years imprisonment each.[16] The remaining seven were acquitted. Compared with the terrible tortures, suffering and agonized deaths of fifteen innocent civilians from Changi Jail, as well as the horrendous abuse inflicted on those other internees and civilians who survived the Double Tenth inquisition, Sumida and his men were given relatively humane and quick deaths at the end of a rope. It was not however a fate shared by many of the thousands of other Kempeitai who engineered abuse and murder across Asia, and the vast majority would unfortunately escape justice at the war's end.

Notes

1. *World War II through the eyes of a teenager* by Chua Mui Hoong, *The Straits Times*, 13 August 2007.
2. Peter Thompson & Robert Macklin, *Kill the Tiger: Operation Rimau and the Battle for Southeast Asia* (Dunshaughlin, Maverick House Publishers, 2007), p. 107.
3. Ibid: p. 107.
4. For more information see the author's *Yanagi: The Secret Underwater Trade between Germany and Japan 1942–1945* (Barnsley, Pen and Sword Books Limited, 2005).
5. Peter Thompson & Robert Macklin, *Kill the Tiger: Operation Rimau and the Battle for Southeast Asia* (Dunshaughlin, Maverick House Publishers, 2007), p. 108.
6. *A Shameful Past in Human Memory: A Verbal Account by Elizabeth Choy, The Price of Peace* (Singapore Chinese Chamber of Commerce and Industry).
7. Ibid.

8. Zhou Mei, *Elizabeth Choy: More than a War Heroine: a biography* (Singapore, National Volunteer & Philanthropy Centre and Beaumont Publishers, 2004), p. 78.

9. *A Shameful Past in Human Memory: A Verbal Account by Elizabeth Choy, The Price of Peace* (Singapore Chinese Chamber of Commerce and Industry).

10. Ibid.

11. Ibid.

12. Zhou Mei, *Elizabeth Choy: More than a War Heroine: a biography* (Singapore, National Volunteer & Philanthropy Centre and Beaumont Publishers, 2004), p. 78.

13. Peter Thompson & Robert Macklin, *Kill the Tiger: Operation Rimau and the Battle for Southeast Asia* (Dunshaughlin, Maverick House Publishers, 2007), p. 108.

14. Ibid: p. 109.

15. *The Double Tenth Trial* by Henry Wong, 7 May 1999, National Library Board, Singapore.

16. Double Tenth Trial Judgments, 15 April 1946: Lieutenant-Colonel Haruzo Sumida (death); Warrant Officer Tadamori Monai (death); Sergeant-Major Masuo Makizono (death); Sergeant-Major Tako Terada (death); Sergeant Toichiro Nozawa (death); Sergeant-Major Shiger Tsujio (death); Sergeant-Major Shozo Morita (death); Interpreter Tok Swee Koon (death); Warrant Officer Shigeru Sakamoto (life imprisonment); Sergeant Hideo Kashara (life imprisonment); Interpreter Masyoshi Nigo (life imprisonment); Interpreter Kasuo Miyazaki (15 years imprisonment); Sergeant Kozo Sugimoto (8 years imprisonment); and Interpreter Chan Eng Thiam (8 years imprisonment). P.R. Piccigallo, *The Japanese on Trial: Allied War Crimes Operations in the East, 1945–1951* (Austin, University of Texas Press, 1979), p. 110.

Chapter Seven

Sex Slaves

When we got to the house, we were told we were there for the sexual pleasure of the Japanese military ... we started protesting straightaway. We said that we were forced into this, that they couldn't do this to us, they had no right to do this, it was against the Geneva Convention, and that we would never do this. But they just laughed at us, you know, just laughed. They said they could do with us what they liked.

Jan O'Herne, Dutch 'Comfort Woman'

The crowd was getting uglier by the minute. Hundreds of gaunt white women in thin summer dresses and worn-out straw hats shouted for the release of the young women and girls the Japanese had imprisoned inside the church. Mixed in with the women were dozens of teenage boys equally furious and shouting at the tops of their voices. Japanese soldiers clad in beige uniforms, their shaved heads bearing forage caps with a single gold star, eyed the growing crowd with uncertainty. Normally Allied prisoners, and certainly civilian internees, were cowed and terrified creatures that did everything they could to avoid the interest of their guards. Here at Muntilan Internment Camp on the Dutch island of Java in January 1944 it was the prisoners who were doing all the shouting.

Japanese officers ran about grasping sheathed katana samurai swords in their right hands and nervously fingering holstered automatic pistols, as the prisoners screamed harder. Inside the church located in the camp, a place of sanctuary and safety in better times,

Kempeitai officers had gathered dozens of young women. Their intention was to pick the most attractive and force them to become sex slaves in one of several military brothels catering to Japanese troops on the island. The near riot outside was the collective fury of mothers, brothers and friends determined that the Japanese would not be successful in executing this final disgusting assault upon the helpless.

To say that the Japanese military had no respect for women would be a vast understatement. In the Japanese military mind women served but one purpose – to provide entertainment and/or sport for Japanese soldiers. The methods used by the Japanese to procure this entertainment for their troops were illegal in the extreme and barbarous by nature. Rape was the Japanese soldier's primary relationship with women in the Occupied Territories. The taking of sex by force was not an individual pursuit, but a group exercise encouraged by senior officers in all theatres.

Japanese soldiers had begun brutalizing civilian populations before the Second World War in China in 1937. Mass rape and mass murder had been practised upon the Chinese populations of cities and villages in front of the world's media. Foreign journalists had reported what was being done to Chinese women and girls, but the Western Powers had easily dismissed the evidence as a reflection of Asians making war upon Asians. Westerners commonly portrayed Asians as cruel and heartless people who viewed life cheaply.

The greatest sexual crime in history was committed by Japanese troops in the Chinese capital city of Nanking (now Nanjing) in 1937–8 when hundreds of thousands of women and girls were raped, tortured and murdered by entire regiments of Japanese troops, without any sanction from senior officers. The army that unleashed itself upon the rest of Asia on 8 December 1941 consisted in large part of young men who thought rape and brutality were normal expressions of soldiering, as normal to the Japanese as cutting the heads off prisoners-of-war or killing oneself to avoid the disgrace of capture. Morality was perverted beyond recognition, and immense suffering was inflicted upon innocents as a result.

As well as simply raping women that they encountered in towns and villages across Asia, the Japanese military also instituted a form of organized prostitution and/or slavery to give all Japanese troops access to women. Known as 'Comfort Women', they came from a variety of different nationalities and found themselves involved in this sex trade through a variety of different paths. In the occupied Netherlands East Indies Dutch women and those of mixed race parentage were forced into sexual slavery, the details of which are only now beginning to emerge in the early twenty-first century, such was the degree of abuse and the shame attached to it. The treatment these women endured was appalling in the extreme. Some of their stories follow later in this chapter, and it is easy to see why after being released so many never spoke of their terrible experiences at the hands of the Japanese. The role of the Kempeitai in creating this human misery was vital, yet another example of the actions of an organization completely devoid of morals, scruples or humanity.

It was the responsibility of the Kempeitai to procure 'prostitutes' for Japanese units, to establish and run brothels, and to control those unfortunate women who were imprisoned within them. It was part of the wartime mission of the Kempeitai. During the course of the war between 60,000 and 200,000 young women were forced into sexual slavery in military brothels. The majority were Asians and they would come from Korea, China and other occupied territories. Initially at least, some were recruited by offering attractive wages to actual prostitutes. In the later stages, women were deceived or simply forced into prostitution, some even being kidnapped or 'bought' from their parents for this purpose.

The young Japanese soldiers who raped and abused women, and often used brothels, came from a country where prostitution was well organized and carried on quite openly. A huge industry catered for the sexual desires of Japanese men and it still does today – if one visits the central entertainment districts of Tokyo it is clearly apparent. Women were not considered equal to men in or out of marriage. Prostitution did not carry with it the stigma or shame associated with the sin-based Christian morality of the Western nations. Sex, both marital and extra-marital, was viewed as natural and something to be enjoyed, and paying for sex carried no taboos.

It was perhaps unsurprising that the Japanese military believed that organized prostitution would serve the Emperor's soldiers well. Once the initial terrorization of a civilian population had passed and the occupation began, Japanese soldiers still wanted access to women. Providing easy access to prostitutes would improve the morale and military effectiveness of Japanese soldiers, so the logic went. Institutionalized brothels would also help the army control the spread of sexually transmitted diseases and so improve the health of its soldiers. The British had organized military brothels for soldiers in India during the nineteenth century with these very ideas in mind, but outrage at home had forced their closure, leading to a massive increase in sexual diseases among soldiers as they were forced to go to unregulated brothels once again.

The Japanese military was not completely ignorant of the damage inflicted on relations with civilians of the occupied territories by the sexual brutality of Japanese soldiers who had raped and pillaged extensively during the initial invasions. 'Comfort Stations', as the Kempeitai called brothels, would prevent Japanese soldiers from raping civilians and thus prevent the rise of hostility among the peoples of occupied areas. The Kempeitai was responsible for rooting out all anti-Japanese plots, so not providing ammunition for such plots in the first place was naturally a concern for the military police. Comfort women appeared to provide the answer. In this the comfort stations failed, for Japanese troops continued to prey on women throughout the war. Their attitude was based upon a belief in their own racial superiority. '[It] didn't matter to us whether women lived or died,' said Japanese veteran Anji Kaneko in 2007. 'We were the Emperor's soldiers. Whether in military brothels or in the villages, we raped without reluctance.'[1]

Initially, the army placed advertisements in newspapers in Japan, Korea, Taiwan and Manchukuo (occupied Manchuria) to recruit prostitutes. These sources rapidly dried up and created a shortage of prostitutes elsewhere, particularly back in Japan. The army moved to procure more women, the vast majority of whom had never been involved in the sex industry, from the territories that Japan had recently conquered. It was in this operation that the Kempeitai used all of its nefarious talents for intimidation and violence to force native women into sexual slavery. What occurred in occupied Java went even further, with the Kempeitai targeting white women for the first time. Although only about 300 Dutch women were forced to become comfort women, representing a tiny percentage of the tens of thousands of native females coerced into sexual slavery, their stories have been practically unheard until quite recently, and have sparked an outcry in the Netherlands and elsewhere.

In January 1942 Japanese troops staged amphibious landings on the island of Java, the administrative capital of the Netherlands East Indies (NEI). Borneo and the Celebes were also invaded. At the same time British resistance north in Singapore was coming to an end, and in the Philippines American efforts to stop the Japanese had been roundly defeated and their forces bottled up in the Bataan Peninsula and on Corregidor Island. Java was the headquarters of ABDA, the American-British-Dutch-Australian Command headed by British General Sir Archibald Wavell. Defended by a mixture of British, Dutch and American troops, backed up by the hotchpotch of locally raised Indonesian home guards of untested ability the Japanese quickly overwhelmed Allied resistance and occupied the island. Wavell and his staff fled to India, and the NEI were abandoned to the Japanese. On 8 March 1942 the Dutch formally surrendered. The Japanese made further landings on Timor, Sumatra, the Moluccas and the Sunda Islands and after fierce engagements with local Allied forces captured all of these places as well.

Dutch and other Allied soldiers were rounded up, disarmed and sent to prisoner-of-war camps where thousands would die from disease, starvation, physical abuse and arbitrary executions. By the latter half of 1942 the Japanese had also interned Allied civilians living in the NEI, sending men, women and children to dreadful internment camps where conditions were almost as bad as those reserved for military prisoners. Java was the centre of this gulag, as the island had had the biggest white population before the war. More than 150,000 Europeans were interned either as prisoners of war or civilian internees throughout the NEI, while a further 22,000 mainly mixed-race Indo-Dutch living on Java stayed out of the camps. European women who were nationals of neutral countries such as Switzerland and Sweden, or countries that were friendly with Japan, such as Germany and Italy, were not interned. However, everyone, regardless of nationality or status, was subject to the suspicions of the Kempeitai, who viewed all non-Japanese as potential security threats. A Swiss or German passport did not save many from seeing the inside of a Kempeitai torture chamber.

White women had not been safe from rape by Japanese troops during the initial invasion and occupation. Caucasian women and children were sexually assaulted at Tarakan, Menado, Bandoeng, Padang and Flores Island. At Blora, close to Semarang in Java, twenty European women and girls were imprisoned in two houses beside a main road. Over a period of three weeks, as Japanese units passed by these houses, the women and their daughters were repeatedly raped. The older women protested in vain to Japanese officers, who laughed in their faces, until one day a senior Japanese officer happened to pass by the houses and witnessed what his men were doing. He immediately ordered the assaults to cease, and the white women were sent to the relative safety of an internment camp. The Blora rapes highlighted the deplorable state of discipline that existed in the Japanese Army towards the treatment of non-combatants, and the sadism and brutality of the average young Japanese soldier who took part in these assaults with alacrity.

Java was placed firmly under the control of the Japanese Army. Many of the outlying islands that constituted the vast NEI were under Navy control, whose own military police, the Tokeitai, ran brothels and torture chambers in a similar fashion to the Kempeitai. Java was administered by the 16th Army under the control of 7th Army Headquarters in recently captured Singapore. Neither Tokyo nor the 7th Army issued actual orders for the establishment of military brothels to the Kempeitai in Java. Instead, local 16th Army officers took it upon themselves to order the local field Kempeitai to begin establishing Comfort Houses. The commissariat officer of the 16th Army was ordered by the chief of staff to issue licences to brothels. A licence would only be issued if the 'prostitutes' had signed a document that stated that they were working voluntarily for the army as sex workers. In practice, the Kempeitai used coercion and/or violence to obtain the necessary signatures that were passed up the chain of command to 16th Army Headquarters in Batavia.

The girls themselves came from several different national groups. Some were Japanese or Koreans who had been recruited and shipped in to service the troops. Others were Indonesian women who were recruited locally, and they had often been deceived into becoming sex workers by their Japanese procurers. A smaller number were European women who were living in internment camps, and the last group were European women who were still at liberty outside the camps. Up to mid-1943 native and non-interned European women were mainly recruited to act as housekeepers for individual Japanese officers or civilians. When Japanese troops wanted sex they went to local brothels or to individual European or native prostitutes.

The Kempeitai instructed local hotel owners to convert their establishments into brothels in mid-1943. The recruitment of prostitutes was increased. The Japanese decided to set up brothels that contained a particular race or nationality of women in certain areas. There were brothels that contained Chinese women and others that were staffed by Indonesians. Javanese women were transported in from outlying islands to fill others, and European women were targeted in the internment camps. Recruitment turned to physical force as the Kempeitai took the initiative in establishing scores of brothels for Japanese troops in Java. Military brothels, employing European women, were established at Batavia, Bandoeng, Pekalongan, Magelang, Semarang and Bondowoso. 'This change of policy was probably due to the increasing incidence of venereal disease and the inability of the privately run brothels to remedy this problem. In addition, fewer European women were available for work in the brothels, as most of them [living outside the internment camps] preferred to establish a relationship as mistress to one Japanese man.'[2] Such reasons were cited by the Kempeitai in applying force to recruit women from internment camps in the Semerang area. 'They believed that among the twenty thousand women interned in these camps enough volunteers could be found to solve their recruitment problems.'[3]

The use of European women as prostitutes appears to have been fairly widespread in Java. The women fell into three categories. Firstly, there were those women who had been working as prostitutes before the war and who continued in that profession. Secondly, some women volunteered to leave the internment camps after being promised work as barmaids or waitresses and were subsequently forced into prostitution by unsavoury Japanese and Korean pimps. The third group were European women forcibly taken from the internment camps in groups and used as sex slaves by Japanese forces. Among the second group of European women, their stories were quite similar. For example, in June 1943 the Japanese owner of the Akebono restaurant in Batavia was instructed by the Kempeitai to open a brothel. He opened an establishment called the Sakura (Cherry Blossom) Club in new premises on Gang Horning. Of the twenty European women working at Sakura Club, eleven had volunteered for the job to escape Cideng Internment Camp in the city. In late 1943 the Kempeitai ordered the establishment of a second military brothel in Batavia for army officers. Called the Theresia or Shoko Club, it was located on Telokbetongweg, and was run by a Japanese pimp. He used European women as procurers, and in December 1943 the Kempeitai ordered him to obtain more white women. Using his European procurers, the pimp went to Cihapit Internment Camp in Bandoeng and successfully recruited eleven white women to work as prostitutes.

The most infamous of the Kempeitai recruitment drives was conducted at Muntilan Internment Camp near Magelang. In November 1943, a Japanese pimp from Magelang brothel and a local Kempeitai officer drew up a list of women deemed suitable to become prostitutes from among the prisoners held at Muntilan Internment Camp. The Kempeitai officer in turn contacted the camp leaders asking them to recommend any women on the list who would be suitable to work as 'barmaids' in Magelang. Although the offer of work sounded quite innocent, the suspicions of many of the older mothers were aroused and they demanded to see the list. The names were all of young women and girls, and things did not look right to them. On 25 January 1944 some Kempeitai troops arrived at the camp in a bus brandishing a copy of the list. A *tenko* or roll call was immediately called, and the people on the list were ordered to go to the church (the camp being situated inside a monastery) for an inspection. The camp leaders and the camp doctor followed behind, protesting loudly to the Japanese officers. Behind them followed a large crowd of women and teenage boys. When the church door opened and the Kempeitai tried to escort their chosen women to the bus a riot broke out. Furious internees hurled clumps of earth and stones at the Japanese, who immediately turned on the crowd with great brutality, officers even slashing at unarmed civilians with their swords. Through this maelstrom of violence, the young girls were roughly bundled aboard the bus and driven out of the camp.

Three days later the Kempeitai returned to the camp with a proposal that volunteers replace the women who had been forcibly taken. A few women, who had been working as prostitutes before the war, volunteered. On 28 January 1944 thirteen women from the camp, most of who were married, were taken to Magelang. A Dutch woman, who was 25-years-old at the time, recalled: 'We were sent to an asylum from a detention camp ... and underwent a health inspection by Japanese doctors on February 3.' Two women were assigned to each room in the brothel. 'After returning to our room, Ms. Bracker and I closed all our windows and doors. Around 9 o'clock in the evening, we heard a knock. Military police forced us not to close the door. The military police brought a Japanese soldier and we must accept the soldier. The military police forced us to do so saying, "If you do not accept the soldier, your husband will be responsible for that."' The Kempeitai would use any and all methods to force women to comply with their foul plans. 'The brothel was open for officers on weekdays, and for sergeants on Sunday afternoons. Sunday mornings was for private soldiers and sometimes for common Japanese people. We always resisted but it was in vain.'

In February 1944 the Kempeitai visited seven women's internment camps on Java, but the camp authorities and prisoners at three of the camps put up such opposition that the Japanese did not manage to procure a single girl. At the other four the Kempeitai, working with Japanese civilian pimps, managed to obtain some women. Once again, women who volunteered to save others from this horror, or were simply selected against their will, were roughly examined, raped, beaten and forced to service Japanese soldiers. One woman attempted suicide, another faked insanity and was placed in an asylum, while another later had to have an abortion. The experience of one of these women demonstrates the whole sordid, depraved and inhuman nature of the ordeals that decent Dutch women were forced into by the Kempeitai. Jan O'Herne was an attractive young girl, born in Bandoeng in Java 1923. After the Japanese invasion O'Herne, along with her mother and two sisters, was imprisoned in a condemned army barracks at Ambarawa. 'I'd been in the camp two years,' recalled O'Herne. 'They [the Japanese] gave an order that all young girls from 17 years and up had to line up in the compound. These high military officers walked towards us and started to eye us up and down, looking at our figures, looking at our legs, and it was obviously a selection process that was going to take place.'[4]

The girls selected were herded aboard an open truck and 'driven away ... as if we were cattle. And I remember we were so scared and clinging to our little suitcases and clinging to each other.' The seven girls were driven to a large colonial house about twenty-five miles from the camp outside Selarang. 'When we got to the house, we were told we were there for the sexual pleasure of the Japanese military ... you know, our whole world just collapsed from under out feet. And we started protesting straightaway. We said that we were forced into this, that they couldn't do this to us, they had no right to do this, it was against the Geneva Convention, and that we would never do this. But they just laughed at us, you know, just laughed. They said they could do with us what they liked.'[5]

The Japanese took portrait photographs of the girls that day, and these were displayed on the veranda to allow Japanese troops to pick the girls they liked. The brothel was sarcastically named 'The House of the Seven Seas' by the Kempeitai. 'We were given flower names and they were pinned to our doors,' recalled O'Herne. 'They started to drag us away one by one. And I could hear all the screaming coming from the bedrooms, you know, and you just wait for your turn ... And there stood this large, fat, bald Japanese officer looking at me, grinning at me, and I put up an enormous fight, but he just dragged me to the bedroom.'

O'Herne and the other girls were all virgins when they were assaulted. 'I said, "I'm not going to do this." And he said, "Well, I will kill you. If you don't give yourself to me, I will kill you." And he actually got out his sword. I went on my knees to say my prayers and I felt God very close. I wasn't afraid to die.' The Japanese officer had no intention of killing O'Herne. 'He just, you know, threw me on the bed – got hold of me, threw me on the bed and just tore off all my clothes and most brutally raped me. And, I thought he would never stop. It was the most ... the most horrendous ... I never thought suffering could be that terrible.' The Japanese officer left. 'I thought, "I want to go to the bathroom. I want to wash this all away. I want to wash away all the shame, all the dirt. Just wash it away, wash it away." '[6]

When O'Herne got to the bathroom she found the other girls already there. 'We were all there in the bathroom, you know, all totally hysterical and crying and just trying to wash away the dirt, you know, the shame. Within one night, we lost our youth. We were just such a ... such a pitiful little group of girls, and we were just embracing each other. And how many times was each one raped that night? You know, I shall never forget that first night. And we felt so helpless. This was going to happen from now on, night after night.'[7]

The ordeal these young Dutch girls were subjected to by the Japanese lasted for four long months. They lived tortured lives in a state of constant fear. 'I'll never forget that fear,' said O'Herne. 'You know, it runs right through your body like electrical currents. And it's a fear that has never left me. It's been with me all my life. I can feel that fear sometimes at night ... Because when it's dark, it means I'm going to be raped over and over again.' The fear drove O'Herne to take an extreme measure in 1944. 'You come to a stage where you think, "I've tried everything. What can I do? What can I do next?" I cut off all my hair. I thought if I made myself look as ugly as possible, nobody would want me ... It turned me into a curiosity object. And they wanted me even more because I was the girl that cut her hair off ... "We all want the bald girl." '[8]

The girls were checked weekly for venereal diseases by Japanese army doctors. Doctors take an oath to help people, and O'Herne thought that a doctor would help her. 'When the doctor came, I went to him and I said, "Look, I want you to know we're here against our will. Use your influence. Go to the highest authority, report this, that we are forced into this." ' The doctor's response was the opposite of what O'Herne and the other girls expected. 'He just laughed and he ended up raping me himself. And from that time onwards, every time the doctor came for his regular visit, he used to rape me first.'[9]

The Dutch girls were not only raped, but they were also beaten. Those who became pregnant were kicked in the stomach or thrown down the stairs to induce miscarriages. The Japanese soldiers enjoyed humiliating the girls, and sadism was part and parcel of the sexual assaults that they endured. 'This just went on, you know, week after week, month after month. We were total wrecks. I'd been beaten up so many times.'[10]

Suddenly, the rapes ended and the girls were sent back to their internment camp to be reunited with their families. The Kempeitai warned the girls not to speak of what had been done to them; otherwise they and their families would suffer the consequences. The Japanese closed brothels employing European women in the last week of April 1944. A colonel from the Ministry of War in Tokyo had been making a routine inspection tour of civilian and military prison camps on Java. 'One of the camp leaders of Ambarawa 9 whose daughter had been taken away managed to arrange a meeting with the Japanese colonel to tell him what had happened. The colonel informed Batavia, Singapore [Southern Area Army HQ] and Tokyo of his findings and recommended the immediate closure of the Semarang brothels. The headquarters at Batavia responded immediately by sending orders to this effect to the general responsible in Semarang.'[11] Many of these brothels later resumed operations, but instead of using European women they forced mixed-race girls to become 'comfort women'. O'Herne and her comrades were suddenly and expectedly reunited with their mothers back at the camp:

[That] first night [back at the camp], I couldn't even talk or say anything to her. I just ... I can feel it now, laying in my mother's arms, you know, in the hollow of her arms ... her arms around me ... And then the next day, I told her what had happened to me and so did the other girls. We had all these girls with all these mothers ... And the mothers just couldn't cope with this story, this happened to their daughters, you know. It was too much for them – they couldn't cope with it. And we were only to ever tell our mothers just once. And it was never talked of again – it was just too much for them.[12]

After the war a Kempeitai major in charge of the forced recruitment of European women for Japanese brothels was sentenced to death for war crimes. Others went to prison, and one Japanese officer killed himself before he could be tried. The Dutch women were deeply scarred for life. Jan O'Herne married a British soldier who was part of a unit protecting the camp from Indonesian nationalists after the Japanese surrendered in 1945 and later moved to Australia where she currently lives. She and several other Dutch women survivors, particularly one woman named Ellen van der Ploeg, have been vocal in calling for an apology from the Japanese government alongside one for the thousands of Asian women impressed as prostitutes, but the Japanese government has refused to recognize what occurred, stating that 'comfort women' were merely prostitutes who had volunteered to service Imperial troops. And although this is clearly a lie, no one can force the Japanese government and people to recognize the myriad crimes committed all across Asia and the Pacific by wartime Imperial forces. The Japanese continue to laugh in the face of all those who demand recognition and compensation for the horrors that they endured.

According to recent research, out of 200–300 Europeans who worked as 'comfort women' in the Netherlands East Indies, at least sixty-five, like O'Herne, were forced into this work by the Kempeitai. 'It's absolutely appalling,' said O'Herne in 2007. 'I am so angry that after all these years and so much proof ... Japan is not owning up to their historical responsibilities.'[13] It remains extremely doubtful whether Japan or the Japanese people ever will.

Notes

1. 'Japan's Abe: no proof of WWII sex slaves', *Washington Post*, 1 March 2007.
2. Bart van Poelgeest, *Report of a Study of Dutch Government Documents on the Forced Prostitution of Dutch Women in the Dutch East Indies during the Japanese Occupation*, Unofficial Translation, 24 January 1994.
3. Ibid.
4. *The Forgotten Ones*, transcript of television documentary on Australian Story, produced by Margaret Parker, Australian Broadcasting Corporation, http://www.abc.net.au/auhistory/transcripts/s351798.htm.
5. Ibid.
6. Ibid.
7. Ibid.
8. Ibid.
9. Ibid.
10. Ibid.
11. Bart van Poelgeest, *Report of a Study of Dutch Government Documents on the Forced Prostitution of Dutch Women in the Dutch East Indies during the Japanese Occupation*, Unofficial Translation, 24 January 1994.
12. *The Forgotten Ones*, transcript of television documentary on Australian Story, produced by Margaret Parker, Australian Broadcasting Corporation, http://www.abc.net.au/auhistory/transcripts/s351798.htm.
13. 'Our forgotten shame of wartime sex slavery', *Brisbane Times*, 23 June 2007.

Chapter Eight

Slaughter of the Innocents

She returned to Dinawan Island and there found 2 graves containing a number of decapitated bodies and 37 heads. She recognized one of the heads as being her husband.

Sujiang, Dinawan Island

The screaming of women and children was deafening. They were local natives, twenty-five in all, and their pain was intense. Lieutenant Shimizu of the Kempeitai stood watching as his men hanged the women and children by their wrists from the pillar of a white-painted mosque. Grasping his sword scabbard in his right hand, he drew an automatic pistol from a brown leather holster on the left of his belt and bellowed a series of commands to his men. As the figures writhed and screamed on the ends of their ropes a couple of light machine guns were brought into position before the mosque and cocked. Shimizu raised his pistol and aimed at one of the swinging figures, his finger closing over the trigger as he raised his voice and shouted 'Fire!'

Wherever the Japanese went their treatment of local inhabitants soon bred deep-seated discontent. Although they spent a lot of time and effort trying to convince the Asian populations of the Occupied Territories that Japan was their friend and had 'liberated' them from the grasp of white colonialists, the actions of the Japanese spoke much louder than their kind words. A virtually identical situation developed in the Ukraine and other areas of the Soviet Union when the Germans invaded. Masses of the population initially welcomed German troops who appeared to be liberating them from Stalin's tyrannical and racist rule, only to find their goodwill was misplaced as the SS and *Einsatzgruppen* began a reign of terror behind the advancing army divisions. It soon became very clear in Asia to the Malays, Indonesians, Filipinos, Indians, Polynesians and innumerable small tribes from Borneo to New Guinea that the Japanese viewed their fellow Asians as cheap labour to be exploited for the benefit of Japan. The Chinese, who were found living in all of the Occupied Territories, had long harboured a deep-seated distrust and hatred of the Japanese that had been reciprocated in spades for generations; and events in mainland China from 1937 had proved to the Chinese that their opinion of the 'shrimp barbarians', as they called the Japanese, was well-founded. Most Chinese thought that the Japanese were beyond the pale, that they were a sadistic, cruel and militaristic people who were racially chauvinistic and violently xenophobic and had 'borrowed' most of their culture from China in the first place (writing, government models, literature, folklore and myths, architectural styles, and Imperial system). Indeed, it was galling to most Chinese, and still is, that Japan 'borrowed' so much from China, modified those 'gifts' and then claimed that they were in some way superior to their fount of origin. The Chinese felt somewhat superior themselves to the cultures of former vassal states like Korea and Japan, and this feeling remains a strong undercurrent in Sino-Japanese relations today. It was the Chinese who bore the brunt of Japanese efforts to intimidate and control the populations of conquered Asia, and the Japanese were straightforward in dealing cruelly with their 'blood enemies'.

Among the many other nationalities of Asia, some believed the propaganda claptrap which portrayed the Japanese military as a liberating force. Many believed that Asians would not subjugate other Asians, but all those who dreamed of liberation and independence were to find those dreams smashed by Japanese oppression. Certainly the Japanese attempted, in a rather half-hearted manner, to encourage independence movements and to raise 'national' armies to fight the British; but the conquerors could never fully trust anyone or any organization that was not Japanese, and so these experiments all failed miserably. At the end of the day, the Japanese were using Asian independence aspirations for their own malevolent ends, rather than for any altruistic reasons.

One of the major problems for the Japanese in trying to win the trust and respect of their fellow Asians was the behaviour of the Kempeitai. To be a member of the Kempeitai, one had to believe implicitly in the Imperial Way, and this meant a belief in the racial superiority of the Japanese above all other peoples. Therefore, rather than ambassadors of Japanese culture and thought, the Kempeitai were the very worst examples of Japanese racism and intolerance – and the parallels with the SS again are striking. The Kempeitai viewed all native peoples with great suspicion, and they assumed that everyone was fundamentally anti-Japanese, and therefore plotting the destruction of the sacred Empire. Pragmatically, the Kempeitai was not far off the mark, for in the period following the conquest many native peoples stood by and watched as the Chinese and whites among them were victimized and killed. But the Kempeitai did not stop with just the Chinese, and they soon began to believe in their paranoid delusion that 'everyone' was out to get the Japanese, and that the Kempeitai was the only force standing between order (and the ultimate victory of Imperial Way thought) and absolute defeat. This institutionally ingrained distrust and contempt for all things 'foreign' made the Kempeitai violently reactive and heavy-handed. Kempeitai paranoia increased steadily as the war turned inexorably against Japan after defeat at the Battle of Midway in June 1942.

There are a multitude of examples of Japanese military paranoia, but one instance from the island of Borneo exemplifies the indiscriminate fury of the Kempeitai, and their woefully medieval techniques used to reveal the 'truth'. The consequences for native people were devastating, and the effects of Kempeitai pogroms are still felt in the region today.

On 9 October 1943 a violent anti-Japanese revolt suddenly erupted in the sleepy port town of Jesselton, now Kota Kinabalu, in the British colony of North Borneo on the South China Sea. The Japanese were stunned by the uprising. The majority of the rioters were ethnic Chinese who had suffered over a year of persecution and violence at the hands of vindictive Japanese officials, and they had decided to fight fire with fire. It was a hopeless cause from the very beginning, for the rioters were deep inside enemy territory and could expect no help from the Allies. In fact, their only real friends were small bands of guerrillas operating in the jungle hinterland with which the Chinese, led by Albert Kwok, had established contact.

The rebellion occurred on the 'Double Tenth', the night of 9–10 October, and guerrillas led by a Lieutenant-Colonel Suarez did a great deal of the fighting with Japanese forces. Forty Japanese soldiers were gunned or hacked down by furious Chinese, and several buildings used by the Japanese were burned. For a few hours Jesselton was free, but the Japanese response to this challenge to their power was typically harsh, indiscriminate and cruel.

Japanese aircraft soon appeared over the town and began bombing and strafing anything seen moving in the streets, as well as in neighbouring villages. Most of the people killed or made homeless had not been connected with the rising in any way, but the Japanese determined to impress upon *all* of the inhabitants, Chinese or not, who was in charge and the huge power of the Japanese military should anyone dare to challenge that authority. By 10 October the revolt was over, crushed by the weight of Japanese airpower and the damage inflicted upon the town and its peoples. The guerrillas retreated inland and fought another small battle with Japanese ground forces six miles from Jesselton before they were tricked into surrendering. The Japanese now instigated phase two – a violent campaign of repression led by the Kempeitai.

Large numbers of Kempeitai were immediately dispatched in trucks from the capital, Kuching, with orders to seek out, arrest, interrogate *and* execute all those implicated in the anti-Japanese revolt. Because it was known that the revolt had been planned and led by local Chinese, the Kempeitai simply assumed that *all* Chinese were guilty of insurrection and arrested every one they could lay their hands upon. It was also an excuse for the Japanese to kill Chinese, an activity they relished at all times throughout the war. Hundreds of men and women were dragged from their homes in the middle of the night by groups of Kempeitai soldiers and thrown into overcrowded and filthy jails throughout the town. All of the suspects were tortured; the usual panoply of Japanese cruelty was displayed, including the water treatment, beatings, starvation, electrocution and so on. Once they had been broken under interrogation and given the Kempeitai more names, further arrests were made and the jails and torture chambers fed with more individuals. Those who had confessed, either truthfully or falsely, to having taken part in the revolt were denied any recourse to the law before being sentenced to death. The number of Chinese killed was huge – on one occasion alone 189 men and women were executed.

The Kempeitai soon began to look further afield than just the Chinese of Jesselton. Malays were also implicated and hauled away to uncertain fates. Even local indigenous peoples were suspected, including a group known as the Suluks who inhabited a cluster of small islands off the coast near Jesselton. A British officer who investigated the large-scale atrocities committed against the Suluks believed that their part in the anti-Japanese revolt was minimal. Captain M.J. Dickson said that the 'Suluk people seem to have taken part in it only on the first night.'[1] They were to pay a frightful price for that minimal support.

The Suluks had moved to the islands under the protection of the Sultan of Brunei in the late nineteenth century to escape Spanish persecution. They occupied islands including Mantanani and Mangalum off the west coast of Borneo. Both Borneo and Brunei were under British control, and so the Suluks lived peacefully under the protection of the Crown. They were primarily fishermen who lived in small coastal villages consisting of wooden houses built out over the beach on piles. As the Suluks were Muslims, villages usually contained a mosque with a small school attached. As well as fishing, the Suluks cultivated coconut palm, and exchanged fish for rice and cloth in the coastal villages of Borneo, including trading bird's nests with local Chinese in Jesselton. A British report noted that the Suluks were 'vigorous, bold and independent people, holding themselves inferior to no man and generally liked by the British and native peoples of Borneo.'[2] By 1941 the Suluk population was noted as approximately 838 men, women and children. They were about to be swept up in a storm of blood and violence that would reduce their population to only 288 when the war ended in 1945.

The Japanese found the Suluks too independent for their liking. The Suluk chieftains had made it plain to the Japanese that they would not be providing their men folk as cheap labour and they had refused to cooperate with Japanese fishing firms that tried to muscle in on their trade. In the Japanese mind this meant the Suluks were troublemakers and would have to be watched carefully. Their suspicions were confirmed during the Double Tenth rebellion when a small group of Suluks 'from Sulug Island, near Jesselton, landed on the night of the rising near the Malay Kampong at Jesselton, armed with parangs and spears, and burned down the Customs shed and some supplies of rubber and rice.'[3] One of the Chinese ringleaders arrested by the Kempeitai, Dr Lou Lai, broke under torture and named most of the other leaders of the rising, including several Suluk chiefs. His forced confession incriminated all of the Suluks in the eyes of the Kempeitai, and the Japanese determined to have their revenge.

Japanese troops and Kempeitai clambered aboard small boats and were taken out to the islands inhabited by the Suluks on the pretext that they were searching for a Chinese guerrilla named Lin Tin Fat who had managed to avoid the roundup following the rebellion. The Japanese believed that Lin was hiding on Mantanani Island twenty miles off the Borneo coast and sixty miles by sea from Jesselton. On 13 February 1944 twelve Kempeitai soldiers stepped ashore on the island, accompanied by twenty-four Japanese troops from the local garrison, six Native Police and two Chinese interpreters. The Kempeitai orders were simple: find Lin. If Lin could not be found, arrest all those Suluks who could have information concerning his whereabouts and the extent of Suluk involvement in the rebellion. The local chief denied any knowledge of Lin, so the Kempeitai ordered the local troops to arrest fifty-eight Suluk men and take them back to Jesselton.

The fifty-eight Suluks were all horribly tortured at Jesselton. A local imprisoned alongside them, Bachee bin Hassan said that when the Suluks were first taken to the Kempeitai prison 'they were each given a slip of paper with their name on it. I was with them then.'[4] Each day Kempeitai soldiers would select several Suluks and take them from the prison to the nearby Kempeitai office for questioning. Hassan was sometimes forced by the Japanese to act as an interpreter, and so witnessed terrible scenes of torture. 'The K.T. [Kempeitai] used to ask them what they had done in the rising,' recalled Hassan, 'whether they had attacked the Custom House or burnt the rubber. If the Suluk said 'No', he was beaten with a stick about 4 foot long, as thick as a police baton. They were beaten all over the body.' Many of the Suluks gave false confessions under such terrible duress. 'Sometimes I saw Suluks tied and water poured down their throats till their stomach was full,' recalled Hassan. 'Then the K.T. would jump on the man's stomach or kick it.'

Every one of the Suluk prisoners from Mantanani Island died in the Kempeitai prison, mostly from beatings administered by Japanese investigators or starvation in the cells. Those who managed to survive these twin horrors were later executed secretly by the Kempeitai and their bodies hastily buried. The Kempeitai, however, was not satisfied with the information they had gleaned from repeatedly interrogating the Suluk men from Mantanani. Even while the first group of fifty-eight was still alive in the prison, Japanese launches arrived off the island's beaches on 15 February. Led by Lieutenant Shimizu of the Kempeitai, they came to kill the rest of the people on the island. Shimizu strode with his unit into the main village and began rounding up the remaining men, along with several women. The remaining Suluk men could see what was about to happen and tried to defend their loved ones armed only with crude spears and parangs. Immediately, Shimizu ordered light machine guns to open fire into the group, and many were mown down as they tried to flee.

When the smoke cleared many Suluks lay in pools of their own blood, moaning and crying out for help, while all around lay dead relatives and friends. Shimizu ordered his men to finish off the wounded. The Japanese soldiers strolled among this carnage, occasionally driving their long bayonets into writhing bodies on the sand or dispatching individuals with a single rifle shot to the head. As the Japanese finished this massacre Shimizu ordered his men to reform and then started to corral a large group of terrified women and children. Shimizu ordered their hands bound behind their backs, and in a display of considerable sadism he ordered them hanged from the mosque, thereby insulting their religion as well as abusing condemned civilians. At his command the guns opened fire again and twenty-five women and children were dispatched. The Japanese then burned the village and the Suluk fishing boats before boarding their own boats and sailing back to Jesselton. In a couple of hours the Japanese had eradicated an entire community for no apparent reason except cruelty and revenge. Shimizu was later arrested by the British at the end of the war and was tried as a war criminal in Singapore.

Horror was followed by horror. One month later eight or nine Suluks were caught on the mainland and detained by the Kempeitai at Kota Belud. 'Two of them were men, the remainder women and children, the youngest a baby in arms ... They were kept in prison for about six weeks, and then executed one evening. A hearsay report says that they were offered the choice between shooting and beheading, and chose the former.'[5] British military intelligence believed that the killing of these women and children, as well as the women and children on Mantanani, indicated 'a policy of extermination'[6] on the part of the Japanese. The population of Mantanani was about 430 when the Japanese first arrived. In 1945 only 125 remained, 'of whom not more than 20 or 25 are adult males.'[7]

Japanese crimes were not confined to Mantanani Island. In February or March 1944 the Kempeitai visited the small island of Dinawan, where 120 Suluks lived. They arrested all males over the age of twelve, a total of thirty-seven. These suffered a similar fate to the men of Mantanani. Their wives and children, totalling ninety-one people, were removed and transported to Gaya Island, where twenty-seven died of starvation before the end of the war. One of the wives named Sujiang wanted to know what had happened to her husband. After the Japanese surrender 'she returned to Dinawan Island and there found 2 graves containing a number of decapitated bodies and 37 heads. She recognized one of the heads as being her husband.'[8] In 1945 the British noted that the entire population of Dinawan was fifty-four people, all of them adult women and children under sixteen years of age. Not one man ever came back from Jesselton.

On Sulug Island Chief Panglima Ali and all the other men and teenage boys, twenty-nine in total, were arrested and died in unknown circumstances in Kempeitai custody in Jesselton. About forty women and children were also removed from the island and sent as slave labourers to the Bangwan Estate in North Borneo where twenty-five died from hunger, disease or exhaustion. Udar, consisting of two small islands off Mengattal, was also devastated. All the adult males were executed by the Japanese, while forty-five women and children were enslaved and removed to Kimanis Estate in North Borneo where eleven perished. Other islands suffered a similar fate. Maarof bin Abdullah was imprisoned at Jesselton Prison between May and June 1944, and he stated that 258 Suluk men and women were locked up there. 'All died by beatings, from disease, by being dried in the sun, and about 100 were removed at

1 a.m. on 17th June 1944 by the Japs to Mile 5 and there shot,' related Abdullah to British investigators.[9]

Captain Dickson, of the British Army's No. 8 War Crimes Investigation Team was not convinced that the Kempeitai were actually trying to exterminate the Suluks, even though their heavy-handed tactics contained grounds to make such a charge. 'The killing of women and children on Mantanani Island was, in my opinion, the result of anger, amounting to hysteria, at the resistance offered by the Suluks,' wrote Dickson. 'The deaths of so many Suluk men are to be attributed to the methods employed by the Kempei Tai rather than to an official intention to exterminate the race.'[10]

Planned extermination or not, British investigators were concerned that so many Suluk men and boys had been killed by the Kempeitai that their population would never fully recover in peacetime, and that the unique Suluk culture would disappear as their remaining women married men from different tribes. It was another sad tale of the Kempeitai destroying the lives of ordinary people, in this case on a large scale and with huge ramifications for the future of an entire and unique way of life.

Notes

1. International Military Tribunal for the Far East, Box 256, Exhibit 1654, Prosecution Document No. 5334: *Report of Captain M.J. Dickson of the British Army*, MacMillan Brown Library, University of Canterbury, Christchurch, New Zealand.
2. International Military Tribunal for the Far East, Box 256, Exhibit 1659, Exhibit No. 1659A: *Atrocities Committed Against The Suluk Peoples of North Borneo During Japanese Occupation*, MacMillan Brown Library, University of Canterbury, Christchurch, New Zealand.
3. Ibid.
4. International Military Tribunal for the Far East, Box 256, Exhibit 1654, Prosecution Document No. 5209: *Affidavit of Bachee bin O.K.K. Hassan of Inanam*, MacMillan Brown Library, University of Canterbury, Christchurch, New Zealand.
5. International Military Tribunal for the Far East, Box 256, Exhibit 1659, Exhibit No. 1659A: *Atrocities Committed Against The Suluk Peoples of North Borneo During Japanese Occupation*,

MacMillan Brown Library, University of Canterbury, Christ-church, New Zealand.

6. Ibid.
7. Ibid.
8. International Military Tribunal for the Far East, Box 256, Exhibit 1654, Prosecution Document No. 5211: *Affidavit by Sujiang, a Suluk woman of Dinawan Island*, MacMillan Brown Library, University of Canterbury, Christchurch, New Zealand.
9. International Military Tribunal for the Far East, Box 256, Exhibit 1659, Exhibit No. 1659A: *Atrocities Committed Against The Suluk Peoples of North Borneo During Japanese Occupation*, MacMillan Brown Library, University of Canterbury, Christ-church, New Zealand.
10. International Military Tribunal for the Far East, Box 256, Exhibit 1654, Prosecution Document No. 5334: *Report of Captain M.J. Dickson of the British Army*, MacMillan Brown Library, University of Canterbury, Christchurch, New Zealand.

Chapter Nine

Asian Auschwitz

We removed some of the organs and amputated legs and arms. Two of the victims were young women, 18 or 19 years old. I hesitate to say it but we opened up their wombs to show the younger soldiers. They knew little about women – it was sex education.

Akira Makino, March 2007

In China there is a place located in the northern city of Pingfang near Harbin in Heilongjiang Province that sums up today for many Chinese the true face of Japanese occupation. It ranks alongside the massacre at the memorial hall in Nanjing as representative of all of the sufferings heaped upon the Chinese people by Imperial Japan between 1937 and 1945.

At Pingfang a series of nondescript but well built red-brick structures surrounded by parkland are the remains of a gigantic experiment in biological and chemical warfare conducted by the Japanese military in occupied Manchuria. Many thousands of innocent people, from babies and young children to Allied prisoners of war were put to death at the Pingfang facility in the name of spurious science. Japanese military doctors, under the control of the Kempeitai, were permitted to conduct on live human beings every sort of perverted medical experiment normally banned by morality and political and public revulsion. They were as free to play with lives as SS doctors in the Nazi extermination camps, to push the boundaries of our understanding of human anatomy and of human resistance to disease, infection and extremes of temperature, altitude and privation. The Japanese desperately tried to cover up their crimes when the war came to an end, but much of their facility, too well-built to be easily demolished, survived to stand testimony into the twenty-first century of Japan's own Holocaust upon the innocent. It is another, and perhaps the greatest, chapter of shame that continues to sour Sino-Japanese relations in the present day. The Japanese deny what happened at Pingfang and elsewhere, while the Chinese are determined that their people should never forget what happened. The title of the Japanese organization that operated at Pingfang has entered the general consciousness as an evil name to rank alongside Belsen and Auschwitz. The name is Unit 731.

In 1905 the Russians, after being defeated in a short war with Japan, had ceded southern Manchuria to the Japanese. In 1931, the Japanese had expanded their control over the rest of Manchuria and the following year that had created a puppet state they named Manchukuo to try to legitimize their invasion and occupation of Chinese territory. To further cement their control over Manchuria they placed the last Chinese emperor, Pu Yi, on the throne of Manchukuo, the former Qing Dynasty of China having originated in Manchuria hundreds of years earlier. The Japanese, however, exercised real control over the province. The territory was garrisoned by the Japanese Kwantung Army quite independently of control from Tokyo, and this army was eventually to engineer, with Kempeitai assistance, a plot to invade the rest of China.

In 1932, Lieutenant General Dr Shiro Ishii was placed in command of a new Japanese facility constructed in the village of Beiyinhe, about sixty miles south of Harbin. Ishii was a physician and expert on biological warfare. He had initially been attracted to germ warfare after he discovered that it had been specifically banned by the 1925 Geneva Protocol. Ishii reasoned that if germ warfare had to be banned under international law, it must be very powerful and he determined to secretly develop these weapons for his nation. Ishii had powerful friends in the Japanese government and military, and under their protection his research flourished. When he was not working in his laboratories, Ishii could be found in one of the famous Geisha houses in Tokyo where he was known as somewhat of a swashbuckling womanizer. He was also a daring inventor. He created a revolutionary new water filter for the Japanese military and was invited to demonstrate his new product before Emperor

Hirohito himself. Ishii urinated into the filter and offered the results to the Emperor to drink. Hirohito not unnaturally declined, but Ishii drank the purified liquid before his sovereign, this stunt earning him further exposure and generating interest in his secret work.

The occupation of the whole of Manchuria provided a vast secret testing area for Ishii's new weapons programme, directly financed and supported by the Japanese government. Kempeitai troops built Zhong Ma Prison Camp, and railway lines were extended directly into the camp, linking it with the entire South Manchurian Railway network. Materials and equipment were shipped directly to the camp, and Chinese prisoners were herded into the prison. Ishii organized a secret research group of doctors and scientists codenamed 'Togo Unit' who would conduct research into chemical and biological weapons for the army. In 1935 Ishii shut down Zhong Ma and moved all his researchers to a much bigger facility being constructed at Pingfang, a dozen miles south of Harbin.

In order to build the Pingfang centre, Ishii ordered the razing of eight Manchurian villages. With a perimeter fence encompassing a camp of over four square miles, the Pingfang facility contained an airstrip, railway station and sidings, Kempeitai barracks, prison camp for test subjects, underground bunkers, dungeons and gas chambers, science laboratories and operating theatres, and crematoria used to dispose of prisoners' bodies. In total there were about 150 structures on the site, many of which survive to this day due to their solid and expensive construction. To keep the scientists entertained there was a bar and a cinema, and even a Shinto temple within the grounds.

The unit was an integral part of the Kwantung Army and used the cover name 'Epidemic Prevention Department'. In reality, Dr Ishii and his peers were busy developing lethal weapons and conducting inhuman experiments on people, experiments that plumbed the very depths of depravity and sadism. The people who were gathered at Pingfang were men and women, children and infants. They were mostly Chinese, but also included some Koreans, Russians and Allied prisoners of war from the United States and Britain. The Japanese called the prisoners *maruta*, meaning 'logs', an in-joke among the staff after the Japanese had told the local population that the facility was a lumber mill.

Research by Chinese academics at the Harbin Academy of Social Sciences has identified the names of 1,463 people who were secretly transported to Pingfang for medical research, and a conservative figure of between 5,000 and 12,000 people is the number the Japanese probably murdered at Unit 731. General Ishii believed that the results of the research at Pingfang would far outweigh the cost in human lives and the doctors' disregard for their Hippocratic Oath. 'A doctor's God-given mission is to block and treat disease,' Ishii said to his staff of scientists, 'but the work on which we are now to embark is the complete opposite of those principles.'[1]

People who were sent to Pingfang had their files marked 'Special Deportation' by the Kempeitai, who often added other comments like 'incorrigible', 'die-hard anti-Japanese' and 'of no value or use' when describing the prisoners.[2] The 'special deportations' were begun on the orders of General Ishii on 26 January 1936, as the scientist demanded increasing numbers of human test subjects. In 1941 the facility was renamed the 'Epidemic Prevention and Water Purification Department of the Kwantung Army', or Unit 731 for short. Support for the experiments being conducted at Pingfang came directly from Japanese universities and companies in the Home Islands, as well as from the Kempeitai and the Japanese government. The work undertaken by Unit 731 was seen as vital to the Japanese war effort, and no expense was spared in making the facilities as up to date as possible.

Unit 731 was divided into eight divisions, under General Ishii's overall command. Division 1 conducted research into bubonic plague, cholera, anthrax, typhoid, and tuberculosis, using live human subjects. These guinea pigs were drawn from a special camp that held around 300–400 prisoners on site, and was kept fully stocked by the Kempeitai. Division 2 conducted research into biological weapons used by troops in the field and concentrated particularly on inventing new devices to release germs and infected parasites. Division 3 ran a factory that actually produced artillery shells containing biological agents and was based off-site in the city of Harbin. Division 4 produced other lethal agents, while Division 5 was responsible for training personnel. Divisions 6–8 looked after equipment, medical supplies and camp administration.

Allied to Unit 731 were a number of test sites or sub-units located throughout Asia. About eighty miles from Pingfang there was an open-air testing site at Anta. At Changchung was located Unit 100, codenamed the 'Wakamatsu Unit', under the command of veterinarian Yujiro Wakamatsu. This unit was dedicated to developing vaccines to protect Japanese livestock, and developing lethal animal diseases to be used against Chinese and Soviet livestock. Biological sabotage was an important duty of Unit 100.

At Beijing, the Japanese had established Unit 1855, an experimental branch of Unit 731 with a research facility at Chinan in Hopei Province. There scientists conducted research mainly into bubonic plague and other diseases. At Nanjing, earlier devastated by Japanese actrocities in 1937–38, Unit 731 maintained another satellite station, Unit Ei-1644, codenamed the 'Tama Unit' after its commander, which collaborated with Pingfang on many joint projects and experiments. In southern China, at Canton (now Guangzhou) near Hong Kong the Japanese established Unit 8604 which they codenamed the 'Nami Unit'. This unit was the main rat farm for the Kwantung Army, breeding millions of the animals for use in biological warfare applications. Also at Unit 8604 the Japanese conducted human deprivation experiments and research into water-borne viruses like typhus and cholera. Unit 200 was based in Manchuria, and again worked closely with Unit 731 on plague research. The Japanese were not seeking a cure for plague, but rather to develop new and considerably more lethal strains that could be unleashed on the Chinese population. There was also another facility in Manchuria, Unit 571, closely associated with Pingfang, but the site of its headquarters is currently unknown and the nature of the research conducted there remains a mystery.

Outside of China, Unit 731's tentacles stretched deep into the rest of Asia. The biggest unit was based at the prestigious Raffles Medical University in Singapore. Established in February 1942 soon after the British surrender, Unit 9420 consisted of about 1,000 personnel under the command of Major-General Masataka Kitagawa and under the operational day-to-day control of Lieutenant-Colonel Ryoichi Naito. It was divided into two parts: 'Kono Unit' specialized in research into malaria, while 'Umeoka Unit' was interested once again in plagues. Evidence has come to light that Unit 9420 operated another sub-unit in Thailand during the war, but for what purpose it is not known, the Japanese having partially destroyed records of their medical research before Allied war crimes investigation teams arrived in September 1945. General Ishii's empire of death also extended into Japan itself, to the oldest facility located in the southern city of Hiroshima. Here the Japanese had established their first chemical weapons factory in 1928, manufacturing mustard gas, but it later moved on to producing much more lethal poisons for military use. During the 1930s the Japanese government ordered the removal of the factory and research facility from all maps of the area to preserve secrecy and security.

The kinds of experiment conducted on live human subjects were numerous and terrible. Vivisection was practised with alacrity by Unit 731 medical staff. No anaesthetics were administered to victims before they were sliced up and dismembered because doctors believed that the drugs would interfere with their research results. 'The fellow knew that it was over for him, and so he didn't struggle when they led him into the room and tied him down,' recalled a 72-year-old former medical assistant at Unit 731 when describing a 30-year-old Chinese male victim. 'But when I picked up the scalpel, that's when he began screaming.' The horror of the event was simply routine procedure at Pingfang. 'I cut him open from the chest to the stomach, and he screamed terribly, and his face was all twisted in agony. He made this unimaginable sound, he was screaming so horribly. But then he finally stopped. This was all in a day's work for the surgeons, but it really left an impression on me because it was my first time.'[3]

The prisoners were shackled hand and foot, but they were well fed and exercised regularly. 'Unless you work with a healthy body you can't get results,'[4] explained one former member of Unit 731. Prisoners were deliberately infected with various diseases and then dissected while alive so that doctors could observe the results of the diseases on the human body. Men, women and children were used. Other examples included doctors raping female prisoners to make them pregnant, then several months later these same women were dissected and their foetuses removed while alive. Limbs were often amputated to study the effects of blood loss. Sometimes, Japanese surgeons would reattach the severed limbs to different parts of the body, for example sewing legs into arm sockets and so on. Freezing experiments were conducted, where limbs were frozen and then amputated, while others were defrosted intact to study the effects of gangrene on live tissue. In fact, this research turned out to be among the most useful conducted at Pingfang and is still informing medical opinion regarding frostbite injuries today. The methods used were, however, extremely cruel. During the winter prisoners were staked out in fields and their bare arms drenched in cold water to accelerate the freezing process. Scientists would strike the arms with a stick to test whether they were frozen – if they heard a hard, hollow sound the freezing was judged to be complete. Defrosting caused the onset of gangrene, as well as intense pain, which was studied carefully.

Some prisoners had their stomachs removed and the oesophagus reattached to the intestines. Others were tied down, and parts of various organs, such as the brain, liver, kidneys, lungs and so on were removed. Some of these experiments were conducted on infants who lay screaming for their mothers, their short lives abruptly terminated by doctors who viewed these little children as nothing more than live flesh to play with.

One former Unit 731 medic, Takeo Wano, said that he once saw a six-foot-high glass jar in which a Western man was pickled in formaldehyde. The man had been cut into two pieces, vertically. Specimens like these abounded. A Japanese man, who remained anonymous when interviewed in 1995, said he saw specimen jars containing human internal organs, all neatly labelled. 'I saw labels saying "American", "English" and "Frenchman," but most were Chinese, Koreans and Mongolians. Those labelled as American were just body parts, like hands or feet, and some were sent in by other military units.'[5] Another story tells of when General Ishii one day demanded a human brain to experiment on. A group of Kempeitai guards 'grabbed a prisoner and held him down while one of them cleaved open his skull with an axe. The brain was removed and rushed to Ishii's laboratory.'[6] Dozens of former medical staff who were employed at Unit 731 remain alive in Japan today, and several have come forward to talk about what they did to prisoners in the name of science. One, surnamed Kamada, recalled his dissection of a live *maruta* (or log, as the Japanese referred to their victims), who had been deliberately infected with plague bacteria. 'I inserted the scalpel directly into the log's neck and opened the chest,' stated Kamada. 'At first there was a terrible scream, but the voice soon fell silent.'[7]

Testing the effects of battlefield weapons on live human targets was considered important research by the Japanese, not least in the area of battlefield medicine. Prisoners were tied to wooden stakes on special ranges, and grenades exploded at different distances from them to study the effects. Some prisoners were shot and the resultant wounds examined before the prisoner was killed. Flame throwers were used on human subjects to test the most effective range for use of the weapon, and other poor souls were taken to the open-air testing facility at Anta and exposed to biological and chemical weapons to test their effects.

Disease research was at the centre of Unit 731's operations. Prisoners were told they were receiving vaccinations, when in reality the Japanese deliberately infected them with all sorts of fatal diseases to study their effects on human subjects. Sexual diseases, such as syphilis and gonorrhea, were introduced to males and females via rape, and left to fester so that the results could be studied before the patients were executed.

Huge numbers of fleas were applied to infected patients so that the Japanese could breed billions of infected insects for use in biological warfare bombs. These weapons were later used on the Chinese population. Low-flying Japanese aircraft released special canisters containing plague-infected fleas over Chinese cities, including Ningbo in 1940 and Changde in 1941. The resulting epidemics killed upwards of 400,000 Chinese civilians. In fact, infections from these experiments, and others like them, were still killing people in northern China in 1948, three years after the war had ended.

Other human experiments were bizarre. Prisoners were hanged upside down to see how long it would take for them to die. Air was injected into arteries to induce fatal blood clots. Horse urine was injected into human kidneys. Special high pressure chamber experiments were conducted as Japan developed jet aircraft in cooperation with the Germans, whose doctors were also conducting high altitude tests on Jewish prisoners in the concentration camps. Extremes of temperature and their effects on humans were studied, alongside water and food deprivation.

Giant centrifuges were built to test how much G-force the human body could withstand, and these experiments were naturally fatal to the test subjects as the speed was increased and increased. X-ray radiation was administered to prisoners, including lethal doses. The Japanese constructed gas chambers where chemical weapons were tested on live prisoners. The list of atrocities and crimes is nearly endless, and each experiment breached just about every ethic known to medical science. Some of the experiments produced no scientific

General Hideki Tojo, wartime Japanese Prime Minister and Minister of War. Earlier, Tojo had
en in command of the Kempeitai in Manchuria and helped to engineer the undeclared war
ainst China. Later, he was responsible for the terrible conditions throughout Japanese prisoner-of-
ir camps in Asia, as the Kempeitai took charge

2. American soldiers, their hands tied behind their backs, await an uncertain fate after being taken prisoner at Bataan, Philippines in 1942. The Kempeitai and Japanese army forces killed thousands unarmed, surrendered Allied personnel

3. Indian prisoners-of-war, probably captured in Malaya or Singapore, about to be used by the Kempeitai as live targets on a rifle range. The Kempeitai also organized the Indian National Army, group of renegade Indian nationalists, against the British and Imperial forces in Burma

Allied prisoners transporting their sick comrades. The brutality of Japanese prison camps was directly attributable to their being under the auspices of the Kempeitai

Kempeitai officers organizing the beheading of suspected guerrillas in the occupied Philippines. The Kempeitai was obsessed with 'anti-Japanese' plots and murdered hundreds of thousands of largely innocent people throughout the occupied territories

6. Sergeant Leonard Siffleet, an Australian coast watcher captured on New Guinea, about to be beheaded by a Kempeitai officer, 1943

The Kempeitai maintained its own commando forces. Pictured here are *Giretsu* commandos ▸arding a plane for an attack on American-occupied Leyte, December 1944. In 1945, a *Giretsu* unit ▸ade a daring and suicidal attack on American airfields on Okinawa in a vain effort to neutralize ▸merican aircraft

9. An RAF officer questions a recently liberated 'comfort woman'. Japan was guilty of the enforced sexual slavery of tens of thousands of young women across Asia, all of it organized and administered by the Kempeitai

10. Pregnant comfort women liberated by American forces, 1945

11 A group of Kempeitai officers accused of murdering 637 civilians by the British, in the dock in Rangoon, Burma, March 1946

data, but many did advance human knowledge. It is a sad fact that when Japanese and German doctors were permitted to do as they pleased with patients, to play God, the terrible suffering produced data that was invaluable after the war in developing the weapons of the Cold War and for sending Man into space. Without German and Japanese research into jet engines and the human body's endurance, the United States would never have reached the Moon in 1969. It was the United States that cynically protected German and Japanese scientists and doctors who had been involved in these crimes against humanity in order to give America the technological edge over the Soviet Union in the Cold War.

Knowledge of what was happening at Pingfang was widely held throughout the highest echelons of the Japanese government, who sanctioned it. Even the Imperial Family was familiar with Unit 731's activities. Prince Mikasa, Emperor Hirohito's younger brother, actually toured the Unit 731 facility where he was shown films of Chinese prisoners 'made to march on the plains of Manchuria for poison gas experiments on humans'[8], as he noted in his memoirs. General Hideki Tojo, who was Prime Minister of Japan and War Minister for most of the conflict, was so pleased by General Ishii's test results that he saw to it that the Emperor awarded Ishii a high decoration.

When the Soviet Union entered the war in Asia on 8 August 1945, they rapidly overcame the worn-out Kwangtung Army as Operation Autumn Storm swept all before it. The Soviets occupied Manchuria and Korea. General Ishii ordered the scientists and doctors evacuated to Japan before the Red Army arrived at Pingfang, and the destruction of the facility. Although most of the scientists managed to escape, the Kempeitai troops left behind tasked with destroying the facility were largely unsuccessful because the buildings had been so well constructed before the war, and there was no time to make a thorough job of it. Important evidence was thus left behind, and it did not take long for the Allies to figure out what those red-brick buildings had been used for.

Before his research team had been broken up, Ishii had held a meeting at which he had warned his staff never to speak about what they had done, and he ordered every member 'to take the secret to the grave.' Ishii threatened them, that if they did not keep their silence, his associates would find them in Japan and kill them.

Finally, Ishii warned all of them to keep out of public life and maintain low profiles. However, it did not take too long for Allied military investigators to begin the process of hunting down those responsible. Incredibly though, the Americans had no intention of punishing Ishii and his men when they located them – instead they were to offer them jobs. In one of the great scandals of the Second World War, the military ruler of occupied Japan, General Douglas MacArthur, granted Ishii and his associates immunity from prosecution in return for cooperating with the Americans and turning over to them their research results in human experimentation and biological and chemical warfare. The research material was too valuable to the Americans to risk letting it fall into Soviet hands or be exposed to the world's judgment. That was why there was never any mention of Unit 731 at the International Military Tribunal for the Far East, more commonly known as the Tokyo War Crimes Trials. The American Office of Strategic Services (OSS), the forerunner of the postwar CIA, made sure that Ishii and his associates were secretly smuggled into America, alongside dozens of Nazi scientists and technicians. The exigencies of the Cold War meant that the United States could ill afford to waste any opportunity for knowledge that could give them the edge over Stalin.

In 1949 the Soviets convened a trial at Khabarovsk of some members of Unit 731 that the NKVD had managed to snatch, but the most prominent scientists and officers had long ago been smuggled to America. The Soviet trial did manage to reveal the inner workings of the Pingfang facility, even if it failed to bring to justice the main war criminals. The court's report was released in 1950.[9] Dr. Shiro Ishii settled in Maryland where he worked on bio-weapons research for the American military until he died of throat cancer in 1959. Others slipped back into Japan once their work was completed in America, including a prominent Unit 731 doctor, Masaji Kitano, who went on to be president of Japan's largest pharmaceutical company, Green Cross.[10] This would be the equivalent of Auschwitz war criminal Dr. Josef Mengele sitting on the board of directors of Bayer Healthcare or GlaxoSmithKline. Other Japanese officers who were active in Unit 731 went on to fabulously successful careers, including one who became Governor of Tokyo, another who was President of the Japan Medical Association and one who was head of the Japan Olympic Committee.

Unit 731 has cast a very long shadow over modern China. People are still injured by the detritus of Ishii's mad experiments, even today in the early twenty-first century. In August 2003, twenty-nine local people living in Heilongjiang Province were taken to hospital after a construction crew accidentally uncovered artillery shells loaded with chemicals from the Unit 731 factory. The Japanese had buried them at the war's end in an attempt to cover their trail. This incident opened up another row between China and Japan over Japan's wartime record, an issue that simmers away just below the surface between the two powerful neighbours and threatens to erupt into protest and violence at any time.

The repercussions of the activities of Unit 731 are also felt in the United States and Britain. It was long suspected that Allied prisoners of war were experimented on by Japanese doctors at Pingfang, and perhaps elsewhere as well. A little evidence for this assertion has surfaced in the last decade that seems to show that Japanese medical teams from Unit 731 conducted tests and experiments on American and British prisoners held at a camp outside the city of Mukden (now Shenyang) in Manchuria. The camp, located at the town of Fengtian near Shenyang, was named Prisoner of War Camp No. 1 Hoten. On 11 November 1942 fourteen American officers led by Major Stanley H. Hankins, and 1,188 American enlisted men arrived at the camp from the Filipino capital Manila via the port city of Pusan in Korea. They were herded into a former Chinese Army barracks and joined later by eighty-five British and fifteen Australian and New Zealand prisoners of war whose senior officer was Major Robert Peaty, Royal Army Service Corps. Peaty and an Australian military doctor named R.J. Brennan kept secret prison diaries written on scraps of toilet paper. Peaty described Hoten Camp thus: 'I was reminded of Dante's *Inferno* – abandon hope all ye who enter here ...'[11]

Peaty recorded in his diary for 13 February 1943 that 'about 10 Japanese medical officers and 20 other ranks arrived today to investigate the cause of the large number of [POW] deaths.' The Japanese doctors allegedly injected some of the remaining prisoners with smallpox, typhoid and so on, as part of a Unit 731 experiment on Caucasian prisoners. It appears that the experiments were presented to the Allied prisoners as 'innoculations'. For example, Peaty records in his diary for 30 January 1943: 'Everyone received a

5cc typhoid-paratyphoid A inoculation.'[12] On 23 February Peaty recorded the results of the Japanese 'inoculations': 'Funeral service for 142 dead. 186 have died in 5 days, all Americans.'[13] Further 'inoculations' followed that led to many more deaths.

Several crucial pieces of evidence corroborate Major Peaty's claim that Japanese medical officers were present in the camp in large numbers. A document discovered in the archives of the International Military Tribunal for the Far East, dated 17 February 1943, records: 'For some purpose unknown, the POWs were sent to this [Hoten] concentration camp. Three months after their arrival, a department chief named Nagayama made a report on the conditions of prisoners and lack of nutrition adjustment in the camp.' The Japanese medical officer named in the report was Dr. Saburo Nagayama, clinical department chief at Unit 731. Kwantung Army Operational Order No. 98, issued by Commander-in-chief General Yoshijiro Umezu provides further corroboration. It reads, in part, 'Assign 32 medical officers to go to the concentration camp for prisoners of war at Mukden.' Lieutenant-General Ryuji Kajitsuka, chief of the medical department of the Kwantung Army and General Ishii's boss, immediately ordered Unit 731 to carry out the assignment on 1 February.

More evidence for the use of white prisoners of war for human experimentation comes from the proceedings of the Khabarovsk War Crimes Trial convened in the Soviet Union in 1949. One defendant, Major Tomio Karasawa, stated: 'Blood of human species of all peoples was tested for the study of immunity. Minato, a researcher, was sent to study the blood of American POWs.'[14] This indicates that Dr. Minato was among the medical officers who came to Hoten Camp and injected prisoners with various diseases in February 1943. Another Japanese who stood trial at Khabarovsk, Kiyohito Morishita, said in court: '[The] Soviets and Americans can be distinguished in appearance. Among the *maruta*, I saw Americans or British. I also heard some *marutas* speaking English to each other.'[15] Morishita was referring to the Unit 731 facility at Pingfang where he worked, and not Hoten Camp. His testimony suggests that Allied POWs were taken from Hoten to Pingfang and killed. Australian Army doctor R.J. Brennan may have corroborated this assertion when he recorded in his diary an incident where 150

American prisoners were force-marched out of Hoten Camp and never seen again.

Some British veterans insist that they were the victims of Unit 731 experiments, but at present, because of a lack of conclusive evidence since most Unit 731 files were voluntarily returned to the Japanese in the 1950s by the Americans (who failed to make any copies), the Ministry of Defence denies that British personnel were involved. The curator at the Unit 731 museum in Pingfang summed up the significance of both the facility and the atrocities carried out by the Japanese in its buildings when he said: 'This is not just a Chinese concern; it is a concern of humanity.'

Notes

1. 'Doctors of Depravity' by Christopher Hudson, *Daily Mail*, 2 March 2007.
2. 'Archives give up secrets of Japan's Unit 731', *China Daily*, 3 August 2005.
3. 'Unmasking Horror – A special report: Japan Confronting Gruesome War Atrocity' by Nicholas D. Kristof, *New York Times*, 17 March 1995.
4. 'Doctors of Depravity' by Christopher Hudson, *Daily Mail*, 2 March 2007.
5. 'Unmasking Horror – A special report: Japan Confronting Gruesome War Atrocity' by Nicholas D. Kristof, *New York Times*, 17 March 1995.
6. 'Doctors of Depravity' by Christopher Hudson, *Daily Mail*, 2 March 2007.
7. Ibid.
8. 'Unmasking Horror – A special report: Japan Confronting Gruesome War Atrocity' by Nicholas D. Kristof, *New York Times*, 17 March 1995.
9. *Materials on the Trial of Former Servicemen of the Japanese Army Charged with Manufacturing and Employing Bacteriological Weapons* (Moscow, Foreign Languages Publishing House, 1950).
10. See: Sheldon H. Harris, *Factories of Death: Japanese Biological Warfare 1943–45 and the American Cover-up* (New York, Routledge, 1994).

11. 'Doctors of Depravity' by Christopher Hudson, *Daily Mail*, 2 March 2007.
12. Ibid.
13. Peter Williams & David Wallace, *Unit 731: The Japanese Army's Secret of Secrets* (London, Hodder & Stoughton, 1989), pp. 53–4.
14. *Beijing Bright Daily*, 1 June 1994.
15. Ibid.

Chapter Ten

The Bomber Boys

*Enemy flyers who have raided Japanese territories,
Manchukuo, or our operational areas, come within our
jurisdiction, and violated wartime international law shall
be tried by court martial and sentenced to death or heavy
punishment as important war criminals.*

Japanese *Regulations for Punishment of Enemy Air Crews*
13 August 1942

The Philippine city of Cebu, 26 March 1945. The two American
flyers looked incongruous next to their Japanese guards. Both men
stood head and shoulders above the impish figures of the guards
with their long rifles and fixed bayonets. The airmen's flight suits
were dirty and stained with blood, and each man had his hands tied
behind his back with wire. The Americans stared blankly ahead of
them as the Japanese shoved them along with the butts of their rifles
towards a recently dug hole close to the school where they had been
imprisoned and tortured for several days. A Japanese Kempeitai
officer stood stiffly beside the hole, identified by the white armband
worn on his left arm with its printed Japanese characters and his
dark green cavalry uniform and riding boots. One hand rested on his
pistol holster. Beside him stood a Japanese sergeant with a sheathed
katana sword in his hands.

The two Americans were roughly knocked to their knees and a
guard jerked their heads forward, exposing their grimy necks. The
officer nodded to the sergeant, who stepped forward and unsheathed
his sword with a flourish. He lined up the blade on the first American's

neck, and then raised his arms high over his head and with a loud bellow brought the sword down in a devastating cut, the American tumbling forward into the hole twitching feebly. The sergeant then repeated his actions on the second American. The officer flipped the catch on his holster, drew out his Nambu automatic pistol and fired several shots into the bleeding bodies that lay side-by-side in the dirt hole.[1]

A few yards away there was another hole already filled with its human debris – the bodies of five Filipinos the Kempeitai had bayoneted to death before they had executed the American airmen. Why the Filipinos had been killed is lost to history, but the Japanese occupation of the Philippines was one long catalogue of brutality, much of it stemming from the behaviour and activities of the Kempeitai.

Around noon the Japanese returned to where they had executed the two American flyers, and soldiers piled wood over the bodies of the Americans lying in the foxhole. But the job was not quite finished. Evidently, one of the Americans was miraculously still alive after the sword cut to his neck and the pistol shots the Kempeitai officer had fired into the pit. He had 'managed to crawl out of the foxhole and was seen sitting on the ground attempting to wave to an American plane overhead.'[2] Japanese soldiers threw him back into the hole, piled on more wood, then a couple of green painted army jerry cans of petrol were brought up and the wood was thoroughly soaked in gasoline. A Japanese soldier lit a rag soaked in petrol with his lighter and quickly cast it onto the makeshift bonfire. The petrol ignited with a loud 'whump!' and the grisly deed was finally completed.

The two American airmen were killed, along with hundreds of other Allied flyers, on the direct orders of the Japanese government. One event above all others persuaded the Japanese to abandon all notions of civilized warfare. After Pearl Harbor, the United States was desperate to get back into the war and hit the Japanese. President Roosevelt gave the green light to an ambitious plan to bomb Tokyo and show the Japanese that the United States had a long military reach and was undefeated. On 18 April 1942 that idea became a reality when sixteen B-25 Mitchell medium bombers were launched from the aircraft carrier USS *Hornet* several hundred miles from the Japanese mainland. Each of the planes was stripped of armament and most of its fixtures and fittings so they could carry more fuel and bombs for what many in the army believed would be a one-way mission. Led by Lieutenant-Colonel Jimmy Doolittle, each plane dumped one ton of bombs over Tokyo and other targets, and although the physical effects of the air raid were negligible, the psychological effect on the Japanese was astounding. The government had led its people to believe that the Home Islands were safe from enemy incursion, and the fact that so many American bombers had penetrated Japanese airspace and dropped bombs near the Imperial Palace was cause of great shame and loss of face.

The Doolittle Raid confirmed in the minds of the Japanese government, military and public the vulnerability of Japan's cities. Even Tokyo was largely constructed of wood, and the small Doolittle attack showed how easy it would be to destroy Japan's infrastructure and economy through the use of air power. Harsh new laws would be promulgated ordering the treatment of captured flyers to be the same as the treatment of war criminals. Coupled with the refusal of the Japanese government to ratify the 1929 Geneva Convention which their diplomats had signed, the chances of surviving after being shot down over Japanese occupied territory was slim at best for most Allied aircrew. The Japanese believed that such harsh treatment of Allied airmen would discourage enemy bombing raids upon its territory, since they believed that the Allied nations placed great store in the numbers of their own casualties and the manner of their men's treatment after capture. This was certainly true, but Japan's illegal treatment of prisoners did not prevent British, American, Australian, Dutch and New Zealand aircraft from attacking targets across the Empire.

Doolittle's aircraft were supposed to fly 1,200 miles across the East China Sea to friendly airbases in Chinese-controlled territory on the mainland after striking Tokyo, but many ran out of fuel and crashed in Japanese-controlled areas. Sixty-four American airmen bailed out over Chekiang in eastern China, and eight were captured and turned over to the Kempeitai. The remainder escaped to freedom with the assistance of Chinese guerrillas, and one B-25 landed in the Soviet Union where the aircraft and its crew were interned for the duration. Those eight Americans captured at Chekiang were cruelly tortured by the furious Kempeitai, and the decision was taken at the highest levels to 'punish' all Allied airmen who in future dared to attack Japanese targets.

On 13 August 1942, the Japanese hurriedly sanctioned a new law making air-raids on any territory controlled by the Japanese a 'war crime.' Captured Allied airmen were to be denied prisoner-of-war status and instead would face a military court martial. 'Death shall be the military punishment,' read the Japanese order, and 'shall be by shooting.'[3] Mitigating circumstances were occasionally allowed by the Japanese, and instead of a horrible death some airmen were instead sentenced to inhuman imprisonments in circumstances of the greatest cruelty. Conveniently, the Japanese had ignored the fact that they had been the first modern power to use air attacks on populated areas when Japanese Navy seaplanes had bombed Shanghai in 1932, killing thousands of innocent civilians.

The new regulation was in total violation of International Law as it meant that airmen faced death sentences for attacking viable industrial targets that supplied the Japanese war machine, and it was contrary to the expected treatment of captured enemy personnel. The results were predictable. The Kempeitai was able to torture captured airmen and then court-martial them in spurious legal circumstances at show trials. Executions smelled distinctly of revenge killings. Three of Doolittle's men suffered this fate when they were court-martialed and shot as 'war criminals' by the Japanese. The Kempeitai, however, was only just getting warmed up. The Japanese instituted one of the biggest war crimes in history throughout Chekiang and Kiangsu Province. Any village or town that was suspected of having harboured downed American flyers was razed to the ground and its inhabitants massacred. By mid-August 1942 the Japanese had murdered 250,000 men, women and children. It was an appallingly high price to pay for what had been a propaganda attack on the Japanese mainland almost completely devoid of military results.

On 28 July 1942, the commander of the China Expeditionary Army, General Shunroku Hata, ordered that all US airmen currently held in Japanese custody be put on trial as war criminals. This was a retroactive order, as they were already in prison in China. The Kempeitai had already beaten and tortured these men so thoroughly that when the Americans were brought to court most were in no fit state even to stand and answer the charge. They were offered no defence representation whatsoever, and were duly found guilty of war crimes; three of them were sentenced to death, while the other five were given life imprisonment. The death sentences were carried out in October 1942.

Following Doolittle's daring raid the Japanese Home Islands were to remain impervious to attack until late in the war. The Americans lacked an aircraft with the range to reach targets in Japan until they had captured bases closer to the Home Islands. The introduction of the Boeing B-29 Superfortress and the capture of the Mariana Islands brought Japan in range of regular air attack. From June 1944 Japan was bombed by B-29s, but these were low intensity raids involving only a few dozen aircraft flying from bases in Chengdu in China. The raids were expensive to mount because all the supplies needed for the bases, aircraft and personnel had to be flown into China from British India, and involved aircraft crossing the formidable 'Hump', as pilots soon christened the Himalayas. The first B-29 raid on Japan was flown from Chengdu on 15 June 1944 when forty-seven Superfortresses attacked a huge iron and steel works at Yawata.

For airmen shot down in occupied China, the Kwantung Army reserved particularly fierce retribution. The executions were always conducted by the Kempeitai in full view of the local Chinese population, to serve as a warning and to demonstrate that the Japanese were 'protecting' the Chinese from bombing raids on Chinese cities. Certainly, the Americans struck several Chinese cities where the Japanese had munitions factories or other belligerent facilities, and Chinese people were unfortunately killed because so many lived and worked in close proximity to the targets. In the city of Hangzhou near Shanghai in December 1944 an American aircraft was forced down and three airmen taken prisoner. The Kempeitai arrested them, beat them severely and then paraded the terrified and bleeding men through the city streets. A large crowd of local Chinese peasants gathered to watch and jeer at the Americans. The Kempeitai forced the American flyers to run through the hostile crowd, where they were struck by fists and beaten with any object to hand, before the Japanese finally doused them with petrol and burned the airmen alive in the street.

Once the Mariana Islands had been captured by American amphibious forces huge numbers of B-29s were sent to five new airbases on the islands of Tinian, Saipan and Guam. Japanese industry could now be systematically reduced and cities and towns razed. These islands were easily supplied by ship, unlike the airbases in free China. The first combat mission against Japan was launched from Saipan on 24 November 1944 when 111 B-29s attacked Tokyo. Thereafter, ever more intense raids were launched until the end of the war, resulting in an inferno of destruction and loss of life not witnessed before or since in the history of air warfare. For Allied aircrew shot down over Japanese-occupied territory or the Home Islands after the Doolittle Raid in April 1942 and the beginning of the B-29 raids, the prospects of surviving were extremely dim indeed; and some of the stories of those who were spared death but instead imprisoned by the Kempeitai are among the true untold stories of the Second World War. 'From the time of the Doolittle raid in April 1942, the Japanese called them war criminals, and flyers coming down in Japanese-held territory were marked men.'[4] People often forget that the strategic bombing campaign against Japan cost the lives of many Americans, and that Japanese air defences, though nowhere near as good as the German *Luftwaffe*, were not idle in trying to knock B-29s out of the skies by any and every means to hand.

Fire was the key to defeating Japan. Admiral Isoroku Yamamoto, architect of the Pearl Harbor attack in 1941, had little faith in the ability of the Home Islands to stand up to a modern war. In 1939 he tried to warn his people, commenting that 'Japanese cities, being made of wood and paper, would burn very easily. The Army talks big, but if war came and there were large-scale air raids, there's no telling what would happen.'[5] Incendiary raids meant the effective destruction of Japanese cities, along with the death of huge numbers of civilians.

The first great firebombing raid on Tokyo was launched on the night of 23/4 February 1945 when 174 B-29s destroyed one square mile of the city. On the night of 9/10 March 334 Superfortresses started a huge firestorm that consumed *sixteen* square miles of Tokyo and killed over 100,000 people. Over the following weeks 1,600 sorties against Japan's six principal cities (Tokyo, Nagoya, Kobe, Osaka, Yokohama and Kawasaki) devastated over forty per cent of the urban area. A fleet of 600 B-29s flattened dozens of smaller cities over the coming months. Every Japanese city except Kyoto was hit, the damage varying in scale from 20–30% of the urban area destroyed to almost total eradication of the settlement, for example Toyama (99% destroyed), Fukui (86%), Tokushima (85.2%), and Fukuyama (80.9%). Although American aircraft dropped leaflets on cities targeted for destruction in advance of a raid urging citizens to escape, civilian casualties were massive and the hatred of the Japanese people for American flyers was intense and understandable.

Elsewhere in the war against Japan the British were slowly advancing through the jungles, plains and steep hills of Burma. The Royal Air Force was intimately involved in the advance to victory, not only in supplying British and Indian troops on the ground but in driving the Japanese from the air and bombing Japanese supply depots, rail yards and troop concentrations. RAF aircrew who fell into the hands of the Kempeitai met equally grisly fates to those of US airmen shot down over Japan. In February 1945 an RAF Liberator bomber was shot down in southern Burma near Pypon. The six crew all bailed out successfully, but they were soon picked up by the Kempeitai and taken to Myanaung on the Irrawaddy River for interrogation. The two RAF flying officers and four flight sergeants faced hours of torture, but they all refused to divulge anything of use to the Japanese. The flight sergeants were then taken six miles into the jungle and again brutally interrogated. Again, the Kempeitai did not manage to extract any useful information. Frustrated, the Kempeitai forced the beaten and bruised men to march another five miles along a jungle track. There they found another party of Japanese soldiers waiting for them next to a recently excavated trench. Each British NCO was forced to kneel in front of the trench, blindfolded and then decapitated by a Kempeitai officer with his sword. Afterwards, the Japanese soldiers used the headless corpses for bayonet practice before the remains were kicked into the trench and the rich red jungle earth piled on top of them. This was but one of dozens of similar incidents.

On the night of 24/5 May 1945 Tokyo burned. The city glowed orange in the darkness, flames leaping and twisting themselves into great columns of fire that stretched up into the smoke-blackened sky. The temperature was tremendous, a searing heat whipped into a howling wind that destroyed whole city blocks in an instant, turning people into blazing torches that struggled helplessly for a moment before collapsing into blackened shapes that melted into the boiling pavements. The Japanese had sowed the wind in December 1941, now they were reaping the whirlwind. Above the city roared huge silver aircraft, their bomb-bay doors hanging open like obscene gashes as more incendiary and napalm bombs tumbled to earth, the drone of the aerial engines a constant background refrain to the carnage below. At the Imperial Palace complex Emperor Hirohito and his family sat stiff-backed on chairs inside the protective concrete shell of an air-raid shelter deep underground listening to their capital being gutted, the emperor's eyes darting nervously towards the dusty ceiling while thump followed thump as bombs crawled their way towards his home.

Not far from the Palace voices were raised in terror, some in Japanese and some in English. Guards ran around a large jail complex bellowing orders in Japanese, jangling keys in locks and herding prisoners towards air-raid shelters as they cast terrified glances over their shoulders at the huge firestorm bearing down upon them. One block of the jail was in an uproar. White faces, many with blackened eyes or split lips, clamoured at the cell windows and doors, calling, screaming and pleading in English to be released before it was too late. The commandant, his orders clear, had released some 450 of his fellow countrymen held as military prisoners in the jail. He glanced back contemptuously at the white men screaming for mercy and hurried his remaining staff into the shelters as the first incendiaries began bursting across the jail. He felt no sympathy for the white prisoners, and had callously abandoned them to a fate he believed they richly deserved.

The white prisoners, sixty-two of them, were all American airmen captured when their B29s had been forced down over the Tokyo area during previous raids. They had been beaten, humiliated and denied medical treatment since capture and were now left to perish at the hands of their comrades high above, raining fire and death on the city as they themselves had done before. The Japanese hated the American flyers more than any of their tens of thousands of brutalized prisoners spanning the length and breadth of their slave empire, for the B29s brought America's revenge to the very shores of the sacred Home Islands and even threatened the life of the God-Emperor himself.

When the fires abated a few hours later the guards emerged from their bunkers and surveyed the scene before them. The jail was severely damaged, with many small fires still burning in the early morning haze. The block where the Americans were held was also a ruin, but some of the smoke-blackened prisoners were miraculously still alive. Stretching away in all directions was a barren, smouldering ruin of a city, unrecognizable and uninhabitable. The officers and their guards felt their hatred intensify against the Americans who had committed this outrage, an impotent anger that they could no longer militarily express against the high-flying B-29s. Seizing their rifles and fixing their bayonets, the infuriated Japanese guards dashed in among the dead and dying Americans and began to smash skulls, break arms and legs and stab the bodies over and over again until all of them were dead.

The greatest air-raid of the war so far was over. A force of 558 B-29s had levelled half of the city of Tokyo, 56.3 *square miles* reduced to rubble, ash and twisted metal. It was the third gigantic air attack on Japan's capital and signalled that the final endgame for the Japanese had arrived. A few more of these raids and Japan would be reduced to a smoking ruin. Over a million Japanese were now homeless in Tokyo and over 100,000 lay dead. The remaining city hospitals were overwhelmed with 40,000 injured. Fourteen wrecked B-29s lay among this carnage like giant beached whales, a small price for the Americans to pay for so great a result. But the Japanese would not surrender. They determined to fight even harder for their Emperor and to exact a terrible toll in blood from the hated Allied nations as the front line crept ever closer to the Japanese homeland. The cold-blooded murder of the American flyers in Tokyo that morning by the Kempeitai was part of the hardening of the Japanese spirit. Many believed that they would not leave any of their prisoners alive to be liberated should they lose the war.

At Omori Prison Camp on the outskirts of Tokyo, the American prisoners held there were spared the wrath of the Japanese and survived the war to be liberated. They were all aircrew, and had been shot down either over Japan, or earlier on in the war over the Occupied Territories, and transported to Omori as slave labourers. Among them was 39-year-old Colonel Richard T. King, commanding officer of the 500th Bombardment Group who had been shot down over Tokyo on 3 December 1944 and 22-year-old Lieutenant Raymond 'Hap' Halloran, a B-29 navigator who had bailed out over Tokyo on 27 January 1945. Their stories are typical of the brutalization Allied airmen were subjected to and the state of constant tension and fear they felt as prisoners of the Kempeitai. They had all feared falling into enemy hands, but they were also confident of their aircraft and the righteousness of their mission. 'We were proud of our assignment as B-29 crew members,' said Halloran. 'Had no personal concerns – War at 32,000 feet is impersonal.'[6] Halloran was about to discover that war at ground level was to prove considerably more personal.

Colonel King was flight commander of a twelve-aircraft formation of B-29s on 3 December 1944 at 32,000 feet over Tokyo. His aircraft, which he piloted, was nicknamed '*Rosalie Rocket*'. Their mission was to attack an aircraft engine plant, and they were engaged by Japanese fighters shortly after dropping their bombs. 'Although we shot down some of the fighters, they hit our left inboard gasoline tank so seriously that it sprayed gasoline all over the aircraft and the entire ship began to burn,' recalled King. 'By the time the ship had lost altitude to 29,000 feet I baled out. At that time I did not realize that I was injured in any way. Immediately after baling out I counted at least eight and possibly nine chutes as I floated earthward myself [a B-29 had a crew of eleven].'[7]

King landed in an open field and cut the shroud lines to his parachute canopy. He discovered that he had been burned on one leg and across his face. 'Since Japanese fighters were diving down directly over the field and it seemed they might be looking for me, I walked over under the trees at one side of the field and waited there a few moments.'[8] A quick inventory showed that his Colt .45 automatic pistol had been torn off when he jumped, so he was unarmed and in very hostile territory.

Hap Halloran was only on his fourth mission on 27 January 1945 when his squadron of B-29s was attacked by a pair of Japanese fighters. Halloran's aircraft, *Rover Boy's Express* was hit. 'Suddenly we were trailing smoke and fire with a full load of bombs and half our fuel,' recalled Halloran. 'We fell below and behind the rest of the B-29s in our squadron. There was nothing they could do to help us; it was a sad feeling.'[9] Fire from the Japanese fighters had ripped through the Superfortress's fuselage and shot out the electrical controls and the intercom system. The pilot controlled the rudder and control surfaces of the aircraft through electrical cables, and the turret-mounted defensive armament was also electrically controlled.

The B-29 was going to crash, so the only option was to dump the bombs and get the crew of eleven out through the bomb-bay. 'As we baled out through the bomb-bay my feet, hands and face froze,'[10] said Halloran. The B-29 was pressurized and was flying at 32,000 feet when it was hit, and the sudden drop in temperature had been dramatic, from a pleasant 70 degrees to minus 58 degrees Fahrenheit, a change of 127 degrees in less than a second.

Halloran was in free fall over Japan. 'I didn't want to let my silk out too fast and fell free to somewhere between three and four thousand feet over Chiba Prefecture East of Tokyo.' He was concerned lest roving Japanese fighters machine gun him as he floated helplessly beneath his parachute canopy, and 'I wanted to get out of the extreme cold and rarefied air to warmer air near the ground.'[11] Halloran popped his chute, but 'three Japanese fighters headed directly for me as I hung helpless in the sky. They came in very close, throttled back and circled me in a counterclockwise direction, very close in. Two left after the initial circling. The third plane returned for a second pass, very close in. I feared the worst. He throttled back, was very close in just below me. I raised my hands over my head – I was frightened. The pilot was very visible to me.' At this point the Japanese pilot did something quite extraordinary: 'he saluted me and pulled off,'[12] said Halloran.

As the young American officer continued drifting down towards earth, he could see Japanese civilians following his descent on the ground. A large group was gathering, and an ugly reception committee was waiting for him when Halloran landed heavily in a residential area east of Tokyo. It was the moment many American aircrew failed to survive, and being shot down and bailing out over Japan was one of the greatest fears faced by the flyers. As Halloran remarked to this author: 'Fears – yes, sir. Being shot down over Japan and captured.' He believed that 'we would be killed by civilians or military.'[13] That many Americans expected death in Japanese hands was because it was logical. 'They hated us for good reason – we were destroying their country – they were starving.'[14] Colonel King also faced a hostile reception when a group of Japanese civilians found him in the countryside. They 'not only handcuffed me but also bound me with my own shroud lines.'[15]

Ironically, it was the Kempeitai who actually saved Halloran's life. As Halloran drifted closer to the ground he could see the angry upturned faces of local Japanese civilians, and hear their excited screams. He could also see the many weapons they carried in their hands. 'I felt helpless and feared the worst. I hit very hard in a strong wind,' recalled Halloran. 'The civilians followed the flow of my chute. They were extremely hostile and beat me with clubs, rods, rocks and many other objects. I blacked out from the beatings. I felt I would die that afternoon on enemy soil.'[16]

As soon as it was reported by Japanese air defences that enemy planes had been shot down and crewmen had been observed baling out, Kempeitai squads were sent out in any available transport to track the white parachutes as they came to earth and capture the airmen before enraged civilians killed them. Halloran was lucky, for a group of Kempeitai soldiers quickly arrived on the scene and wedged themselves between the prone Halloran and the mob, ordering them back.

The Kempeitai knew the value of enemy airmen and the military intelligence they could torture out of them before they were court-martialed and executed or imprisoned under the instructions of 13 August 1942. For some Americans, the Kempeitai arrived just in the nick of time as they were only seconds away from death. Lieutenant Delbart W. Miller of the 40th Bombardment Group was shot down on 26 May 1945 over Tokyo. Shortly after he landed a group of Japanese civilians had beaten him and thrown a rope noose around his neck and were about to lynch him from the nearest lamppost when the Kempeitai intervened.

Colonel King was not beaten by the crowd of civilians who captured him, but instead they marched him to the local police station 'where I waited for two hours until two Japanese soldiers came to pick me up.'[17] King and another downed airman, Colonel Bryon Brugge from Wing Headquarters, were blindfolded, loaded on to a truck and driven into central Tokyo.

'I was tied and thrown into a coal truck and taken to a briefing room at a fighter base where the beatings continued,' recalled Lieutenant Halloran.[18] He was then transferred to a Kempeitai prison close to the Imperial Palace, where he was extensively maltreated. 'They wanted to know about the B-29 aircraft,' said Halloran. 'It was a charade. One day they showed me a large blueprint of the aircraft and I found out that they knew more about the technical aspects of the plane than I did.'[19] All bomber crews flying missions over Japan had been told to cooperate with the Japanese if they fell into enemy hands. Halloran and his crew were briefed one week before their final mission by a US Marine officer from Washington DC who instructed them to forget earlier briefings regarding capture and interrogation and 'tell them answers to all questions,' as the standard 'name, rank and serial number' routine 'only resulted in instant death when captured.'[20] The Japanese wanted to know all about Saipan, the island base the Americans used to launch B-29 raids on Japan. Saipan had a large Japanese population, and had been captured after fierce fighting with Japanese forces. 'They would grill me about Saipan,' said Halloran. 'How many Japanese prisoners were held there? I told them I didn't know the difference between a Japanese and an islander. That was the wrong answer and I would be knocked down again. I would tell them that I didn't see any Japanese after being accused of killing Japanese as they tried to surrender when the island fell in 1944. With that answer I would be hit again. Well, maybe I saw a few, I would say and then they would beat the hell out of me and say that their people would never surrender. It was a no-win situation.'[21]

King had been subjected to a similar interrogation to Halloran several weeks before. The Japanese demanded his name, rank and serial number, which he gave as this was not in contravention of the Geneva Convention. However, 'they went on to request our home addresses and other information. When I asked why they wanted this information, they said they needed it so they could notify our families. This, of course, was never done.'[22] King was stripped, but some of his clothing was later returned to him. He was then subjected to a 'severe interrogation', as he put it, concerning Saipan. 'When I answered many of their questions (truthfully) that I did not know, they attempted to force me to answer by slapping my face and other minor abuse.'[23]

Lieutenant Halloran spent sixty-seven days in Kempeitai custody, where he was kept in a horse stall in solitary confinement, was interrogated and beaten virtually every day and was offered no medical treatment for his injuries. The last two days were truly bizarre. The Japanese took some American flyers to Ueno Zoo in Tokyo, where the men were stripped naked, and in their filthy, bruised and bearded state, placed into animal cages and displayed to the public. Members of the public filed past the cages, laughing and jeering at the prisoners. It reveals a truly bizarre and sadistic streak rooted in the Japanese character – similar in many ways to the present delight in ritual humiliation and torture to be found in many modern Japanese game shows on television. Even at the height of the fire-bombing campaign against German cities and industry in 1944–45, downed British and American aircrew were usually accorded prisoner-of-war status and treated well. There were cases where enraged mobs beat Allied airmen to death soon after they landed by parachute or strung them up from the nearest lamppost, but there was never this level of sadistic cruelty and denigration officially organized by the German authorities. Aircrew prisoners fell under the jurisdiction of the *Luftwaffe*, not the Gestapo, and they were treated as fellow professional airmen by their captors. One could only imagine the outcry among the British if the government had ordered downed *Luftwaffe* airmen to be publicly exhibited naked in cages at Regents Park Zoo, even at the height of the Blitz.

When Halloran arrived at Omori Camp on 1 April 1945 he discovered thirty-one other flyers, including five members of the crew of the *Rover Boy's Express*. By far the most prominent prisoner held at Omori was 33-year-old Lieutenant-Colonel Gregory 'Pappy' Boyington, a Sioux Indian and a decorated Marine Corps fighter ace with twenty-six confirmed aerial victories to his name. Boyington was one of the famous 'Flying Tigers', the American Volunteer Group that flew combat missions against the Japanese in China before the Pacific War began and later commanded Marine Corps Squadron VMF-211, famously called 'The Black Sheep Squadron'. Boyington had been shot down over Rabaul, New Britain, during a massive dogfight with Japanese aircraft on 3 January 1944, during which he had personally dispatched three enemy fighters. He bailed out into the sea and was picked up by a Japanese submarine and taken prisoner. Immediately after the war Boyington was awarded the Congressional Medal of Honor and the Navy Cross by President Truman.

Halloran got to know Boyington well during their imprisonment together, recalling that he 'had maintained a sparkle in his eyes and the look and mannerisms of a natural leader.'[24] Boyington was tough, 'he instilled confidence in us in a quiet way and I knew I would be OK as long as Pappy was there.' Even the Japanese were impressed to have such a famous prisoner. 'Boyington would give the Japanese guards demonstrations of the number of Japanese planes he had shot down. Strangely, most of the guards respected and sometimes applauded him.'[25]

Boyington fared better than many other American pilots and aircrew captured by the Japanese at Rabaul. In early 1944 the Japanese had several dozen American airmen from the 13th Air Force and 1st and 2nd Marine Air Corps as prisoners inside a former tailor's shop in Rabaul's Chinatown. The building was the head-quarters of the 6th Field Kempeitai. Rabaul was under incessant air attack at this time, and the prisoners were moved to an air-raid shelter across the street where others were brought in to join them. Eventually, the Kempeitai had a total of sixty-two American flyers in their hands. It was as well that the Japanese moved the Americans, for a direct hit from an American bomb destroyed the Kempeitai headquarters building in early March.

On 3 March the prisoners were loaded aboard trucks and driven to a tunnel-like cave at Tanoura, located by the sea a few miles from Rabaul. Guards packed the prisoners tightly into the tunnel, where they suffered greatly from overcrowded conditions and lack of water, food and sanitation arrangements. The men were given two buckets of water a day – but only after their guards had washed their dirty dishes in them.

Kempeitai Warrant Officer Zenichi Wakabayashi ordered twenty names to be called out on 5 March. These prisoners boarded trucks and were never seen again. A second group of eleven was similarly selected and disappeared. Those who survived by remaining at the cave told Australian investigators that Wakabayashi had informed the men that they were being transferred to a camp on Watom Island, a few miles offshore.

According to the Japanese version of events, thirty-one American airmen had been assembled on Tanoura Beach awaiting sea transport to Watom Island when American aircraft bombed them. The prisoners and their guards took cover in separate shelters, but Wakabayashi reported that a bomb scored a direct hit on the prisoners' shelter, killing all but five of the men inside. The five survivors were all so badly injured that they died shortly afterwards. That evening the Kempeitai guards cremated the bodies in a huge funeral pyre on the beach (a rather strange thing to do considering the area was under constant aerial attack). Human ashes were later given to Australian investigators as 'proof' by the Japanese. At the Rabaul War Crimes Trial immediately after the war, the Australians raised some serious questions regarding the Japanese version of events. They wanted to know why the bodies were cremated when other Allied deaths usually resulted in burial in mass graves. They also wanted to know why the commandant of Watom Camp, Colonel Kahachi Ogata, had not been informed of the imminent arrival of thirty-one prisoners. It was suggested at the trial that Wakabayashi had deliberately ordered the execution of nearly half the prisoners held at the Tanoura cave simply to ease congestion, and he had ordered all forensic evidence destroyed by burning the bodies afterwards. There was no real evidence, and although Wakabayashi was questioned for a second time in 1948 he maintained that his version of events was the truth. After what we now know of the treatment of Allied prisoners by the Kempeitai, we should view Wakabayashi's testimony with a great deal of suspicion.[26]

Even the end of the war brought only more death to captive Allied aircrew. The city of Hiroshima was strictly off-limits for Allied bombers, even as a secondary target, because the Americans wanted it preserved intact to test the effectiveness of the atomic bomb against a fully populated and pristine Japanese city. Hiroshima was a major military base (the stated reason for its destruction by the Americans) and because it was one of the last major cities undamaged by the B-29 raids, its Kempeitai unit was fully operational and based at Hiroshima Castle.

On 28 July 1945 a group of American B-24 Liberator bombers had attacked the huge Japanese naval base at Kure with the aim of damaging or sinking the battleship *Haruna* at anchor in the harbour. Passing over Mount Futaba the American aircraft drew considerable anti-aircraft fire and planes were hit. Ironically, although the bombers successfully sank the *Haruna*, the battleship's fuel tanks had been pumped dry so the ship was already immobilized before the attack.

The first B-24 to go down was nicknamed *Taloa*. Very few of the crew got clear of the stricken aircraft. 'A second plane ... was hit but was able to fly to an island short of Okinawa,' recalled Second Lieutenant Thomas Cartwright, piloting *Lonesome Lady*. Suddenly, Cartwright's plane was struck by flak and badly damaged. 'I did not realize how badly we were damaged and planned to head for the open sea where there was hope that our Naval seaplanes would spot us and pick us up if we ditched and survived,' wrote Cartwright. 'We started losing altitude and the controls were becoming less responsive and I could not head out to sea – the plane flew back toward land on its own.'[27] With one engine on fire, Cartwright ordered his crew to jump for it. One crewman perished when his parachute failed to open, but the other seven made it safely to the ground, finding themselves spread out over several miles.

All but one of the American flyers was quickly picked up by the local Kempeitai, though a Japanese civilian was shot dead by two of the Americans when he approached them with a rifle. The Americans were taken to Chigoku Military Police Headquarters in Hiroshima and roughly interrogated. At this stage of the war American airmen were instructed to cooperate fully with their captors in the hope of saving their lives as the war appeared to be almost over. The Kempeitai did not believe most of what the airmen told them, and continued to beat and torture them for information. In total, the Kempeitai picked up fifteen Americans from *Taloa* and *Lonesome Lady*. The Kempeitai dispersed these men into individual cells at three locations around Hiroshima.

On the morning of 6 August two silver B-29 Superfortress bombers appeared above the untouched city of Hiroshima. One carried an atomic bomb, the other cameras to film what followed. At 8.16am nuclear destruction flattened most of Hiroshima, killing around 140,000 people. Most of the Americans in the city, including two US Navy flyers, were vapourized. Evidence suggests that some survived the initial blast only to be murdered by vengeful Kempeitai officers and local civilians. Two were probably dragged from their cells at Hiroshima Castle and clubbed to death in the grounds by the furious Kempeitai, while two others were tied to lampposts in the devastated city and stoned to death by mobs of disbelieving civilians. Lieutenant Cartwright survived and was taken to Tokyo for further interrogation about the new American wonder weapon, while tail gunner Wilbur Abel had managed to hide in the hills around Hiroshima when he had first landed by parachute, and had thus avoided capture. The day after the atomic bombing Abel gave himself up. The Kempeitai tortured him badly, but he did manage to survive the war along with Cartwright, one of only a handful of American airmen captured by the Kempeitai who did.

Notes

1. Box 252, Exhibit 1461, General Headquarters United States Army Forces, Pacific, Office of the Theater Judge Advocate, War Crimes Branch, Document 2837: *Murder of two American PW's at Cebu City,* 16 October 1945, MacMillan Brown Library, University of Canterbury, Christchurch, New Zealand.
2. Ibid.
3. Box 263, Exhibit 1991, Japanese Expeditionary Forces in China, Document No. 626-A: *Regulations For Punishment of Enemy Air Crews,* 13 August 1942, MacMillan Brown Library, University of Canterbury, Christchurch, New Zealand.
4. Gavan Daws, *Prisoners of the Japanese: POWs of the Second World War in the Pacific* (London, Pocket Books, 2007), p. 321.
5. Ronald Spector, *Eagle Against The Sun* (New York, Vintage Books, 1985), 503.
6. Halloran to author, 27 July 2005.
7. *A Prisoner of War Remembers* by Colonel Richard T. King, Jr., http://www.powmiaff.org, accessed 19 August 2008.
8. Ibid.
9. 'Time heals everything – almost' by William H. Stewart, *Saipan Tribune,* 27 July 2005.
10. Ibid.
11. Ibid.
12. Ibid.
13. Halloran to author, 27 July 2005.
14. Ibid, 27 July 2005.
15. *A Prisoner of War Remembers* by Colonel Richard T. King, Jr., http://www.powmiaff.org, accessed 19 August 2008.
16. 'Time heals everything – almost' by William H. Stewart, *Saipan Tribune,* 27 July 2005.
17. *A Prisoner of War Remembers* by Colonel Richard T. King, Jr., http://www.powmiaff.org, accessed 19 August 2008.
18. 'Time heals everything – almost' by William H. Stewart, *Saipan Tribune,* 27 July 2005.
19. Ibid.

20. Halloran to author, 27 July 2005.
21. 'Time heals everything – almost' by William H. Stewart, *Saipan Tribune*, 27 July 2005.
22. *A Prisoner of War Remembers* by Colonel Richard T. King, Jr., http://www.powmiaff.org, accessed 19 August 2008.
23. Ibid.
24. 'Time heals everything – almost' by William H. Stewart, *Saipan Tribune*, 27 July 2005.
25. Ibid.
26. Another case bearing remarkable similarities to Tanoura Beach occurred on Wake Island and is recounted in Chapter 6 of the author's book *Slaughter at Sea: The Story of Japan's Naval War Crimes* (Barnsley, Pen and Sword Books, 2007).
27. 'Date with the Lonesome Lady: A Hiroshima POW Returns', http://www.canyoncountryzephyr.com, accessed 31 October 2008.

Chapter Eleven

Kempeitai Kamikazes

Born of Desperation. With their air force in tatters and their navy cut to shreds, the enemy was preparing for a last-ditch defense by any means at hand. And to the Japanese, that meant murder and suicide.

Time magazine, June 1945[1]

The large, camouflaged twin-engined bomber lay at a crazy angle across the runway, smoke and dust rising from where it had come to rest. Large blood-red Japanese roundels were displayed prominently on its wings and fuselage. Muffled sounds of shouting and violent movement emanated from inside the aircraft, which had landed wheels-up with a screeching of metal a few moments before. Suddenly, the aircraft's Perspex nose-cone was kicked away and out crawled several Japanese soldiers dressed in beige uniforms blackened with soot and soft forage caps, their web equipment festooned with weapons. Beneath their caps most wore white *hachimachi* head-bands just like their Kamikaze brothers in the Army Air Service, emblazoned with Japanese characters or the red rising sun. More soldiers flung open the fuselage doors and tumbled out on to the tarmac. Quickly sorting themselves out, they ran off in small groups screaming and shouting and firing their rifles and machine guns in all directions, while others ran along carrying long poles and lengths of rope, their faces blackened with camouflage cream. Tracer rounds whipped across the airfield, and the dull boom of anti-aircraft guns provided a cacophony of noise as the Japanese soldiers raced determinedly through the darkness and set about their destructive tasks.

The unrelenting B-29 bomber offensive against the Japanese Home Islands in 1944/5 led the Japanese to attempt to deny the Americans the use of their new airfields in the Mariana Islands. A daring commando operation was dreamt up by the Kempeitai's special services department to rival some of the great raids launched by the British and Americans during the war. The only difference to Allied commando operations was that this great Japanese raid was designed as a one-way mission in the finest spirit of the Kamikazes.

The Kempeitai was a huge organization that administered a myriad of different departments. One of its areas of speciality was the launching of commando-style reconnaissance and sabotage missions, using units drawn from the regular army with attached Kempeitai specialists. Three such organizations were created in the latter part of the war. *Matsu Kikan* (Pine Tree) undertook, as we shall see shortly, secret reconnaissance missions to Australia; *Minami Kikan* (Little Tree) was a secret unit attached to the puppet Burmese National Army; and *Giretsu* Airborne Unit was a specialist kamikaze raiding force assembled to neutralize American B-29 bomber bases. All three came under the command of Japanese Army Intelligence, the Japanese Army Espionage Service and the Kempeitai Intelligence Unit.

By late 1944 B-29s were flying in force against targets in mainland Japan, and Japanese air defences were inadequate to stop them flattening cities virtually at will. Desperate times called for desperate measures. The B-29s flew from a handful of large airbases on Okinawa, Saipan, Tinian, Guam and the Ryukyu Islands. The Kempeitai, working closely with army intelligence, decided that the best way to neutralize the B-29 threat was not by trying to knock them out of the skies over Japan, but to destroy the aircraft at source – that is, on their newly operational airfields. The Japanese had already tried launching conventional bombing missions against these airfields, but the results had been negligible as American fighter cover and anti-aircraft defences were extremely strong and Japanese losses in men and planes made the missions pointless. The Kamikaze operations around Okinawa had, however, borne some fruit for the Japanese, and it was becoming clear to the high command that the only way to strike the Americans hard was to send young, determined, and brave men on one-way missions. They would sell their lives dearly for their Emperor and nation without harbouring thoughts of survival, making such men formidable and determined adversaries. The Japanese plan called for a new kind of Kamikaze unit – a commando force able to land by sea or by air to physically destroy the parked B-29s on the airfields and cause as much damage and confusion as possible before they were killed in action.

The Japanese Army already had a division-sized force of paratroopers that had been raised in 1941 and formed part of the Army Air Service. The Imperial Navy also maintained Marine Parachute Units. The army paratroops were divided into raiding brigades and regiments, and they had first seen action in 1942 when they dropped on the oil fields at Palembang in Sumatra during the Japanese invasion of the Netherlands East Indies. The 1st Raiding Regiment under Colonel Seiichi Kume and elements of the 2nd Raiding Regiment under Major Niihara had quickly overwhelmed the enemy and achieved all of their objectives. The idea of taking out American airfields using special raiding forces had also already been attempted by the Japanese. On 6 December 1944 a 750-strong detachment from the 2nd Raiding Brigade had dropped on American airfields in the Burauen area of Leyte in the Philippines. They had managed to destroy some aircraft and inflicted casualties on the Americans, but ultimately the entire Japanese force had been wiped out.

Now, in late 1944, the Japanese searched for a man to lead a new Kempeitai-controlled commando unit and discovered Captain Michiro Okuyama, the commanding officer of the 1st Raiding Regiment's Engineer Company. He and his men were highly trained in sabotage and demolition, and Okuyama had been the first member of the original army parachute training unit. He was known as an outstanding officer and leader of men and he was highly respected by his superiors. Headquarters ordered Okuyama to select 126 men to form the new *Giretsu* (Respect for Faith) Airborne Unit, making it clear that the mission they would be training for was a suicide assault from which none were expected to return alive.

Okuyama selected his men, most of whom were fellow combat engineers and sabotage experts from his own regiment. Okuyama would lead the Command Section, while the assault groups were divided into five platoons. 1st Platoon was led by Lieutenant Utsuki, 2nd by Lieutenant Sugata, 3rd by Captain Watabe, 4th by Lieutenant Murakami and 5th Platoon was under the command of Lieutenant Yamada, all experienced and respected officers. On 5 December 1944,

Giretsu Airborne Unit was assembled at the Army's Air Academy at Saitama. Okuyama's unit was joined by ten Kempeitai intelligence officers from the Nakano Intelligence School, two officers being assigned to each assault platoon, bringing the unit's strength up to 136 men.

At the academy a mock-up B-29 was constructed and two new explosive devices quickly developed to deal with the American aircraft. The first was a 2kg explosive charge on the end of a pole. On top of the charge was a rubber suction cup. The saboteur pushed the pole under the B-29's wing, the explosive charge stuck to the aircraft skin, and then a cord was pulled to ignite a delay fuse. The second new weapon was a chain charge. It consisted of a rope measuring 13–16 feet in length that was fitted with explosive charges along its length. A small sandbag weighted one end. The weapon could thus be thrown over a B-29's wings or fuselage and ignited to cause maximum damage to the aircraft.

The training was intense. Captain Okuyama ordered that each commando must try to destroy at least three enemy aircraft, regardless of the risk to his own life. The hours spent making dummy attacks on the mocked-up B-29 soon turned the unit into an efficient raiding party, with each man sure of his job and the unit able to operate in the dark against its targets. This was demonstrated to invited senior officers on the night of 22 December, and the observers were mightily impressed. A mission was planned almost immediately on the basis of the demonstration, but the availability of aircraft to transport the commandos to their target was to cause a delay. The air squadron assigned to transport the commandos to their target was Captain Suwabe's 3rd Independent Flying Unit which transferred on to the Mitsubishi Ki-21-II 'Sally' bomber in readiness for the mission.

The plan was deceptively simple. The *Giretsu* Airborne Unit would board a collection of Ki-21 bombers and fly south from Japan to the lonely volcanic island of Iwo Jima where they would be refuelled. The planes would then fly on to the American-occupied Mariana Islands and crash-land on selected B-29 airfields. The commandos would then storm the parked B-29s and destroy as many aircraft and crewmen as possible before taking up positions close to the airfields to deny their use by the enemy with small-arms fire. The attack was scheduled for 17 January 1945, and would be launched from Hamamatsu Airbase on Honshu Island.

American air attacks on the airfields located on Iwo Jima intensified before the *Giretsu* attack was launched, as part of the softening up of Japanese defences before a full-scale invasion was launched. America wanted to use Iwo Jima as a kind of lifeboat anchored in the Pacific between the bases in the Marianas and Japan, so that damaged B-29s could divert and make emergency landings. The American bombardment of the Japanese airfields on Iwo Jima meant that refuelling the Ki-21 medium bombers to be used by the *Giretsu* Unit was out of the question. On their own, the Ki-21s lacked the range to fly directly from Japan to the Marianas, so the operation was cancelled.

US Marines captured the airfields on Iwo Jima in March, and it was proposed to use the *Giretsu* Unit to effect their recapture, but the island's garrison fell before the plan could be put into operation. The commandos waited in a state of readiness for another mission to present itself. They did not have long to wait. On 1 April a massive American amphibious assault hit the big island of Okinawa, south of Kyushu. American forces captured the Japanese airfields at Yontan and Kadena on the island's west coast, and fighter interceptors shot down many of the Japanese Kamikaze aircraft that launched massed attacks on American and British shipping supporting the invasion. Although the Kamikazes managed to sink several ships and damaged many others, their tactics were being seriously disrupted by American fighters flying from the two recently captured airbases. Suddenly, the solution presented itself to the Japanese High Command on 15 May – use the *Giretsu* Airborne Unit to neutralize Okinawa's airfields.

Codenamed Operation *Gi*, the plan had a distinct advantage over the former operation planned against the Marianas. The Ki-21 medium bombers would be able to fly directly from Japan to Okinawa without requiring any refuelling. The *Giretsu* Unit and the 3rd Independent Flying Unit were immediately moved south to Kengun Airfield on Kyushu. Preparations were hastily made for the assault on the two American bases. 3rd Flying Unit was equipped with sixteen Ki-21s, with a further four in reserve. All of the bombers were stripped of their guns to save weight. Captain Okuyama with the Command Section and 1st, 2nd and 5th Platoons would fly in eight Ki-21s and assault Yontan Airfield. Captain Watabe with the 3rd and 4th Platoons would take four aircraft and attack Kadena.

The *Giretsu* Unit would take off from Japan in the evening, timing their arrival at the American airfields just before midnight. Just before the commandos landed, fifty army and navy Kamikazes would launch a mass attack on the airfields to provide a diversion, allowing the bombers to glide in and make wheels-up crash-landings. The Japanese commandos would storm from the bombers, using their pole and chain charges to cripple American aircraft and destroy vital facilities before taking up positions overlooking both bases, where their small-arms fire would disrupt the bases' effective operation. The following day, Operation *Gi* called for a mass Kamikaze attack by 180 Japanese aircraft on the enemy fleets off Okinawa, supported by thirty conventional attack aircraft including a few fitted with the *Ohka* jet-powered flying bomb (which was also a suicide weapon). If all went well, the American fighter defences should be severely damaged, and their remaining planes grounded by *Giretsu* commandos firing across the runways. Imperial General Headquarters in Tokyo believed that Operation *Gi* could mean the defeat of the American invasion of Okinawa. It was a good plan, and although the American and British fleets had rapidly become accustomed to Kamikaze air attacks on their ships, no-one was expecting over 130 heavily armed and well trained Japanese commandos to suddenly appear, all of them expecting to die in the course of the mission.

Captain Okuyama's men were well armed and psychologically prepared for a bitter fight. They were armed with Type 99 rifles, sub- and light machine guns, grenade dischargers and the specialist explosive devices invented for the unit. Additionally, each commando also carried an automatic pistol and high explosive and white phosphorous grenades. X-day was set for 23 May, but bad weather over Okinawa led to the operation being postponed for a day. On the evening of the 24th a short and moving ceremony was held at the airfield at Kengun as the men raised cups of *sake* arranged on long wooden trestle tables on the airfield and shouted 'Banzai!' twice before taking a final sip. Captain Okuyama then gave the men a final rousing speech before they boarded their aircraft and made ready for departure. At 6.50pm the first of the twelve bombers roared down the runway and took off, heading the 480 miles to Okinawa and what the men hoped would be a glorious death in battle. They were seen off by the ground crews who furiously waved Japanese flags as the bombers powered down the runway.[2]

Four of the planes aborted the mission with engine trouble and returned to Kengun. The remaining eight flew on in formation before arriving over Okinawa. A radio message from the lead aircraft was picked up at Kengun, but nothing further was then heard from the *Giretsu* Unit as the planes began to make their descent into Yontan Airfield. The diversionary attacks had been launched by seven waves of conventional bombers that had started a large fire on the base, but without causing any significant damage. Marine Corps and US Army anti-aircraft gunners shot down eleven Japanese bombers. At 9.25pm a Type 97 approached the airfield much lower than the conventional bombers and was immediately shot out of the sky. At 10.30pm three Ki-21 bombers appeared to be trying to land at Yontan, but their slow air speed, low altitude and regular course made them easy targets for the anti-aircraft batteries. These three all carried *Giretsu* commandos, and were among only four aircraft that actually got on to the airfield, the other four being shot down by American fighters. The pilots of the three damaged Japanese bombers attempted to use their aircraft as a giant Kamikaze vehicle, and with their commandos still aboard they slammed into the ground. A number of the commandos actually survived the crashes and rushed out of the wreckage firing their weapons into parked aircraft and setting demolition charges. Only one of the *Giretsu* Unit's aircraft actually landed as planned. It swung in low through a hail of flak and, wheels-up, safely skidded across the runway coming to rest only eighty yards from the control tower before ten commandos poured out from its nose cone and doors and began to attack American aircraft.

As soon as it became clear that Japanese troops were on the ground, the American forces defending the airfield panicked and began firing literally in all directions. It has been surmised that some of the damage inflicted on the airfield facilities and aircraft, and some of the American casualties, were the result of this indiscriminate firing. All across the base weapons were being discharged by both Americans and Japanese, and planes and vital facilities were going up in smoke. The next morning a Marine Corps unit was hastily dispatched to the airfield to hunt down and kill the remaining *Giretsu* commandos. The Japanese were all dead by 12.55pm, when the last one was shot whilst hiding in some brush. Many of the Japanese airmen from the 3rd Independent Flying Unit had taken their own lives while the commandos had gone about their mission. Altogether, the Americans collected together sixty-nine dead Japanese from the wrecked planes and strewn about the airfield. The Japanese commandos had managed to destroy four F4U Corsair fighters, and to damage a further twenty-two. They had also destroyed two four-engined PB4Y Privateer patrol bombers and four Dakota transport planes. Damaged aircraft included three F6F Hellcat fighters, two Privateers and a pair of Dakotas. The *Giretsu* commandos also set on fire a massive tank containing 70,000 gallons of precious aviation fuel. American losses were three killed and eighteen wounded.[3] All this destruction was caused by only ten *Giretsu* commandos from the one intact Ki-21 that had belly-flopped on Yontan's runway, and a few survivors from the crash-landing of another. If the entire team of 136 men had successfully landed, the damage they would have caused and the confusion they would have sown in the enemy's ranks does not bear thinking about. Perhaps also if the *Giretsu* Unit had parachuted onto the target rather than attempted the assault by crash-landing planes, more would have survived to continue with the mission.

The mass Kamikaze attacks were launched against the Allied fleet on 25 and 27 May, the Japanese not knowing if the *Giretsu* Unit had successfully silenced at least one of the enemy's airfields. Unfortunately for the Japanese, Yontan was fully operational again by the afternoon of the 25th and the Kamikazes were heavily defeated. The *Giretsu* commandos were undoubtedly brave and resourceful soldiers who died for a cause they believed in implicitly, but ultimately their sacrifice did not save Japan from inevitable defeat.

The Kempeitai was to have little success with its other special operations units, in particular with one named *Matsu Kikan* or Pine Tree. This little unit went into action some time before the *Giretsu* Airborne Unit, and before Japan's position was completely desperate. In January 1944 Japanese Naval Intelligence suspected that the Americans were constructing a new naval base at Admiralty Gulf on the north-west shore of Western Australia. Although cooperation between the Imperial Army and the Imperial Japanese Navy was best described as difficult both before and during the war, on this occasion the navy made a request to the closest military forces to Western Australia to conduct a reconnaissance to confirm or deny their suspicions.

Based on Ambon Island, the Japanese 19th Army contained the commando-style *Matsu Kikan* under the command of Captain Masayoshi Yamamoto of the Kempeitai. The *Matsu Kikan* contained graduates of the Army Intelligence School at Nakano in Japan (who would later feature prominently in the *Giretsu* Unit), and they performed the function of an elite reconnaissance force. Yamamoto detailed one of his subordinates, Lieutenant Susuhiko Mizuno, to put together a small team ready for insertion into Western Australia. Mizuno's mission briefing contained three specific tasks: firstly, he was to investigate the possibility of effecting a landing in Australia by a large Japanese force. Secondly, Mizuno was to find a good location where such a force could be put ashore; and thirdly, he was to scout around and try to find any Australian or American military establishments in the region, such as the suspected naval base.

Lieutenant Mizuno's party departed on their mission from Koepang in Timor (in the Japanese occupied Netherlands East Indies) aboard a tiny 25-ton fishing vessel called the *Hiroshi Maru* on 14 January 1944. The rest of Mizuno's team consisted of two sergeants, a superior private who would act as a radio operator, six Japanese sailors, and fifteen local Timorese disguised as fishermen. The Timorese would sail the vessel to Australia, and if any Allied aircraft or ships encountered the *Hiroshi Maru* their presence would hopefully deter a more thorough investigation of the boat.

The first attempt to carry out the mission was scrubbed when the tiny fishing boat was caught in a ferocious storm that forced Mizuno to return to base on the morning of 15 January. The Japanese waited out the storm and then set out again on the evening of the 16th. Strangely, although the Japanese had already disguised their activities with the addition of the Timorese fishermen, they now took the contradictory step of providing the *Hiroshi Maru* with air cover for the voyage. Any Allied plane or ship that encountered a small fishing boat with its own dedicated aerial cover would immediately be suspicious. 19th Army Headquarters had instructed the 7th Air Division at Kendari Airfield to release an aircraft for the operation, and Staff Sergeant Aonuma found himself flying his

Type-99 light bomber on circuits around the *Hiroshi Maru* as she motored towards Australia.

On 16 January, as the fishing boat approached Cartier Islet, Aonuma spotted a submarine running on the surface. Knowing that the submarine could only be an enemy boat, Aonuma decided to dissuade it from making a closer inspection of the *Hiroshi Maru*, and he dove in to attack. Lookouts aboard the submarine had already spotted the Japanese bomber, and the submarine immediately crash-dived, followed under the waves by two bursts of machine gun fire from the Type-99. As Aonuma passed over the white swirling water marking where the submarine had vanished he dropped six 50kg bombs. The bombs detonated underwater, throwing up great geysers of water and spray at the surface as Aonuma circled over the spot several times. He later reported that the submarine had probably been damaged by his attack.

The Type-99 bomber continued to fly top cover for the *Hiroshi Maru* as the vessel approached the deserted Australian coast. A radar system monitored the airspace over the coastline, and Staff Sergeant Aonuma had already been briefed about its existence so he took his aircraft down low well out at sea. Moving swiftly ahead of the fishing boat, Aonuma located Cartier Islet, and he returned to guide the *Hiroshi Maru* in.

The first 'landfall' made by the Japanese was at 9am on the morning of 17 January when they reached East Island. The island is actually a coral reef that is exposed during low tide. Twenty-four hours later the Japanese reached Browse Island, and here Lieutenant Mizuno and his men went ashore, the first Japanese forces to land in Australia. Browse contained nothing except a ruined watchtower, but the island did provide the Japanese force with a suitable laying-up position. Timing his mission carefully, Mizuno wanted the force to land on the mainland on the early morning of 19 January.

After three hours on Browse, the *Hiroshi Maru* weighed anchor and sailed through the night to the mainland, entering an inlet on the coast of Western Australia at approximately 10am. A light mist concealed the Japanese landing party as they quietly collected tree branches with which to camouflage the *Hiroshi Maru*, then the men ate a cold breakfast before beginning their mission. Mizuno divided his command into three parties that was each tasked with exploring different areas of the wilderness. Mizuno commanded one, while his two sergeants, Morita and Furuhashi, each led another, and it was agreed that all the parties would rendezvous back at the boat after two hours. Mizuno even had an 8mm movie camera with him to record anything of interest.

The Japanese were to discover nothing of any military value, all the parties reporting finding only old campfires along the coast. After a night aboard the boat, Mizuno ordered another series of patrols on 20 January, but by 2pm, and with nothing to show for their labours, Mizuno decided to end the mission and return to Timor. The Japanese landings near Cartier and Browse Islands in Western Australia remain the only confirmed presence of enemy troops in Australia during the Second World War, though many locals and amateur historians insist that Kempeitai reconnaissance parties undertook several similar missions to Australia, and that Japanese submarine crews also came ashore in quiet localities to replenish their stocks of fresh water. Either way, Japan's interest in Australia was soon forgotten as events closer to home drew their attention.

The Kempeitai's attempts at creating special forces units were rather haphazard and not very successful. None of the missions undertaken were successful, and in the case of the *Giretsu* assault on Okinawa in 1945, entailed huge loss of life and equipment by the Japanese.

Notes

1. 'Murder and Suicide', *Time*, 11 June 1945.
2. Film actually has survived that shows the *Giretsu* Unit's departure from Japan: *Japanese newsreel No 262 – Giretsu Parachute corps*, http://www.youtube.com.
3. Richard O'Neill, *Suicide Squads: The Men and Machines of World War II Special Operations* (London, Salamander Books, 1999), pp. 234–5.

Chapter Twelve

Leave No Survivors

Upon returning to the camp I immediately reported to Major Sadakichi that the mine had been totally destroyed and all 387 POWs entombed in its depths.

Lieutenant Yoshiro Tsuda,
Deputy Commandant, Aikawa POW Camp Japan, 1945

There can be no excuse for a nation which as a matter of policy treats its prisoners of war in this way, and no honour to an army, however brave, which makes itself an instrument of such inhumanity to the helpless.

Field Marshal Sir William Slim, 1945

Two British soldiers sat on the dusty road, a bewildered, hunted expression on their faces. Their uniforms consisted of nothing more than ragged shorts and torn, sweat-stained shirts. They wore hats woven from palm fronds, but beneath the wide brims their faces were unshaven and sickly looking. They were walking skeletons, and though still young men, their sun-blackened skin hung loosely over their bones. Their feet, wrapped in rags, were swollen and discoloured by beriberi, and their bellies clung to their backbones with starvation. The beriberi had also caused unsightly lumps to appear elsewhere on their bodies. Beside them were sticks they had used to support themselves on the endless trek. These two young soldiers simply could not go any further and had been left behind by their Japanese guards.

165

Beside the road was a small hut. A well-fed Japanese sergeant emerged from the hut, a rifle clasped in his hands, and began to walk impatiently towards the British soldiers, thumbing off the rifle's safety catch as he moved. He was muttering under his breath as he strode towards them, the kind of muttering sounds people make when they have been roused from a place of comfort to perform an unwanted task. The two soldiers looked up at him, their grimy faces streaked with sweat, their eyes sunken and resigned. They both knew what was about to happen, and they were probably well beyond caring. The Japanese cursed loudly and raised his rifle, aiming at the first white soldier's head just a few feet away. The gunshot reverberated across the mountainous country, as the soldier was flung violently backwards, blood and brains spraying across the dusty surface of the road like obscene paint. The soldier's body twitched several times before it was still. The Japanese recycled the bolt action rifle with a metallic click, an empty cartridge case tumbling into the dirt while a thin whisper of cordite smoke drifted from the rifle barrel. The Japanese raised the rifle to his shoulder again and fired. Then he turned abruptly away from the two corpses that lay like discarded laundry in the road and marched back to his hut. This little scene of horror was just one of hundreds of similar vignettes of death played out along a trail on the jungle-covered island of Borneo in 1945, beginning at a small town whose name today is a testament to Japanese cruelty and barbarity towards Allied prisoners of war: Sandakan.

The fate of prisoners became a pressing concern for Allied war planners as they framed the final destruction of the Japanese war machine. The Japanese had been notoriously unpredictable and capricious throughout the war, and a final mass killing of all Allied POWs seemed inevitable to most, as indeed it did to the Japanese themselves. Camp commandants anxiously awaited instructions about what to do with their prisoners if the Allies proved victorious.

At his headquarters at Kandy in Sri Lanka, the tall and elegant Vice-Admiral Lord Louis Mountbatten, King George VI's cousin and uncle to the present Duke of Edinburgh, carefully considered the situation. 'Dicky' Mountbatten carried the exalted title of Supreme Allied Commander, South East Asia (SEAC). Winston Churchill had ordered Mountbatten to liberate all colonial territories in Asia lost to Japan by Britain, France and the Netherlands at the beginning of the war. It was a tall order, but Mountbatten appeared to be just the man for such a task. He had previously commanded Combined Operations in Europe, although he had also been the brains behind the debacle at Dieppe in 1942, when thousands of Canadian troops had been sacrificed in a dry run for D-Day. Many deeply distrusted Mountbatten, and others believed him to be dangerously incompetent, including the Chief of the Imperial General Staff and Britain's top soldier, Field Marshal Sir Alan Brooke. Many thought he owed his exalted position more to his royal connections and social position rather than to any real competence in command. However, the King's cousin was popular with the Americans, which probably explained his appointment in August 1943 to so senior a post as SEAC at the age of only forty-two.

Churchill primarily wanted a military commander out east who was capable of dealing with the Americans, and Mountbatten fitted the profile perfectly, but his remit to recapture European colonies was to prove an almost impossible assignment. His second-in-command was an American, Lieutenant General Joseph W. Stilwell, nicknamed 'Vinegar Joe' because of his permanently bad mood. Stilwell's loyalties did not lie with Mountbatten and SEAC but rather with his own countrymen in Washington, and he was to prove a thorn in the side of the British.

The real power in the region was America's General Douglas MacArthur, the vainglorious leader grandly titled the Supreme Commander, South West Pacific Forces. He had been based in Australia since Roosevelt had ordered him out of Corrigedor in 1942. The line of demarcation between Mountbatten's and MacArthur's competing spheres of influence ran through Japanese-occupied Saigon in French Indochina. Everything to the west of this line was under Mountbatten's, and therefore British, control. The British effort was, however, primarily focused on the recapture of Burma, whereas MacArthur, with the massive support of Admiral Chester Nimitz's Pacific Fleet, had considerably more wide-ranging goals in mind – nothing less than an eventual invasion of Japan itself. It was all a question of numbers and logistics. The Americans were more numerous in the Pacific theatre, better equipped and supplied, had more aircraft and aircraft carriers, and an unequalled fleet train stretching across the Pacific from California. President Roosevelt and his military chiefs were determined that the Pacific and Asia would be a purely American affair, and they had actively stymied virtually every British effort to take an active part in recovering lost colonies and re-establishing British regional hegemony. Those in power in Washington believed that Britain, with its new socialist government and virtually bankrupt economy would have to give way after 1945 to a strong and prosperous United States. The *Pax Britannica* that had ruled the globe for over 150 years would be replaced by a new *Pax Americana*. Even the issue of saving starving prisoners of war caused great dissension between the two allies as the new replaced the old in Asia; this ultimately allowed the Kempeitai and other Japanese forces to kill thousands of prisoners while the British and Americans squabbled.

The end of the war may have been close, but it was not close enough for the tens of thousands of emaciated and diseased prisoners of war in Japanese captivity. The white prisoners taken earlier in the war had not waited out the duration in prisoner of war camps, but on the direct orders of General Hideki Tojo, Prime Minister and Minister of War, they had been forced to slave for the Emperor and were shipped about the occupied territories as free labour. And labour they had. In mid-1943 the Japanese High Command had ordered a railway built from Thailand into Burma, the labour to be provided by British and Commonwealth prisoners held at Changi Camp in Singapore. Shipped north, formerly healthy young men were stripped of their health, dignity and pride, and eventually their lives, as they laboured in atrocious conditions to build the infernal 'Railway of Death' through miles of trackless jungle. Tens of thousands of native coolies were enslaved alongside them in equally appalling conditions by the desperate Japanese. A total of 46,000 Allied prisoners went to work, and 16,000 never came out of the jungle alive. Each mile of track that was laid had cost the lives of sixty-four Allied prisoners and 240 native coolies.

As elsewhere across its gigantic empire, the Japanese needed labour to construct airfields and other military installations on Borneo. Native labour was insufficient, while since the fall of Singapore in February 1942 tens of thousands of white prisoners were languishing at Changi Camp on Singapore Island in relative comfort – tens of thousands of young, strong and fit soldiers from Britain and Australia who could help the Japanese war effort no end by labouring for the Emperor on defence projects the length and breadth of the Occupied Territories. Tojo himself had written instructions to prison camp commandants regarding their captives that ordered in no uncertain terms: 'you must not allow them to lie idle, doing nothing but enjoy free meals, for even a single day. Their labour and technical skill should be fully utilized for the replenishment of production, and contribution thereby made toward the prosecution of the Greater East Asiatic War for which no effort ought to be spared.'[1] Many would eventually be shipped north to Thailand where they slaved to build the Death Railway, while many more ended up in mines in Japan, Manchuria or on the island of Taiwan. Several thousand found themselves packed tightly on to filthy and unmarked steamers and sent to the steamy tropical island of Borneo, occupied by Japan since early 1942 and home to the Japanese 37th Army.

Several POW and civilian internment camps had been established by the Japanese on Borneo. They were located at Batu Lintang, Kuching, Sarawak, Jesselton, Sandakan and briefly on Labuan Island. All came under the control of the Kempeitai, based in Kuching, since prisoner administration was an important department of the military police. The overall commander of the camps on Borneo was the affable and kindly Lieutenant-Colonel Tatsuji Suga, who was noted by the civilian internees at Batu Lintang, where he was based, to be a civilized man and a Catholic convert. Many have suggested that constant interference from the higher and more brutal echelons of the Kempeitai meant that Suga was virtually powerless to prevent the systematic abuse of the prisoners and internees under his command, but that remains debatable.

On 8 July 1942 the first large movement of prisoners to Borneo was made when 'Force B' was shipped out of Changi Camp by the Japanese authorities in Singapore. It consisted of 1,500 fit and healthy Australians under the command of Lieutenant-Colonel Walsh of 2/10th Field Regiment, Royal Australian Artillery. They were sent by ship to the small town of Sandakan in the present-day Malaysian state of Sabah on the north-east coast of the island of Borneo. When the Japanese had invaded, Sandakan was the British colonial capital of North Borneo. The Japanese had established three prison camps outside the town ready to receive the Australians. When they arrived 'Force B' was imprisoned in Camp 1. Lieutenant Rod Wells of the Australian Army recalled his first sight of Sandakan:

169

'From the sea it's lovely. With the red chalk hills on the side of Berhala Island it really is impressive. I suppose for a split moment we thought, with a sigh of relief, that here's some beautiful, peaceful land where there may not be any Japanese.'[2]

The regime in the camps was fairly brutal from the word go, though it really deteriorated after about a year. At Changi, the British and Australians had taken care of themselves. The Japanese had simply ordered the POWs inside the huge Changi Cantonment, a massive and new British barracks complex in the west of the island; they then wired off the perimeter, and apart from supplying food and shooting the occasional escapee had little dealings with the prisoners directly. Some of the guards at Changi were renegade Indians under Kempeitai control. There had been sport, plays, educational classes (the camp was nicknamed 'Changi University' by the inmates) and a hospital. The British had even kept up with foot drill on the parade square, and the men were punished by their own officers for infractions of King's Regulations, instead of submitting to the cruel and unusual punishments the Japanese reserved for offenders. At Sandakan the prisoners found themselves, for the first time, under the direct authority of the Japanese, with disastrous results.

The overall commandant of the three new prison camps in the Sandakan area was Captain Susumi Hoshijima. The Australians were immediately put to work building two airstrips for the Japanese and a system of supply roads through the jungle, as well as aircraft dispersal pens. The typical working day began at 7.30am and continued through to 5.30pm. Although the work was physically demanding, the prisoners were properly fed at the beginning and there was little physical abuse from the guards. Private Keith Botterill of the Australian 2/19th Battalion recalled: 'We had it easy the first twelve months ... we used to get flogged, but we had plenty of food and cigarettes ... We actually had a canteen in the prison camp ... It was a good camp.'[3] In their first twelve months at Sandakan only six prisoners died. When labour was desperately needed it made sense to preserve the prisoners' bodies. However, all that was soon to change dramatically.

During April 1943 776 British prisoners arrived at Camp 2. They arrived in two parties from Jesselton (now Kota Kinabalu), the largest settlement in Sabah, and they were in a generally run-down and poor condition after their long journey. Originally these British had all been prisoners at Changi Camp before being shipped out to Jesselton. The fittest prisoners arrived on the 8th, with the unfit party, numbering 570 men, arriving in camp on the 18th. Two hundred and forty of the unfit were very sick from malnutrition and tropical diseases, and Captain Hoshijima had these unfortunates crowded into wooden huts, seventy-four men to each native building. Formosan Chinese guards from Taiwan also arrived at Sandakan, and their arrival completely changed the character of the camps.

The Japanese regularly employed Formosans and Koreans as prison camp guards and menial labour, and naturally the Formosans and Koreans hated their Japanese colonial overlords. Because they could not vent their frustrations on their masters they instead viciously abused the prisoners in their custody. In fact, Formosan Chinese and Korean soldiers were legendary throughout the Japanese gulag for being even worse abusers of prisoners than the Japanese, which, as one can imagine, took some doing.

With the arrival of the British prisoners and new Formosan guards mass beatings of work details began. Warrant Officer William Sticpewich of the Australian Army Service Corps recalled: 'My gang would be working all right and then would be suddenly told to stop ... The men would then be stood with their arms outstretched horizontally, shoulder high, facing the sun without hats.' The guards would form themselves into two groups, one group covering the prisoners with their rifles 'and the others doing the actual beating. They would walk along the back of us and ... smack us underneath the arms, across the ribs and on the back,' recalled Sticpewich. 'They would give each man a couple of bashes ... if they whimpered or flinched they would get a little more.'[4]

In June 1943 a fresh wave of prisoners arrived at Sandakan. Known as 'Force E', they occupied Camp 3. Consisting of 500 Australian POWs sent directly from Singapore's Changi Camp, when they arrived they were in much better physical condition than the British prisoners. Originally, 1,000 POWs had left Changi, but at Kuching, the capital of Sarawak, 500 former members of Britain's Southern Area Command were transferred to local camps while the Australians were shipped on to Sandakan.

Lieutenant Stephen Day had arrived at Kuching with 500 other British soldiers in November or December 1942. Long before being transferred to other camps he recalled the casual brutality of the Japanese from which not even officers were exempt. Day recalled to investigators his experiences. '[In] this camp for greeting a passing Indian prisoner he was beaten about the face with a hoe handle, knocked down a number of times and kicked in the lower regions and in the stomach whilst on the ground. He was then taken before Colonel Suga and sentenced to five days imprisonment in the cells.'[5] Day recalled that the Japanese also punished the entire camp collectively, a favourite technique being to force all the prisoners to stand with their hands above their heads for two or three hours under a boiling sun. Even army doctors were not safe from physical assault. Lieutenant-Colonel Edmund Sheppard, 2/10th Field Ambulance, Australian Army Medical Corps, was a camp doctor at Kuching. He recorded that between 1 January and 31 August 1945 a staggering 580 prisoners died of deficiency diseases. An awful lot of these men had also been hospitalized by brutal beatings. He himself was struck. According to postwar testimony, 'Bashings of prisoners took place at a rate of 10 a day. Japanese Doctor Yamamoto personally bashed and kicked [Sheppard] and other medical officers including a woman medical officer.'[6] For propaganda reasons the Japanese falsified the conditions inside the camp to portray prisons run in accordance with international law. 'Thus a load of bananas were brought into camp, photographed and then removed from the camp.' Such surreal scenes were played out all over Asia by the strange and cruel Japanese.

At Sandakan, Captain Hoshijima forbade any communication between the prisoners in the three camps, and anyone who disobeyed this order was severely punished. Hoshijima ordered the construction of a special place of torture to punish offenders, known to the prisoners as 'The Cage'. It was placed next to a large tree in Camp 1 and was a wooden structure 130cm high and 170cm long with bars on all sides. Prisoners were forced to sit at attention inside the cage all day and no bedding or mosquito netting was provided. Keith Botterill experienced this horror at first hand: 'The time I was in for forty days there were seventeen of us in there. No water for first three days. On the third night they'd force you to drink till you were sick. For the first seven days you got no food. On the seventh day they started feeding you half camp rations ... Every evening we would get a bashing, which they used to call physical exercise ...'[7]

In August 1943 the majority of the officer prisoners were moved back to Kuching, leaving just nine to manage the other ranks, including one chaplain, Squadron Leader Rev. John Wanless of the Royal Air Force Volunteer Reserve. The reason for this was the ingenuity of Captain Lionel Matthews of the Australian Signal Corps. Matthews was an officer who simply refused to lie down and die as the Japanese evidently intended. He organized a group of twenty officers and NCOs into an *ad hoc* intelligence group. Using native intermediaries, Matthews' group made contact with British civilians being held in an internment camp on nearby Bahara Island. With the help of friendly locals and the internees, Matthews built up a dossier of intelligence concerning the organization and deployment of Japanese forces in the region, their strengths and bases, supply situation and details about the local geography. Matthews wanted to pass all of this information to the Allies in the hope that it would assist them in liberating Borneo. Matthews also learned that a few British nationals, mainly doctors and dentists, had been permitted by the Kempeitai to remain at liberty outside the camps. Matthews' group managed to contact Dr. J.P. Taylor through whom some medical supplies were smuggled into the camps to try to relieve the dire medical situation.

Matthews' group wanted information about the progress of the war, so using their network they managed to smuggle radio parts into their camp and built a simple receiver. What Matthews and his men heard from the BBC was the story of the slow collapse of the Japanese empire, and this emboldened them to make another plan. The network of informers and spies began gathering guns and ammunition for the prisoners, and the prisoners on work details outside the camp managed to cache these weapons near Sandakan. Matthews' idea was that when the Allies invaded Borneo the healthy prisoners (meaning those who could actually walk and had the strength to carry weapons) would rise up in armed revolt, kill or capture their guards and seize the camps. In order to facilitate this, Matthews next decided that the prisoners needed a radio transmitter so they could communicate with the Allies directly. Once again, the parts were smuggled into the camp at great risk to the informers, and Matthews' group almost got away with it. Unfortunately, Joe Ming, a Chinese sympathizer involved in procuring radio parts was betrayed to the Kempeitai by a disgruntled Indian. The Kempeitai tortured Ming and his family until they broke and gave up Matthews and his men. The Allied conspirators were swiftly removed to Kempeitai headquarters at Kuching, where they were tortured for three months until they all confessed to the 'crime' of possessing a radio and plotting against the Japanese. Captain Matthews was executed by firing squad on 2 March 1944 alongside eight of the other ringleaders. He was posthumously awarded the George Cross for his bravery.

Beatings at the Sandakan camps increased in ferocity and number through the rest of 1943 and into 1944, as the Formosan and Japanese guards whaled on the prisoners for the slightest offence. The Japanese knew that they were losing the war, and their frustration and shame was readily transmitted on to the helpless prisoners. In September 1944 Allied aircraft started raiding the Japanese airstrip at Sandakan. The idea was to keep the base out of operation, so it was regularly bombed and strafed. The airstrip was eventually abandoned by the Japanese as unusable, but this meant that they no longer had any use for the Allied prisoners languishing in the three camps at Sandakan. This workforce was now surplus to requirements.

In accordance with the sudden reduction in work the Japanese reduced the prisoners' already meagre rations to only 140–200 grams per man per day from December 1944. The death rate, which was already fairly high from tropical diseases and physical abuse, began to climb rapidly as the men, wracked by malaria, dysentery and beriberi now became seriously malnourished and started to die in large numbers of starvation. To make matters even worse Hoshijima ordered his men to cease feeding the prisoners altogether in January 1945. The only food available was rice the officer prisoners had wisely ordered their men to store, and the prisoners now had to make do on only 85 grams of food per man per day. Without intervention of some kind every one of the thousands of prisoners at Sandakan would die.

And so the depravity and suffering continued as the Allies fought their way closer to ultimate victory over the Japanese. Conditions for prisoners in the outlying territories deteriorated dramatically as the Japanese garrisons found themselves cut off by the Allied advance, bypassed and allowed to 'wither on the vine'. Supply ships no longer arrived with rations and ammunition, which meant that for the prisoners, held on these island fortresses, a period of intense deprivation and suffering had begun, as horrible as that found in the camps at Sandakan.

At Palembang in the Netherlands East Indies all the remaining prisoners had been transferred to a single camp at Soengi Geru in March 1944. The guards were the usual mixture of Formosans and Japanese who took great delight in torturing their charges as often and as savagely as possible. The failure of supplies to arrive meant further reduced rations. In May 1945 the prisoner allowance of rice was cut to only 300 grams per man per day, and actually was considerably lower when issued. Intense hunger drove the British, Dutch, Australian and Malay prisoners to eat snakes, lizards, dogs, cats, worms and insects. The Japanese commandant issued these walking skeletons with picks and shovels and ordered them to construct air-raid trenches against the constant attacks by American and Australian aircraft. When raids occurred the commandant had the prisoners locked inside their huts while he and the camp staff took shelter in the trenches. The commandant ordered British officers to give their words of command in Japanese, and if the slightest error was made everyone was beaten. The camp medical officer, Lieutenant Nakai, took to ordering the beating of prisoners who complained about the appalling conditions inside the camp and the dire shortage of food. Working parties were formed, and the prisoners laboured on airfields, defensive positions and in factories and workshops repairing military equipment. They worked from eight in the morning until one the following morning, and were continually beaten for the slightest misdemeanour. One prisoner recalled a special punishment dreamed up by the camp commandant at Soengi Geru to 'punish' the prisoners further:

[A] barbed wire cage was built with dimensions of six feet by four. It had a flat atap [a kind of grass] roof, no protections at all at the sides, and was situated on top of a red ant's nest. On one occasion there were nine prisoners confined in it at the same time. There was no room for them to move in any direction. They had to stand to attention all day and all night. Two of the nine were supposed to be undergoing a sentence of ninety-six days' confinement, but after sixteen days they were so covered with tropical ulcers that they were taken out and admitted to hospital.[8]

The figures are astounding. During the last three months of the war out of 1,050 prisoners at one camp in Sumatra, 276 perished from malnutrition and disease.

There was another group of men suffering as badly as the British and Australian prisoners on Borneo – Indian soldiers. In some cases they were treated far worse than their European fellow captives. The Indian Army had stood firm alongside its British and Commonwealth allies and provided the majority of troops defending Malaya and a multitude of outlying colonies. The officers were a mixture of British and Indian, and alongside the Gurkha regiments from Nepal, the battalions from the sub-continent provided Britain with a huge pool of manpower to defend its equally huge empire. It is no understatement to suggest that without the Indian Army Britain would ultimately have been defeated.

When the Japanese captured Sarawak on 27 December 1941 they had fought primarily against troops from the 2/15th Punjab Regiment. The Japanese viewed their windfall of strong Indian bodies in the same manner as they viewed their white captives – they were slave labour who would construct much of the new military infrastructure that the Japanese demanded throughout the occupied territories. However, there was also some ambivalence in the treatment of Indian prisoners by the Japanese, for the Japanese always argued that the war they had begun was a war to 'liberate' the oppressed peoples of Asia from the yoke of white imperial domination. Were not Indians oppressed by the British Raj? Indian soldiers were quickly separated from their white officers and actively courted into fighting against their former masters. But the loyalty of most Indian soldiers to their regiments and the British Crown meant that Japanese efforts to subvert them were largely unsuccessful, and they were often accompanied by acts of Japanese brutality towards Indian prisoners that further alienated the two Asian peoples from one another.

Naik (Corporal) Chandgi Ram was captured alongside 212 of his comrades from 2/15th Punjab Regiment at Kuching on 27 December 1941. The Indian prisoners spent two months at Kuching working on an airfield for the Japanese, and they were regularly abused by their guards. 'Implements included rifle butts, sticks, steel rods and boots.'[9] Ram recalled trying to help white prisoners: 'Some Australian and British prisoners were kept in the adjoining cell and we were beaten for giving them food.'[10] Later, Ram and his fellow prisoners were moved to a camp at Seria for a year. 'We were given bad rice mixed with lime in Seria,' recalled Ram. 'At that time we were not used to eating rice and became weak. Those of us who were unable to work were beaten and those who could not carry heavy loads were also beaten.'[11]

The Indian prisoners were later transferred to a camp at Kuala Belait, a small town in Brunei, where they were incarcerated until June 1945 under the command of a Lieutenant Yamaguchi. 'At Seria and Kuala Belat [Kuala Belait] the sick were compelled to work and if too weak to do so were beaten. [Ram] had his teeth knocked out and his collar bone broken as a result of one of these beatings. Others were beaten into unconsciousness and some died as a result of being beaten.'[12] Ram recalled the beatings that he suffered: 'I was beaten with a leather belt, and the Jap also took off a boot and beat me across the face with it.'[13]

Other Indian troops had been captured at the fall of Singapore on 15 February 1942 and later shipped in to Borneo as slave labour alongside British and Australian prisoners. Naik Partip Singh of 17 Field Company, Indian Engineers, was one such unfortunate. He was sent to Lutong Camp in May 1942. Once again they 'were made to work and were beaten with sticks, steel bars and wire pliers.'[14] In May 1943 seventy of these prisoners were sent to another camp nine miles away at the town of Miri. There the Japanese tried to get the Indians to join the Indian National Army (INA), a renegade Japanese-sponsored puppet military force of disaffected Indian soldiers and outright nationalists later sent to fight against the British on the Burma front. Naik Singh was among those sent to Miri, where the Japanese worked them hard before indoctrination began; if their intention was to entice Indian soldiers over to the Japanese side their treatment of Indian prisoners proved to be a rather large disincentive. 'The Indians were put to work loading and unloading ships for nine hours a day,' detail war crimes documents. 'They were beaten as before. On one occasion [Singh] couldn't walk for a month as a result of a beating. He was sick with dysentery, beri beri and malaria.'[15] Naik Chandgi Ram recalled that at Kuala Belait 'Indian officers were put in charge of Indian work parties. I was beaten many times there with sticks and bits of steel pipe ... At first we were given enough rice and vegetables, but when we refused to help them against the British the Japanese reduced our rations.'[16] Two renegade Indians came to the camp and lectured the prisoners about Indian independence and exhorted them to join the INA, but according to Ram, 'this had no result and the two Indians went away again. The Japs reduced the rations more, and we got just a handful of rice a day.' Naik Partap Singh recalled in his testimony that 'we told the Japanese that we would work under them but we would not join the Indian National Army.'[17] The Japanese then tried to force the Indians to learn Japanese. 'We had to count, and when we forgot the numbers we were beaten,'[18] said Ram.

In one month at Kuala Belait fifty-five Indian prisoners died of starvation. 'About 13 or 14 June, 1945, the Indians were ordered to fall in and were then bayonetted or beheaded by the Japanese.'[19] Ram escaped by hiding in some bushes. 'I did not actually see the killing,' recalled Ram, 'but I heard the Indians crying; and in the morning I went in and saw that all of the Indians' heads had been cut off.'[20] Sixty five Indian soldiers were thus executed.

One incident recounted by Naik Ram highlighted how important the issue of 'face' was to the Japanese. The Japanese used to make the Indian prisoners guard themselves at night by issuing one of the NCOs with a wooden rifle. Some refused this duty, and were beaten, including Ram. One night when Ram was being assaulted 'an Indian officer came and asked the Japanese why they were beating the Indians, pointing out that this should not be done. Temporarily the beatings were stopped.'[21] The Japanese guard, Private Atada, had lost face in front of the Indian officer, and so determined to restore his face by once more finding an excuse to assault prisoners. He ordered the Indians to light a fire in their barracks one night soon after to drive away mosquitoes. Later, Atada marched into the barrack and demanded to know who had lit a fire without his permission? 'He called five Indian officers and six Ors [Other Ranks] and beat them with a steel pipe; then the party was taken to the military police [Kempeitai] and beaten again until they fell unconscious. They were badly injured.' The Kempeitai 'beat them with cane sticks. Cold water was poured over the men to restore them, when they again were beaten,' stated Ram. 'After 13 days four Ors were brought back to the camp.'[22] One of the Indian officers, Subadar (Captain) Mohd Anwar was actually beaten to death. Atada was well-known among the prisoners for his sadism. He often accused the prisoners of signalling to Allied aircraft and would beat prisoners accordingly. Lieutenant Yamaguchi, the commandant, ordered his NCOs to beat all of the Indians regularly, seeming to believe that this abuse would make them slave harder.

The Japanese high command believed that Allied aerial assaults on Sandakan that occurred in early 1945 were the prelude to an invasion of Borneo and decided to prevent the remaining Australian and British prisoners from being liberated, which was official Japanese policy. What was set in motion by local Japanese commanders, and overseen by the Kempeitai, was one of the greatest crimes committed by Japan against prisoners during the Second World War. The camps were ordered to be evacuated and the prisoners force-marched 260km inland to the town of Ranau. The POWs were used as pack mules to move food supplies, ammunition and other stores for the Japanese. Any who fell out of the marches were immediately killed by follow-up groups of Japanese soldiers who were ordered to deal with any stragglers terminally.

The mass execution of Allied prisoners was sanctioned at the very highest levels of the Japanese government. During the last six months of the war the Vice-Minister Shitayama at the War Ministry in Tokyo issued clear instructions to Japanese occupation forces across Asia to 'prevent the prisoners of war from falling into the enemy's hands.'[23] The process of moving and killing prisoners of war was further clarified by Allied war crimes investigators who obtained a document outlining Japanese government policy from Sadayoshi Nakanishi, Acting Director of the Prisoner of War Information Bureau in Tokyo, shortly after the war ended. The document reiterated earlier orders that 'Prisoners of War must be prevented *by all possible means* [author's italics] from falling into enemy hands.'[24] It also reiterated that changing the location of POW camps ahead of the advancing Allies was necessary to preserve the prisoners as slave labour for as long as possible, but that prisoners could be released 'In the event of an enemy attack which leaves no alternative.'[25]

Preserving POWs as labour was a primary concern for the Japanese government, and this was highlighted in the document dated 11 March 1945: 'the location of camps will be changed as much as possible, and we shall not let prisoners of war fall into enemy hands until we have got some results from them.'[26] The document also states that when moving prisoners 'emergency measures shall be taken without delay against those of antagonistic attitudes, and we shall hope for nothing regrettable by taking proper measures to suit the occasion.' What this paragraph actually did was to give Kempeitai and army commanders on the ground permission to kill the prisoners in their charge, by substituting the word 'murder' with what had been euphemistically termed 'special measures' by Tokyo. They were to make sure that no physical evidence of these crimes be left for Allied investigators to discover.

The terrain the emaciated and diseased prisoners from Sandakan were being asked to traverse would have taxed even the fittest of soldiers. For the first three miles they waded through a muddy swamp teeming with mosquitoes and snakes, divided by several creeks that had to be forded. There followed forty miles of high ground, which consisted of short, steep hills covered with brush and cut through by several rivers. After this had been negotiated the prisoners faced forty-two miles of serious mountain country before arrival at Ranau. The average daily march was supposed to be six and a half miles, but most of the POWs could barely manage a mile before collapsing with exhaustion. Each group of prisoners was divided into fifty-man parties that were issued a 100-pound bag of rice by the Japanese. A leader, usually an officer or senior NCO prisoner, was issued with a sheet of paper and told to make a roll of the prisoners in his charge. Accompanying each fifty-man party were one Japanese officer, three NCOs and fifteen privates armed with rifles.

The first party to be marched out of Sandakan consisted of 455 Australians split into nine separate groups who left between 29 January and 6 February 1945. They were cynically told by the Japanese that food awaited them at the new camp at Ranau. Each man was to carry four days' rations, and they were also overloaded with rice sacks, ammunition boxes and other military equipment they were forced to haul for the Japanese. Most were barefoot, and began following a trail that had been carved through the jungle by a group of natives. The weather was appalling, heavy rain turning large sections of the path into a muddy quagmire.

The nine separate groups made desperate efforts to reach Ranau, the men exhausted by starvation and disease. Groups 1–5 began the trek with 265 men between them, but seventy died on the journey. Group 3 took seventeen days to reach Ranau and of the original fifty men constituting this group thirty-seven made it. The rest were shot or bayoneted by their guards as they fell out of the column too exhausted or ill to continue. 'When we were about a week away from Ranau we crossed a large mountain,' recalled Australian Private Botterill, 'and while we were making the crossing two Australians, Private Humphries and a corporal whose name I cannot remember, fell out. They were suffering from beri-beri, malaria and dysentery and just could not continue any further. A Japanese private shot the corporal, and a Japanese sergeant shot Humphries. Altogether we lost five men on that hill.'[27] Botterill somehow found the energy to keep going, 'I just kept plodding along. It was dense jungle, I was heartbroken; but I thought there was safety in numbers. I just kept going.'[28]

Quite literally, the march was an exercise in natural selection, with only the fittest surviving. Japanese guards hovered constantly about the columns, waiting to kill on the slightest pretext. 'As we were going along men would fall out as they became too weak to carry on,' recalled Botterill. 'We would march on and then, shortly afterwards, hear shots ring out and the sound of men screaming.'[29] Groups 6–9 marched to Paginatan near Ranau, and only 138 reached their destination. Lance-Bombardier William Moxham, 2/15th Australian Field Regiment, was with Group 7: 'Men from my party could not go on. Boto was the first place where we actually had to leave anyone. They remained there, at this Jap dump. At the next place, at the bottom of a big hill, we left two more men. Later, we heard shots, and we thought the two men must have been shot ... Once you stopped – you stopped for good.'[30]

They were held at Paginatan for one month until ordered to resume the march to Ranau. 'One man was puffed up with beriberi in the legs and face,' recalled Moxham, 'and he was getting along all right on his own and could have made it; but the Japs would not let him alone, but tried to force him along, and eventually he collapsed.' The Japanese guards kicked the man on the ground. 'The

Jap turned and saw the man had gone down, and he struck him over the head with his rifle butt. The soldier was left there. The party marched on.'[31] Only sixty-eight were still alive at this stage, and by the time they struggled into Ranau this number had been reduced to forty-six. Following along behind Group 9 was Lieutenant Kazuo Abe and a group of guards with orders to dispose of any stragglers that they discovered beside the trail. The POWs were simply shot in the head and locals were ordered to bury the corpses beside the trail.

On arrival at Ranau there was little respite for the prisoners. They were herded into insanitary and crowded huts. There was dirt and flies everywhere, and soon a dysentery epidemic struck the already diseased and starved prisoners. 'You'd wake up of a morning and you'd look to your right to see if the chap next to you was still alive,' recalled Botterill. 'If he was dead you'd just roll him over a little bit and see if he had any belongings that would suit you; if not, you'd just leave him there. You'd turn on the other side and check your neighbour; see if he was dead or alive.'[32]

A smaller death march was enacted further to the west in North Borneo, and was unconnected with the Sandakan-Ranau marches, though the outcome was eerily similar. On 23 January Sergeant-Major Tsuruo Sugino of the Borneo Prisoner of War Internment Unit took charge of 157 European POWs on the island of Labuan, located five miles off the coast of Borneo close to Brunei. His orders were to take them to the capital of North Borneo, Kuching. The prisoners, who were British and Australian soldiers, were sick with malaria, dysentery and beriberi. On 7 March, when the prisoners were loaded aboard ships for the short journey to Brunei City, forty-five were missing, having already died from disease. Once at Brunei the POWs remained in the city until 2 or 3 May, and another thirty perished from disease. In a statement Sugino made on 11 October 1945 to war crimes investigators, he falsely claimed that 'I issued medicine for malaria and beri beri to the medical orderlies who in turn issued it to the sic [sic] PWs.'[33] In reality the Japanese guards actively encouraged tropical and deficiency diseases to whittle down the numbers of prisoners in their care as a cost-effective method for disposing of them without having to commit overt war crimes. But allowing prisoners to die from preventable disorders was none-theless a war crime. One POW tried to escape at this juncture, but he was recaptured and hauled away by the Kempeitai to what may be imagined was a cruel and unpleasant fate.

By April only 241 prisoners were still alive at Ranau out of the 455 who had originally left Sandakan. At the end of the month another eighty-nine were dead at the Ranau camp, and another twenty-one perished hauling rice to Paginatan for future evacuation parties leaving Sandakan. Incredibly, the 131 left at Ranau had been reduced to only six survivors by 26 June 1945.

In Brunei on 3 May, Sergeant-Major Sugino departed from the city with eighty-two Allied POWs. They arrived at the town of Kuala Belait in Brunei on the following day. He reported directly to Lieutenant Kamimura of the Kempeitai, who ordered the prisoners placed inside an old cinema that was surrounded by a barbed wire fence. The POWs were held inside this compound until 26 or 27 May, by which time another thirty-seven had perished of disease. They were reinforced by one Indian Army officer and six Indian other ranks, and on 27 May they left for Miri, a town in Sarawak, arriving the next day. This time Sugino reported to Lieutenant Nishimura in the town. The officer told Sugino to take the remaining prisoners to Cape Lobang, and on arrival they camped inside a wooden house surrounded once more by a barbed wire fence. Another four men succumbed to disease over the following weeks. Sugino had the audacity to state to his Australian interrogators that 'Those PWs who were not sick were fat and well,'[34] which, considering that the prisoners under his care had been dying like flies since he had left Labuan Island in January, was nonsense. Sugino's lies became even more far-fetched. On 8 June 1945 a British fleet was spotted by the Japanese approaching Borneo. 'I became anxious for the safety of the PWs,' said Sugino, 'and decided to move to a safer place.'[35] The sick and starving prisoners were herded over three miles inland over a hill to the Rian Road.

The next day fifteen 'fit' prisoners and five Formosan guards returned to Cape Lobang to collect stores. Another prisoner died at this time. Lieutenant Nishimura then ordered Sugino to take the remaining prisoners into the mountains. On 10 June they were all dead. Sugino initially claimed that it was the prisoners themselves who had started the events that led to their deaths. 'At 1900 hours 5 or 6 men lead [sic] by Sjt. ACKLAND jumped up from where they were sitting and started to run away,' recalled Sugino. 'I called the guard to open fire on the escapting [sic] PWs. In the confusion some of the bullets went in the house and caused the PWs to come out. As they came out of the house they were shot and bayonetted [sic] coming out of the house or outside the house.' Sugino said that 'I did not give any orders to cease fire in order to save the sick because I was so excited that I do not know what was happening. Those PWs who were not killed outright were put out of their agony by shooting or bayonetting.'[36] When the shooting stopped Sugino said that he counted thirty-two bodies and ordered some of the guards to hastily bury the corpses beside the road. 'I then heard a burst of firing coming from about 1,000 metres back along the RIAN Rd.,' recalled Sugino. 'I called about 6 guards and ran in the direction of the firing. When I arrived there I found that the PWs were then dead and were being carried to one place for burial by the guards. In addition to the guards I saw 8 men belonging to NISHIMURA TAI [a reference to Kempeitai soldiers under Lieutenant Nishimura's command]'.[37] Sugino asked one of his men, Private Hiroshi Nago', what had happened. '[He] told me that the PWs had been shot trying to escape and that 8 men of NISHIMURA TAI had helped to kill them. I did not ask any further questions because I understood that *the PWs had not been trying to escape when they were killed* [author's italics].'[38] This sentence alerted Australian investigators to dig deeper, and eventually Sugino broke under interrogation and offered up the truth of what really happened on the road.

The reason for the prisoners' deaths was brutally practical. 'I thought at the time that as food was getting short, some of the PW might try to escape and I decided that it would be better to kill them,'[39] Sugino bluntly stated. The Kempeitai soldiers acted on Sugino's direct orders. 'After the PW had been resting about ten minutes, one of the European PW tried to escape by running into the grass. I then gave the order to shoot the whole 15 PW,' stated Sugino. 'After the shooting, some of the PW were not dead, so I ordered that they be shot and bayonetted [sic] as they lay on the ground. The man who had previously run into the grass was also shot.'[40] The Australians charged Sugino with two counts of murder and he was later hanged.

Back at Sandakan Camp, starvation, disease and physical abuse had killed 885 British and Australian prisoners. In April 1945 the Japanese decided to move the remaining 'fit' POWs to Ranau, instituting a second death march. This march began in May when 800 POWs were evacuated from the three camps and the huts burned down. Five hundred and thirty of these POWs were sent on the march to Ranau while the rest languished in the remains of the camps with little to eat and no hope of relief. The second group of marchers was similarly sub-divided into several smaller parties. They were in an even worse state than the first party that had left months before, and the death rate was terrible. Group 2, consisting of fifty men, lost twelve on the very first day of the march.

A Chinese named Chen Kay living beside the trail witnessed some of the atrocities committed by the Japanese as they marched the prisoners past his house at Milepost 15. One morning in early June a large party of British and Australian prisoners stopped beside Chen's house at about 11am and had a meal. At 2pm four Allied aircraft suddenly appeared overhead, and the party was quickly dispersed by the Japanese guards into the nearby countryside amid much shouting and hitting. At 5pm the prisoners were ordered to fall in and the party moved off, leaving behind seven 'who were too ill to walk and had arrived hobbling on sticks.'[41] Two Japanese soldiers and a Malay soldier stayed behind, intending to urge these stragglers along. This they accomplished by 'kicking them and hitting them with their own sticks,' recalled Chen. 'Although they were very weak the Japanese guards succeeded in beating them along for about thirty yards.'[42] Nearby, asleep in a hut, was Kempeitai Sergeant Hositani, who was suffering from malaria. The impatient Japanese guards seized the rifle from the Malay soldier and began shooting the exhausted prisoners where they sat on the trail. Four were killed instantly, two lay on the ground groaning after having been wounded and one managed to summon up enough strength to hobble a few yards down the trail and hide. The guards paused only to order some Chinese men to dig a grave for the prisoners before they hurried on the catch up with the main party.

When Sergeant Hositani awoke he was visited by one of the guards from the party of prisoners that had recently passed by, Corporal Katayama. He asked Hositani to shoot any British or Australian prisoners that he discovered. Hositani quickly discovered two wounded prisoners and shot both of them through the head with a borrowed rifle. Next, he found the prisoner who had managed to hide from the initial massacre. The Chinese heard a single shot and later discovered that the prisoner had been shot in the stomach and died. 'I only shot the prisoners because Corporal Katayama told me to,' said Hositani in his defence. 'I was too sick to bury the bodies so I asked Chen Kay to do so.'[43] It is interesting in this case that a sergeant should obey the order of a corporal.

The adjutant at Sandakan Camp, Lieutenant Watanabe accompanied one of the marches, during which about ninety Allied prisoners were executed because they could not march. He later tried to justify the actions of his colleagues. He said that the prisoners 'were ill and were put out of their misery by being shot. They asked for death rather than be left behind.'[44] This was completely untrue, for we have seen how one man tried to escape from such a massacre. The several Allied prisoners who did manage to escape from the death march also confirm that Watanabe was lying to save his own neck.

It took the second group twenty-six days to reach Ranau. Of the original 530 who had begun the trek, only 183 made it alive (142 Australians and 41 British). The men who died faced their ends bravely, recalled Private Nelson Short of 2/18th Australian Battalion: 'And if blokes just couldn't go on, we shook hands with them, and said, you know, hope everything's all right. But they knew what was going to happen. There was nothing you could do. You just had to keep yourself going. More or less survival of the fittest.'[45]

The killing was not over yet, even as the conflict entered perhaps its darkest final hours – the last weeks of the war in the Pacific.

Notes

1. Lord Russell of Liverpool, *The Knights of Bushido: A Short History of Japanese War Crimes* (London, Greenhill Books, 2002), p. 158.
2. *Laden, Fevered, Starved – The POWs of Sandakan, North Borneo, 1945*, Commonwealth Department of Veterans' Affairs, http://www.dva.gov.au, accessed 6 August 2008.
3. Ibid.
4. Ibid.
5. International Military Tribunal for the Far East, Box 256, Exhibit 1654, Prosecution Document No. 5179: *Affidavit of Lieutenant Stephen Victor Burt Day of the British Army*, MacMillan Brown Library, University of Canterbury, Christchurch, New Zealand.

6. International Military Tribunal for the Far East, Box 256, Exhibit 1654, Prosecution Document No. 5177: *Affidavit of Lt.-Col. Edmund Macarthur Sheppard of 2/10 Field Ambulance*, MacMillan Brown Library, University of Canterbury, Christchurch, New Zealand.

7. *Laden, Fevered, Starved – The POWs of Sandakan, North Borneo, 1945*, Commonwealth Department of Veterans' Affairs, http://www.dva.gov.au, accessed 6 August 2008.

8. Lord Russell of Liverpool, *The Knights of Bushido: A Short History of Japanese War Crimes* (London, Greenhill Books, 2002), p. 184.

9. International Military Tribunal for the Far East, Box 256, Exhibit 1654, Prosecution Document No. 5004: *Affidavit of Naik Chandgi Ram, 2/15 Punjab Regiment*, MacMillan Brown Library, University of Canterbury, Christchurch, New Zealand.

10. International Military Tribunal for the Far East, Box 256, Exhibit 1655, Evidentiary Document No. 5004: *Evidence of Chandgi Ram, taken on 28 September, 1945, at the Prisoner-of-War and Internee Camp, Morotai, before Mr. Justice Mansfield*, 28 September 1945, MacMillan Brown Library, University of Canterbury, Christchurch, New Zealand.

11. Ibid.

12. International Military Tribunal for the Far East, Box 256, Exhibit 1654, Prosecution Document No. 5004: *Affidavit of Naik Chandgi Ram, 2/15 Punjab Regiment*, MacMillan Brown Library, University of Canterbury, Christchurch, New Zealand.

13. International Military Tribunal for the Far East, Box 256, Exhibit 1655, Evidentiary Document No. 5004: *Evidence of Chandgi Ram, taken on 28 September, 1945, at the Prisoner-of-War and Internee Camp, Morotai, before Mr. Justice Mansfield*, 28 September 1945, MacMillan Brown Library, University of Canterbury, Christchurch, New Zealand.

14. International Military Tribunal for the Far East, Box 256, Exhibit 1654, Evidentiary Document No. 5449, *Affidavit of Naik Partap Singh, 17 Field Company*, MacMillan Brown Library, University of Canterbury, Christchurch, New Zealand.

15. Ibid.

16. International Military Tribunal for the Far East, Box 256, Exhibit 1655, Evidentiary Document No. 5004: *Evidence of*

Chandgi Ram, taken on 28 September, 1945, at the Prisoner-of-War and Internee Camp, Morotai, before Mr. Justice Mansfield, 28 September 1945, MacMillan Brown Library, University of Canterbury, Christchurch, New Zealand.

17. International Military Tribunal for the Far East, Box 256, Exhibit 1657, Evidentiary Document 5003: *Evidence of Naik Partap Singh, taken on 27th September, 1945, at the Prisoner-of-War and Internee Reception Depot, Morotai, in the presence of Mr. Justice Mansfield*, 27 September 1945, MacMillan Brown Library, University of Canterbury, Christchurch, New Zealand.

18. International Military Tribunal for the Far East, Box 256, Exhibit 1655, Evidentiary Document No. 5004: *Evidence of Chandgi Ram, taken on 28 September, 1945, at the Prisoner-of-War and Internee Camp, Morotai, before Mr. Justice Mansfield*, 28 September 1945, MacMillan Brown Library, University of Canterbury, Christchurch, New Zealand.

19. International Military Tribunal for the Far East, Box 256, Exhibit 1654, Prosecution Document No. 5004: *Affidavit of Naik Chandgi Ram, 2/15 Punjab Regiment*, MacMillan Brown Library, University of Canterbury, Christchurch, New Zealand.

20. International Military Tribunal for the Far East, Box 256, Exhibit 1655, Evidentiary Document No. 5004: *Evidence of Chandgi Ram, taken on 28 September, 1945, at the Prisoner-of-War and Internee Camp, Morotai, before Mr. Justice Mansfield*, 28 September 1945, MacMillan Brown Library, University of Canterbury, Christchurch, New Zealand.

21. Ibid.

22. Ibid.

23. Lord Russell of Liverpool, *The Knights of Bushido: A Short History of Japanese War Crimes* (London, Greenhill Books, 2002), p. 116.

24. Imperial Japanese Army, Box 263, Exhibit 1978, Document No. 1114-B: *Regarding the outline for the disposal of Prisoners of War according to the change of situation, a notification, Army-Asia-Secret No. 2257, by the Vice War Minister*, 11 March 1945, MacMillan Brown Library, University of Canterbury, Christchurch, New Zealand.

25. Ibid.

26. Ibid.

27. Lord Russell of Liverpool, *The Knights of Bushido: A Short History of Japanese War Crimes* (London, Greenhill Books, 2002), p. 143.
28. *Laden, Fevered, Starved – The POWs of Sandakan, North Borneo, 1945*, Commonwealth Department of Veterans' Affairs, http://www.dva.gov.au, accessed 6 August 2008.
29. Lord Russell of Liverpool, *The Knights of Bushido: A Short History of Japanese War Crimes* (London, Greenhill Books, 2002), p. 143.
30. *Laden, Fevered, Starved – The POWs of Sandakan, North Borneo, 1945*, Commonwealth Department of Veterans' Affairs, http://www.dva.gov.au, accessed 6 August 2008.
31. Ibid.
32. Ibid.
33. International Military Tribunal for the Far East, Box 256, Exhibit 1658, Evidentiary Document No. 5218A: *Evidence of Sgt. Maj. Tsuruo SUGINO of Borneo PW Internment Unit*, 11 October 1945, MacMillan Brown Library, University of Canterbury, Christchurch, New Zealand.
34. Ibid.
35. Ibid.
36. Ibid.
37. Ibid.
38. Ibid.
39. International Military Tribunal for the Far East, Box 256, Exhibit 1658, Evidentiary Document No. 5218A, 25 October 1945, MacMillan Brown Library, University of Canterbury, Christchurch, New Zealand.
40. Ibid.
41. Lord Russell of Liverpool, *The Knights of Bushido: A Short History of Japanese War Crimes* (London, Greenhill Books, 2002), p. 145.
42. Ibid: p. 145.
43. Ibid: p. 146.
44. Ibid: p. 147.
45. *Laden, Fevered, Starved – The POWs of Sandakan, North Borneo, 1945*, Commonwealth Department of Veterans' Affairs, http://www.dva.gov.au, accessed 6 August 2008.

Chapter Thirteen

End Game

One thing we sure are not *fighting for is to hold the British Empire together.*

Life magazine, 1945

The increased ferocity of the Japanese towards their prisoners was a reflection of their shame and humiliation at losing the war, and a desire to make white men pay for this loss of face. The brutality of Sandakan was being played out across the entire Japanese Empire, including in the Home Islands. As the Japanese defensive perimeter began to implode and as Allied victories followed one upon the other, the situation on the Japanese home front deteriorated dramatically as well. Japan had always been almost entirely dependent upon importing raw materials and food, and the American blockade of the Home Islands caused widespread starvation.

Hundreds of Japanese merchant ships were torpedoed and sunk by Allied submarines and aircraft, and Japan soon lost its ability to supply the many hundreds of units defending outlying sections of the Empire's defensive perimeter. At home rice became increasingly scarce, and by late 1944 the daily rice ration for a Japanese soldier was only 400 grams. In 1942 his ration had been 850 grams. The situation was naturally much worse for civilians. There was virtually no petrol left for civilian use, and tobacco became rare, fuelling a massive black market economy. The daily calorific intake for civilians dropped to 2,000. Children as young as ten were drafted as industrial workers, and nearly all university students were called up.

If the situation was bad for Japanese soldiers and civilians, the situation for Allied prisoners held in Japan was truly dire. They existed at the very bottom of the food chain, and although they had never been adequately fed since their capture, by the last year of the war many prisoners were reduced to scavenging for food, often eating meat or fish that had previously been rejected as unfit for human consumption. About the only thing they refused to eat was each other. The Japanese, however, continued to exploit them.

No matter how diseased, emaciated and starving the prisoners were, if they could manage to struggle to their feet the Japanese deemed them fit for work. As the Japanese empire collapsed prisoners were put to work in increasingly demanding physical jobs. They were sent down coal mines in Japan, Manchuria and Korea, or mined metals like lead, copper and zinc. The big Japanese companies, today famous for making cars and televisions, hungrily absorbed white slave labour in their steel mills and factories. Mitsubishi was one of the biggest employers of slave labour, yet this fact is almost unknown today as the company's slick public relations department has air-brushed out the war year's from Mitsubishi's history.

In Japan's ports prisoners of war worked as stevedores, unloading ships and loading boxcars in attached railway yards. All this time the prisoners were subject to beatings and murder at the hands of their Japanese guards, abuse from local citizens, and bombing raids by their own side. The work was unremitting and dangerous, particularly in the mines. 'I was given a lamp and went down the pit and dug coal for a 12–13 hour shift, but if the conveyor belt broke you could be longer,' recalled Gunner Neil Reid of the Royal Artillery imprisoned at Fukuoka mining camp near Nagasaki. 'I sometimes did dynamite, that was hard work, but shorter hours. Other times I shovelled coal onto the conveyor belt, other times timbering (putting props up and then one across the top).'[1] It was intensely gruelling work for half-starved men. 'I worked 7 days a week and had 1 day off a month when the Jap guards took us for a walk,' recalled Reid. 'While we were on the walk the Jap guards went through all our possessions to see if they could find anything.'[2]

The threat of being killed by one's own side was particularly acute for British POWs slaving in the Japanese Home Islands. 'At this time the air raids were becoming more severe, particular damage was caused by fire bombs (napalm),' recalled former prisoner William Mayers. 'Wherever you looked Kobe was ablaze, we began to wonder if we would survive because Kobe was being bombed day and night. We were weaker than ever, our legs like rubber but finally our turn did come ... It's a terrible thing to think that you've gone through years as a POW, starved, beaten, illnesses, used cruelly as slave labour, only to be bombed by your own people and sometimes killed even though they were unaware of it because none of these places were marked by the Japanese.'[3]

The prisoners knew that the war must be going badly for the Japanese, for the character of their guards had changed dramatically over the years. The young men were all gone, sent to die for the Emperor at the front, while older men and soldiers who had been maimed in combat took their places. Guards missing arms, eyes or sporting terrible scars or burns became common. Still their ferocity and sadism remained undiminished.

In the smouldering ruins of the Sandakan camps on the island of Borneo the Japanese still held 288 Australian and British prisoners of war in July 1945. They were left out in the open. Mid-month, the Japanese officer commanding the camp received orders to move the remaining prisoners to Ranau. Most were so ill and emaciated by this stage that they would have to be left behind. The fittest seventy-five were organized into a third group and forced out on to the trail to Ranau. None of them got further than 60km before collapsing. On 13 July the Japanese rounded up twenty-three who had remained behind at Sandakan and took them to the nearby airfield. Captain Takuo Takakuwa had ordered Sergeant-Major Hisao Murozumi to 'dispose' of them, and Murozumi and his men executed them all by firing squad. Private Yashitoro Goto recalled:

> It was Takakua's [Captain Takakuwa] order so we could not disobey. It would be a disgrace to my parents so we carried out the orders. Taking the PWs to the airport near the old house on the drome, all those who could walk ... under Morojumi's [Murozumi] order we lined them up and shot them. The firing party kept firing till there were no more signs of life. Then we dragged the bodies into a near-by air-raid shelter and filled it in.[4]

192

Twenty-nine prisoners were left to starve to death among the ruins of the camp, and by the time Japan surrendered on 15 August 1945 only one Australian prisoner was still alive. On the very day that the war ended Sergeant-Major Hisao had this final prisoner murdered. Wong Hiong, a Chinese worker at the camp, witnessed the grisly scene. According to Wong the Australian soldier's 'legs were covered with ulcers. He was a tall, thin, dark man with a long face and was naked apart from a loin cloth.' The prisoner was taken to a drain. Murozumi 'made the man kneel down and tied a black cloth over his eyes,' recalled Wong. 'He did not say anything or make any protest. He was so weak that his hands were not tied. Morojumi [Murozumi] cut his head off with one sword stroke.' The Japanese then pushed the decapitated corpse into the drain where the soldier's head already lay. 'The other Japs threw in some dirt, covered the remains and returned to the camp,'[5] said Wong.

At Ranau, the death rate among the remaining prisoners had reached seven per day by July 1945. They were subjected to further appalling treatment, including forced labour. They cut bamboo, collected wood and atap for the huts, and carried 20kg bags of food to Ranau from the Japanese supply dump three kilometres away. Some were forced to haul an average of 130 buckets of water up a steep hill each day to supply the Japanese officers' quarters. Rations for the prisoners were deliberately designed to kill them. 'They were given a small cup of rice water a day with about an inch of rice in the bottom,' recalled Private Botterill. 'Plenty of rice was available and the Japanese used to get 800 grams a day themselves, they also used to get tapioca, meat, eggs and sweet potatoes and showed no signs of malnutrition.'[6] Men still died. Sapper Arthur Bird of the Australian Engineers had survived the first forced march to Ranau. On 7 July, he was dragged out of a hut to work by a Japanese guard. Bird tried to explain that he was unfit for labour as he was suffering with beriberi, malaria and tropical leg ulcers. The Japanese responded by kicking Bird on the ground for ten minutes which put him into a coma. Two days later he was dead.

On 27 August 1945, twelve days *after* the Japanese surrender, the last forty survivors at Ranau were each shot in the back of the head. Australian liberation forces were close by the camp when the Japanese committed this final outrage. According to records, 2,776 Australian and British prisoners had been brought to Sandakan in three large shipments as slave labourers. Only *six* survived, all Australians, because they had managed to escape and were sheltered and protected by local people and eventually handed over to the advancing Australian forces. Apart from Warrant Officer William Sticpewich, Lance-Bombardier William Moxham, Private Keith Botterrill and Private Nathan Short the other survivors were Bombardier Richard Braithwaite, 2/15th Australian Field Regiment, and Gunner Owen Campbell, 2/10th Australian Field Regiment. The testimony these six men provided to Australian war crimes investigators ensured that some degree of retribution was taken against the perpetrators of one of the worst cases of mass murder yet committed. Eight Japanese, including Captain Susumi Hoshijima, were found guilty of war crimes at the post-war trial and executed by hanging. A further fifty-five Japanese soldiers were found guilty of lesser counts of brutality and received terms in prison. Lieutenant-Colonel Tatsuji Suga, overall commander of the prison camp system on Borneo, escaped justice by committing suicide in Australian captivity. He stabbed himself in the throat, and then his batman beat him to death with a water canteen half filled with sand.

The bitterest of ironies was discovered by the meagre handful of survivors just after the war. Whilst the death marches were actually underway, the Australian military had planned a rescue operation in March 1945 to liberate the Sandakan camps and the remaining prisoners. Codenamed Operation Kingfisher, it was the brainchild of the Australian version of SOE, Special Operations Australia (SOA), which was confusingly referred to during the war as the Special Research Department (SRD). The operation was hampered by incompetence at the highest levels and a remarkable degree of blundering and indecision. General Douglas MacArthur has footed much of the blame for Kingfisher not being enacted, but this is largely incorrect.

An advance party of Australian commandos was actually landed only thirty miles from the camps in early 1945. 'A month before, MacArthur had given the highest priority to finding and freeing POWs and civilian internees,' writes Gavan Daws in *Prisoners of the Japanese*, 'in the middle of large-scale fighting, and with no expense spared. But that had been in the Philippines; it was part of the grand gesture of MacArthur returning, and the prisoners to be rescued were Americans. The POWs at Sandakan were many times the number at Cabanatuan and Bilibid [the main prison camps in the Philippines], but they were not Americans.'[7]

Daws, and several other historians, have maintained that Kingfisher was scrapped because of MacArthur's huge ego and obvious preference for American forces, and therefore thousands of Australian and British servicemen were abandoned to their deaths. In fact, research by other historians, notably Australian Lynette Ramsay Silver, author of the brilliant *Sandakan – Conspiracy of Silence*, actually places the blame on to the Australians.[8] The Australian chief of staff, General Sir Thomas Blamey, has been revealed as the root cause of the operation's failure as he dithered and prevaricated and made excuses for not involving Australian personnel. Blamey stated that insufficient aircraft and ships were available to support Kingfisher and that all Australian resources were dedicated to supporting MacArthur's final push on Japan.

In the 1970s the declassification of the Kingfisher files revealed that the Royal Australian Air Force had around forty Douglas DC-3 Dakotas and B-24 Liberators in hand and based within easy range of Sandakan. Only some thirty of these aircraft were required to transport an assaulting parachute battalion of 800 men, which had been training extensively in Australia, into Sandakan.

An advance party of SRD commandos was actually put ashore only thirty miles from Sandakan, but then withdrawn when Blamey cancelled the operation. It was not one of the finest hours of the war, not by a long chalk. 'If the March rescue operation had gone ahead, well over a thousand prisoners would still have been alive to be lifted out of Sandakan, with no serious Japanese opposition to be concerned about – on the northeast coast ... there were only about fifteen hundred troops, at the camp itself only a handful of guards.'[9] The paratroopers would have made short work of the small Japanese forces remaining and would have rescued hundreds of men. One might argue that it was almost a war crime not to have launched Kingfisher when the opportunity was there, especially as those in the higher reaches of the Allied command were fully aware of what the Japanese were doing to British and Australian prisoners. Certainly, an element of military incompetence and fears about offending MacArthur and the Americans meant the whole operation was unjustifiably scrubbed. With the cancellation of Kingfisher, the last chance of saving those wretched Allied prisoners was squandered forever.

Both the Supreme Allied Commander, General MacArthur, and his British counterpart Vice-Admiral Lord Louis Mountbatten, Supreme Commander of South East Asia Command (SEAC) were fully aware, because of Allied decryption of Japanese military messages, that the Japanese had issued orders to troops guarding prisoners of war to massacre them if it appeared that the POWs were about to be liberated. Their respective intelligence chiefs had a pretty good idea of the conditions Allied prisoners were enduring across the occupied territories from recent escapees, who were often survivors from the sinking of 'Hell Ship' transports picked up by American submarines, and from local indigenous resistance groups. Both MacArthur and Mountbatten were also aware that the Japanese had killed their prisoners *en masse* before, especially when threatened with imminent invasion and liberation. The name 'Palawan' was well-known among army intelligence types.

General MacArthur's G-2 military intelligence found out about Palawan shortly after the Japanese had completed a terrible crime there. G-2 knew all about the capabilities of the Kempeitai and the Japanese determination to carry out orders that instructed them to kill all prisoners in their charge long before the horrors of Sandakan. Described at the Tokyo Trials as a 'particularly cruel and pre-meditated massacre of American prisoners', 140 were burned alive by the Kempeitai at Puerto Princesa Camp on the Philippine island of Palawan on 14 December 1944. American air raids had begun on Palawan in October 1944 as part of the softening up of the Philippines prior to an amphibious assault, and the Japanese decided to murder the American servicemen at Puerto Princesa as they wrongly believed the invasion was actually imminent. The prisoners, many of whom were survivors of the notorious Bataan Death March in 1942, were herded into air-raid shelters and then the Japanese hurled buckets of petrol over them. Petrol drums were pushed against the entrances and ignited. Any Americans who managed to climb out of the shelters were quickly shot down by Kempeitai soldiers who had surrounded the site with light machine guns.[10]

Another grisly example was the fate of a group of British and American prisoners in Japan who it appears were killed prematurely by the Kempeitai. Five hundred POWs had been shipped over to

Sado Island, lying off the west coast of Honshu in the Sea of Japan, to work a gold mine owned by the industrial giant Mitsubishi. The company owned and operated several mines on the island, all employing slave labourers under the jurisdiction of the Imperial Army and Kempeitai.

A camp for the British and American POWs had been set up in the small town of Aikawa, and this existed outside of the mainstream Japanese slave labour network as the Kempeitai had never considered registering its existence with the International Red Cross in Switzerland (a legal requirement). It was probably this fact that encouraged them to quietly 'dispose' of the mine labourers towards the end of the war.

By August 1945 387 prisoners remained alive on Sado Island under the command of Major Masami Sadakichi. Post-war investigations turned up Sadakichi's second-in-command at Aikawa, Lieutenant Yoshiro Tsuda, who cooperated fully in telling the story of the disappearance of the POWs in his charge. On 2 August Sadakichi ordered Tsuda to kill all of the remaining prisoners. The night before a Japanese detail had entered the mine and placed demolition charges at depths of 100, 200 and 300 feet. The next morning Tsuda was ordered to detail the usual working parties at the nearby mine 'but with special instructions to ensure that every prisoner entered the mine. Usually fifty prisoners remained on top of the mine to empty with rakes the laden steel bins into nearby hoppers.' When Tsuda pointed this out to Major Sadakichi, his remarks were dismissed, the CO stating that the mine was no longer viable and it would be abandoned that day. 'Superior orders decreed that all prisoners of war were to be ordered to the deepest part of the mine, some 400 feet,' recalled Tsuda. 'Major Sadakichi further impressed on me that the guard detail were to carry out their duties in the normal manner, and not to alarm the prisoners.'

The end for the prisoners came swiftly that morning. 'After the prisoners had been set hewing the ore from the marked areas, I was ordered to instruct Sgt. Major Mitsonobu Sakamoto, the NCO in charge of the guards, to ensure their discreet [exit] out of the mine,' said Tsuda. 'The toiling prisoners were to be left to their obvious fate.' All of the guards had emerged from the mine by 9am. They proceeded to push empty steel ore bins down the narrow gauge railway track into the mine, allowing them to gather speed and plunge into the depths on top of the terrified and confused prisoners below. At 9.10 the order was given to detonate the demolition charges. The smoke and dust billowing from the mine entrance had barely settled before the guards set to work dismantling the railway track and dumping the steel rails inside the entrance. Everyone ran for cover as with a loud bang the last charge was ignited. Tsuda recalled 'an avalanche of rock and earth ... completely covering where the mine's entrance had been.' All 387 POWs were entombed in its depths, where their bodies still lie today.

The evident willingness of some Japanese commanders to commit wholesale murder so close to the end of the war was deeply disturbing to Allied military intelligence. Although Operation Kingfisher was shelved for various reasons, other plans were nonetheless sketched out and steps were taken to put them into effect. It was not just the Japanese who were to behave with great brutality in the last weeks of the war. In Poland and Germany in 1945, SS troops forced the inmates of concentration camps into death marches ahead of the rapidly advancing Red Army, and those who were too sick to move were shot, as were those who fell out of the march.

One reason why none of the rescue operations except those in the Philippines ever got off the ground was due to the competitive nature of the Allied intelligence organizations operating in the Far East. MacArthur relied on intelligence from G-2, headed by Brigadier General Charles Willoughby. Willoughby was widely disliked and distrusted by the British and many Americans, and he also controlled the Allied Intelligence Bureau (AIB), an umbrella organization in charge of American, British, Australian and Dutch special operations. Willoughby 'might have enjoyed MacArthur's confidence but to those who knew him best he was a schemer, a bully, a liar, a toady, and a shameless cheat.'[11] Willoughby also controlled the dissemination of vital 'Ultra' intelligence decrypts of Japanese signals traffic through Brigadier General Spencer B. Akin's Central Bureau (CB). CB was a new joint American-Australian signals intelligence unit. The Australians maintained their own intelligence outfit tasked in part with mounting commando raids behind enemy lines called Special Operations Australia (SOA), mentioned earlier. Into this confusion of intelligence units were added the British forces. Mountbatten controlled Force 136, the Far Eastern section of Special Operations Executive (SOE), based in India and headed by 47-year-old Colin

Hercules Mackenzie. Mackenzie had lost a leg serving in the Scots Guards during the First World War and came to military intelligence via business – he was a director of J&B Coats. Mackenzie controlled around 30,000 agents across Asia, and Force 136 had managed to locate around 200 Japanese prison camps within Mountbatten's sphere of influence, but they were located deep behind enemy lines and militarily impossible to get at. The only solution would be the liberation of camps located close to the front line, and for all intents and purposes that meant the *American* front line in the Philippines.

The British had tried to move their own front lines closer to Singapore, with the aim of eventually launching an amphibious assault on the city the Japanese had renamed *Shonan* (Southern Star), when Mountbatten and his staff dreamt up Operation Culverin. If successful, the plan would have led to many hundreds of British POWs being liberated and saved from almost certain death. Culverin involved an amphibious assault by British forces onto the northern tip of Sumatra, west of Java, thereby placing the British in a position to begin advancing north towards Singapore and beyond.[12] It was the kind of dashing amphibious thrust that Mountbatten was famous for, but although Churchill was in support, Culverin never got beyond the planning stage. The British chiefs of staff in London, led by Field Marshal Sir Alan Brooke, rejected the plan because it would have depleted the Allies' supply of landing craft needed for the Second Front in France. Leave amphibious operations to the Americans and concentrate on winning the war in Burma, was the terse message from Whitehall.

The US High Command in Washington had also vetoed Culverin after Mountbatten's American deputy, General Joseph 'Vinegar Joe' Stilwell, had sent a team of staff officers to the American capital to badmouth the whole operation. He detested the British and 'regarded them as effete, defensive and disorganized.'[13] Stilwell did not mince his words: The British were, as he charmingly put it, ' "mother fuckers" who "always try to cut our throats." '[14] Stilwell mounted a successful spoiling operation designed to keep the British as far out of the war in the Far East as possible, and American pressure meant that Culverin was shelved permanently.

The Americans viewed Britain's previous military failures at Hong Kong, Malaya, Singapore and Burma very badly, and the collapse of

British military resistance in 1941/2 had severely damaged the reputation of Britain in Washington. MacArthur and his cronies, known as the 'Bataan Gang' after having escaped with their commander in PT boats before the Japanese captured the Philippines in March 1942, had nicknamed Mountbatten's SEAC 'Save England's Asiatic Colonies'. MacArthur was not the only senior American commander distrustful or hostile towards the British. Admiral Ernest J. King, Chief of US Naval Operations and a member of the US Joint Chiefs of Staff, was a strong opponent of British influence in Southeast Asia, and particularly opposed to any re-assertion of British power. King determined to keep the Royal Navy out of the Pacific War entirely, and almost succeeded. Trashing Operation Culverin was an early victory for American post-war interests. Admiral Halsey was in agreement with King, and privately stated that the Americans 'did not want Britain claiming "she had delivered even a part of the final blow that demolished the Japanese fleet."' Even *Life* magazine was unequivocal regarding British involvement in the Far East. 'One thing we sure are *not* fighting for is to hold the British Empire together.'[15]

The failure of Operations Culverin and Kingfisher undoubtedly cost the lives of thousands of British and Commonwealth POWs who were marginalized in the great American effort to assert its dominance over Asia and secure its position as the major post-war player in the region. Each nation pursued its own agenda, and POWs were often reduced to pawns in the much larger geopolitical game being played out by the Great Powers as each manoeuvred for advantage and hegemony.

As for the Japanese, vengeance against prisoners in their hands was a reflection of their unwillingness to end the war when ordered to do so on 15 August 1945. 'Japanese field commanders, far from the reality of the American pounding of the Japanese mainland, were by turn confused, devastated and recalcitrant at the news of the emperor's surrender. Some wanted to fight on.'[16] The Japanese still had one million men under arms in Southeast Asia when their nation capitulated and they possessed vast resources in the occupied territories that could have sustained a fight for several more months, even years.

Another reason that led to the Japanese killing off remaining Allied prisoners in some areas, the best example being at Sandakan, was a fear that any survivors would inform Allied investigators about the war crimes Japanese commanders and their subordinates had committed. Allied propaganda had made it clear that Japanese war criminals would be punished. Some did fight on. General Seishiro Itagaki, Japanese commander in Malaya and Singapore, 'refused to submit. It was only the arrival of a prince of the Imperial house, with a personal order from Hirohito himself, that persuaded him to summon his officers to his headquarters at Raffles College and order them to surrender.'[17] In the Philippines, Lieutenant General Tomoyuki Yamashita, the man who had defeated the British at Singapore in 1942, fought on until 2 September 1945. Even when General Itagaki surrendered in Singapore he suppressed this important news from most of the troops under his command and the civilian population for a further four days, thus giving his Kempeitai henchmen time to cover up their atrocities while enjoying the powers of an occupying army with the local population. Many more Allied prisoners were 'disposed of' by the Kempeitai *after* the official Japanese surrender, and tens of thousands of incriminating documents that detailed the crimes that they had committed were hauled out of their various headquarters and burned on huge bonfires, crippling the ability of post-war investigators to bring many Kempeitai to justice.

Much of the blame for the Allied failure to save desperate prisoners of war can be laid at General MacArthur's door. He ordered that no Allied troops were to enter Japanese-controlled territories before he had taken the formal enemy surrender in Tokyo Bay. For the British and Mountbatten, this order, born of MacArthur's egotistical desire to be seen as the real liberator of Asia and conqueror of the Japanese, was hard to bear. Mountbatten already had an operation underway to liberate Singapore from Itagaki's surrendered Japanese and take over the prisoner of war camps quickly to prevent further unnecessary deaths. The new operation had superseded Culverin and was codenamed 'Zipper', MacArthur ordered the British fleet to hold its position in the Straits of Malacca on 19 August and not to enter Singapore until he had taken the formal surrender. Mountbatten protested, but MacArthur was not to be moved, replying, 'Keep your pants on.' Mountbatten caustically retorted, 'Will keep mine on if you take Hirohito's off!'[18]

The British were forced to sit idly by while the Kempeitai set its house in order, and while hundreds more British and Commonwealth POWs perished from disease and starvation, not least the poor souls at Sandakan and Ranau. Mountbatten eventually was permitted to take Itagaki's surrender on 12 September 1945. MacArthur's attitude can only be described as disgraceful and callous, but it had been a long war and people had grown hardhearted as the body count had increased daily on the road to ultimate victory over the Japanese. The big players, and MacArthur was about the biggest in the Pacific, were already looking to their post-war roles and gathering as many laurels as possible before the shooting stopped. MacArthur had, after all, the complete backing of the American government that had already made clear that once peace descended it was going to be America, not Britain, that assumed the mantle of regional power broker.

Notes

1. *POW in Nagasaki*, A2715473, BBC People's War, http://www.bbc.co.uk/history, accessed 10 May 2008.
2. Ibid.
3. *A Soldiers Story Taken from his Taped Record: A POW in China and Japan*, A2756360, BBC Peoples War, http://www.bbc.co.uk/history, accessed 10 May 2008.
4. Ibid.
5. Ibid.
6. Ibid.
7. Gavan Daws, *Prisoners of the Japanese: POWs of the Second World War in the Pacific*, (London, Pocket Books, 2007), p. 327.
8. Lynette Ramsay Silver, *Sandakan – A Conspiracy of Silence* (Revised edition: Sally Milner Publishing Pty Ltd, 2000).
9. Gavan Daws, *Prisoners of the Japanese: POWs of the Second World War in the Pacific*, (London, Pocket Books, 2007), p. 327.
10. This massacre is graphically portrayed at the beginning of the film *The Greatest Raid* concerning the US Rangers assault on Cabanatuan POW Camp in the Philippines, 1945.

11. Peter Thompson & Robert Macklin, *Kill the Tiger: Operation Rimau and the Battle for Southeast Asia* (Dunshaughlin, Maverick House, 2002), p. 69.

12. *War Office: South East Asia Command: Military Headquarters Papers, Second World War*, WO 203/4317, National Archives (Public Record Office).

13. Christopher Bayley & Tim Harper, *Forgotten Armies: Britain's Asian Empire & The War With Japan* (London, Penguin, 2005), p. 271.

14. Ibid: p. 271.

15. Arthur Herman, *To Rule the Waves: How the British Navy Shaped the Modern World* (London, Hodder and Stoughton Ltd, 2005), p. 548.

16. Christopher Bayley & Tim Harper, *Forgotten Armies: Britain's Asian Empire & The War With Japan* (London, Penguin, 2005), p. 457.

17. Ibid: p. 457.

18. Peter Thompson & Robert Macklin, *Kill the Tiger: Operation Rimau and the Battle for Southeast Asia* (Dunshaughlin, Maverick House, 2002), p. 249.

Chapter Fourteen

Bearing the Unbearable

It would not be overstating the obvious to suggest that the Kempeitai was a thoroughly rotten and disreputable organization that inflicted tremendous suffering on Allied prisoners of war and internees and on the terrified populations of the territories Japan invaded. Its staff, in the main, consisted of hateful and sadistic men who enjoyed their work immensely, particularly the infliction of pain upon the helpless. Kempeitai operatives literally had blood-soaked hands and the stench of guilt about them, so it was to be expected that these men would be dealt with harshly by the Allies when the war was over. Largely, this was not to be. Most Kempeitai operatives escaped justice – they simply vanished into the millions of demobilized Japanese soldiers making their way back to the Home Islands. Likewise, the victims of Kempeitai activities left the camps and were shipped back to Europe and America, most never returning to the Far East again. The opportunity existed at the close of the war to seize many Kempeitai troops, but the opportunity was largely missed or ignored as the Allies slowly restored their authority over Asia.

At midday on 15 August 1945 Emperor Hirohito's surrender order was played on radios across a stunned Japan. Earlier, General Sanji Okido, the head of the Kempeitai, had gathered together his headquarters staff in Tokyo and told them that Japan was shortly to surrender and that the Emperor himself would make the announcement. Okido had one last task to perform – to prevent a group of army officers led by General Masahiko Takeshita and War Minister Koreichi Anami from trying to assassinate officers advising the Emperor to surrender. In the event, the coup was unsuccessful, and Hirohito's radio broadcast was made, ending the war.

Soon after the surrender broadcast Imperial General Headquarters in Tokyo beamed out coded orders to all Kempeitai commanders in the field to disperse their troops and vanish. Vanish many did, but not immediately. Although Admiral Mountbatten wanted to send in liberating Allied troops to the occupied territories and save thousands of POWs dying of starvation and disease, General MacArthur forbade any such move until he, and he alone, had formally taken the Japanese surrender in Japan itself. This ceremony occurred on 2 September aboard the battleship USS *Missouri* in Tokyo Bay. That gave the Kempeitai in the field roughly two weeks to cover their tracks by destroying records of their activities and eliminating witnesses to their crimes. For two weeks *after* the Japanese capitulation on 15 August, the Kempeitai and camp commandants conspired to keep murdering Allied POWs, and the British and Americans did nothing to prevent them.

In Shanghai, the local Kempeitai troops at Bridge House followed the Imperial General HQ instructions to the letter. Beyond the high wall surrounding the Kempeitai torture centre the city was in an uproar. News of an imminent Japanese surrender had first spread through the city as rumours on 11 August, but the following day's newspapers had carried a proclamation from War Minister Anami that stated that the Japanese would fight on until the bitter end, even if that meant 'chewing grass, eating dirt and sleeping in the fields.'[1] Actual news confirming the Japanese surrender reached Shanghai on 16 August, setting off spontaneous jubilation among locals and a panic among the occupiers.

Thousands of Chinese civilians were loudly celebrating the end of the war with fire crackers and parties, while 15,000 Japanese troops still remained under arms in the city. The Japanese soldiers continued to mount foot patrols, providing the only real order left in the city as corrupt officials associated with the puppet regime of Wang Ching-wei fled from their offices and went into hiding or left the city. Kiangwan Airfield was the scene of frenzied activity as trucks roared up to the dispersal points to off-load wooden crates loaded with looted booty and cash. Japanese aircraft were loaded with stolen property, escaping officials and even the local Japanese military commanders who simply abandoned their units and fled back to Japan ahead of the Allies.

At Bridge House bonfires burned day and night for several days after word had been received that the war was over. Kempeitai soldiers emptied the contents of filing cabinets onto the pyres, carefully combing through tens of thousands of incriminating records from years of investigations, interrogations and executions. Nothing would be left for the Allied war crimes units to use in court. Once the officers were satisfied that the files had all been destroyed, they ordered their men to remove all Kempeitai insignia from their uniforms, and gathering all weapons inside the building, the heavily armed Kempeitai boarded a fleet of trucks and drove quickly away into history.

By the time the Allies occupied Japan and the territories abroad that still contained three million Japanese troops, it was too late to track down many Kempeitai troops. As in Shanghai, elsewhere they had melted away never to be seen again. Allied investigators were soon inundated by stories, statements and affidavits cataloguing horrific tales of torture and murder committed by the Kempeitai across Asia. Bringing those responsible for these crimes to justice would prove to be very difficult indeed. Unless individual Kempeitai could be persuaded to speak out against their former colleagues and corroborate witness statements, achieving a conviction in many cases proved almost impossible.

General MacArthur flew in to Atsugi Airbase in Japan on 30 August 1945 to take command of the occupation forces. On 2 September the formal Japanese surrender was staged in Tokyo Bay, followed on 1 November by the official disbandment of the 36,000-strong Kempeitai. Next, in the New Year, MacArthur authorized the creation of the International Military Tribunal for the Far East, a sort of bargain-basement version of the Nuremberg Trials of Nazi war criminals. In January 1946 the Japanese government was purged of wartime politicians, and the hunt begun for war criminals. MacArthur's legal team decided upon three classes of war criminal. Class A were those who were deemed policy makers who had conspired to wage aggressive war. Their trial, of only twenty-eight men, was held in Tokyo. Among them was the 'father of the Kempeitai' and Japanese Prime Minister Tojo, who was later hanged.

Classes B and C war criminals were defined as those who had ordered atrocities, condoned them and/or actually taken part in them. These trials were held in the countries where the crimes were committed. A total of 5,700 persons were charged and placed on trial, and 3,000 convictions were achieved. Of these, 920 were subsequently executed by hanging or firing squad, among them many Kempeitai. One historian worked out that this equated to one execution for every 250 Allied POWs murdered by the Japanese. Those not executed were given jail terms. However, we can see just from the figures that very, very few Japanese servicemen ever saw the inside of a courtroom, let alone a jail cell; and the overwhelming blizzard of evidence suggests that violence against local populations and Allied prisoners was casual, common and encouraged by senior officers. Even to have tried ten times as many would still have only dealt with a minority of those Japanese guilty of some form of war crime.

Logistically, it was nearly impossible, especially for the cash-strapped British, to hunt down and prosecute so many Japanese, regardless of the evidence against them. In fact, Clement Attlee's new Labour government actually discouraged an extension of the whole trial process that would have led to more Japanese being brought to justice because of the costs involved, and the language and translation difficulties which made the whole process so time-consuming and expensive. They settled, as did the Americans and Australians, for a symbolic trial of Japanese whose guilt was beyond doubt to clear up the whole process and move quickly to the reconstruction of Japan. MacArthur, President Harry S. Truman and Prime Minister Attlee, wanted Japan on their side as the Cold War opened in the Far East and Japan became a bulwark against the spread of communism. Hunting Japanese war criminals was quietly forgotten as the world's attention shifted from a hot war to a cold one, and the twin menaces of Bolshevism and nuclear Armageddon threatened the peace of the world.

In a move of astounding arrogance the Japanese government released all war criminals from Japanese prisons in 1958 regardless of the crimes they had been convicted of. The message was simple – the Japanese did not feel guilty about their wartime record, and they believed those who had been executed and imprisoned by the Allies to be nothing less than the results of 'victor's justice'. It is an idea and an ideology popular in Japan today, where distortion of the nation's war record and arrogance regarding Japan's right to make war have coalesced into a kind of mass denial among the post-war generations regarding Japanese war crimes, and a refusal to pay proper compensation to the living victims of those crimes. The Japanese actually manage to portray themselves as victims of the war, as anyone unfortunate enough to watch the yearly display of national emotion at Hiroshima can see, those taking part in this nauseating ceremony and those supporting the lie of Japanese innocence conveniently forgetting why the atomic bombs were dropped on the country in the first place. It is a disgusting indictment of the moral weakness of modern politicians in the West that none has pointed this fact out to the Japanese, nor has any Western government demanded that Japan pays proper compensation to its victims. The only government that has taken a very strong line with the Japanese over these issues has been China. Western politicians are naturally worried that offending the Japanese will result in them closing down factories in Britain and America, which would cost jobs that democratically elected politicians can ill afford to lose among their constituents. The Western nations may have prevailed over Japan in 1945, but the subsequent peace has belonged to the Japanese who have far surpassed their former enemies economically. Western fallibility was clear within days of Hirohito's surrender, when MacArthur's decision to delay getting occupation forces into Japanese-held territories gave the Kempeitai precious time to complete their escape. In turn, this led to far fewer Japanese war criminals facing justice, which led to the trials coming to an early close and the Japanese being let off the hook of international condemnation. The war, and the activities of the Japanese in that war, was in turn quickly forgotten by both the Japanese themselves and the Western powers. The Kempeitai were but one small part of a vast war for civilization, but an organization whose name deserves the infamy and hatred attached to Germany's Gestapo and SS – a legion of sadists' hell-bent on making Japan the overlord of tens of millions of unwilling subjects by any means possible. The Japanese have forgotten what the Kempeitai was, but should we? For the thousands still alive today who were victims of the Kempeitai, from American airmen to Dutch comfort women, from British journalists to Manchurian peasants, the inquisitors of that organization have never left their nightmares, and probably never will. Japan has never apologized for their treatment, and never will. The victims expected their tormentors to be brought to justice, but we know now that

Britain, the United States and the other Allied nations never will. And of the compensation these elderly people ask of the Japanese government, the chance that they will receive anything is relatively easy to answer – *they probably never will.*

Note

1. Stella Dong, *Shanghai: The Rise and Fall of a Decadent City* (New York, Perennial, 2001), p. 279

Bibliography

Archives

MacMillan-Brown Library, University of Canterbury, New Zealand
1. Box 252, Exhibit 1461, General Headquarters United States Army Forces, Pacific, Office of the Theater Judge Advocate, War Crimes Branch, Document 2837: *Murder of two American PW's at Cebu City,* 16 October 1945.
2. Box 252, Exhibit 1462, Allied Translation and Interpreter Section South West Pacific Area, Document No. 552, Research Report No. 65 (Suppl No. 1), 29 March 1945.
3. International Military Tribunal for the Far East, Box 256, Exhibit 1654, Prosecution Document No. 5334: *Report of Captain M.J. Dickson of the British Army.*
4. International Military Tribunal for the Far East, Box 256, Exhibit 1654, Prosecution Document No. 5209: *Affidavit of Bachee bin O.K.K. Hassan of Inanam.*
5. International Military Tribunal for the Far East, Box 256, Exhibit 1654, Prosecution Document No. 5211: *Affidavit by Sujiang, a Suluk woman of Dinawan Island.*
6. International Military Tribunal for the Far East, Box 256, Exhibit 1654, Prosecution Document No. 5179: *Affidavit of Lieutenant Stephen Victor Burt Day of the British Army.*
7. International Military Tribunal for the Far East, Box 256, Exhibit 1654, Prosecution Document No. 5177: *Affidavit of Lt.-Col. Edmund Macarthur Sheppard of 2/10 Field Ambulance.*
8. International Military Tribunal for the Far East, Box 256, Exhibit 1654, Prosecution Document No. 5004: *Affidavit of Naik Chandgi Ram, 2/15 Punjab Regiment.*

9. International Military Tribunal for the Far East, Box 256, Exhibit 1654, Evidentiary Document No. 5449, *Affidavit of Naik Partap Singh, 17 Field Company.*

10. International Military Tribunal for the Far East, Box 256, Exhibit 1655, Evidentiary Document No. 5004: *Evidence of Chandgi Ram, taken on 28 September, 1945, at the Prisoner-of-War and Internee Camp, Morotai, before Mr. Justice Mansfield,* 28 September 1945.

11. International Military Tribunal for the Far East, Box 256, Exhibit 1658, Evidentiary Document No. 5218A: *Evidence of Sgt. Maj. Tsuruo SUGINO of Borneo PW Internment Unit,* 11 October 1945.

12. International Military Tribunal for the Far East, Box 256, Exhibit 1658, Evidentiary Document No. 5218A, 25 October 1945.

13. International Military Tribunal for the Far East, Box 256, Exhibit 1659, Exhibit No. 1659A: *Atrocities Committed Against The Suluk Peoples of North Borneo During Japanese Occupation.*

14. Netherlands Forces Intelligence Service (NEFIS), Box 258, Exhibit 1746, Document No. 5731: *Statement by Charles JONGENEEL, Capt., RNIA, head of War Crimes Section, NEFIS,* 8 July 1946.

15. Box 258, Exhibit 1749A, Netherlands Forces Intelligence Service (NEFIS), Document No. 5748: *Report on Torture by the Japanese Military Police (Kempei Tai) drawn up by Major ZIMMERMAN R.N.I.A., No. OM/235/E,* 7 June 1946.

16. Netherlands Forces Intelligence Service (NEFIS), Box 258, Exhibit 1752, Document No. 5751: *Letter of Dr. R. Flachs, Bandoeng, Report No. 3: Concerning the third arrestation of Dr. R. FLACHS through the Kempei Dai Nippon and the police of Bandoeng,* 11 June 1946.

17. Netherlands Forces Intelligence Service (NEFIS), Box 258, Exhibit 1760, Document No. 5756: Javint report 3106/3, *Statement of Major Katsumura, Kempeitai,* 20 October 1945.

18. Imperial Japanese Army, Box 263, Exhibit 1978, Document No. 1114-B: *Regarding the outline for the disposal of Prisoners of War according to the change of situation, a notification, Army-Asia-Secret No. 2257, by the Vice War Minister,* 11 March 1945.

19. Box 263, Exhibit 1991, Japanese Expeditionary Forces in China, Document No. 626-A: *Regulations For Punishment of Enemy Air Crews*, 13 August 1942.

The National Archives (TNA): Public Record Office, Kew
1. War Office: *South East Asia Command: Military Headquarters Papers, Second World War*, WO 203/4317.
2. WO 325/151, Statement No. 1504: *Statement of Mr. B.F. Witing*, 13 October 1945.

Published Sources
Bayley, Christopher & Harper, Tim, *Forgotten Armies: Britain's Asian Empire & The War With Japan*, Penguin, 2005.
Bickers, Robert, *Empire Made Me: An Englishman Adrift in Shanghai*, Penguin Books, 2004.
Briggs, Chester M., *Behind the Barbed Wire: Memoirs of a World War II US Marine Captured in North China in 1941 and Imprisoned by the Japanese until 1945*, McFarland & Company, 1994.
Chang, Iris, *The Rape of Nanking: The Forgotten Holocaust of World War II*, Basic Books Inc., 1994.
Dower, John, *War Without Mercy: Race and Power in the Pacific War*, Pantheon Books, 1986.
Felton, Mark, *Yanagi: The Secret Underwater Trade Between Germany and Japan 1942–1945*, Pen & Sword Books Limited, 2005.
—— *The Fujita Plan: Japanese Attacks on the United States and Australia during the Second World War*, Pen & Sword Books Limited, 2006.
—— *Slaughter at Sea: The Story of Japan's Naval War Crimes*, Pen & Sword Books Limited, 2007.
—— *The Coolie Generals: Britain's Far Eastern Military Leaders in Japanese Captivity*, Pen & Sword Books Limited, 2008.
Daws, Gavan, *Prisoners of the Japanese: POWs of the Second World War*, Pocket Books, 1994.
Dong, Stella, *Shanghai: The Rise and Fall of a Decadent City*, Perennial, 2001.
Harris, Sheldon H., *Factories of Death: Japanese Biological Warfare 1943–45 and the American Cover-up*, Routledge, 1994.

BIBLIOGRAPHY

Hasagawa, Tsuyoshi, *Racing the Enemy: Stalin, Truman, and the Surrender of Japan*, The Belknap Press, 2005.

Herman, Arthur, *To Rule the Waves: How the British Navy Shaped the Modern World*, Hodder and Stoughton Ltd, 2005.

Hoyt, Edwin P., *Japan's War: The Great Pacific Conflict*, Da Capo Press, 1989.

Lamont-Brown, Raymond, *Kempeitai: Japan's Dreaded Military Police*, Sutton Publishing Ltd., 1998.

—— *Ships from Hell*, Pen & Sword Books Limited, 2002.

Law Reports of Trials of War Criminals, vol. I, His Majesty's Stationery Office, 1947.

Law Reports of Trials of War Criminals, vol. IV, His Majesty's Stationery Office, 1948.

Lindsay, Oliver, *The Battle for Hong Kong 1941–1945: Hostage to Fortune*, Spellmount Publishers Ltd., 2002.

MacArthur, Brian, *Surviving the Sword: Prisoners of the Japanese in the Far East, 1942–45*, Random House, 2005.

Materials on the Trial of Former Servicemen of the Japanese Army Charged with Manufacturing and Employing Bacteriological Weapons, Foreign Languages Publishing House (Moscow), 1950.

O'Neill, Richard, *Suicide Squads: The Men and Machines of World War II Special Operations*, Salamander Books, 1999.

Perrett, Bryan, *Against All Odds! More Dramatic 'Last Stand' Actions*, Brockhampton Press, 1999.

Piccigallo, P.R., *The Japanese on Trial: Allied War Crimes Operations in the East, 1945–1951*, University of Texas Press, 1979.

Powell, John B., *My Twenty-Five Years in China*, New York, 1945.

Rees, Lawrence, *Horror in the East: The Japanese at War 1931–1945*, BBC Books, 2001.

Russell, Lord, *The Knights of Bushido: A Short History of Japanese War Crimes*, Greenhill Books, 2002.

Shaw, Ralph, *Sin City*, Warner Books, 1997.

Silver, Lynette Ramsay, *Sandakan – A Conspiracy of Silence*, Revised edition: Sally Milner Publishing Pty Ltd, 2000.

Smith, Colin, *Singapore Burning: Heroism and Surrender in World War II*, Penguin Books Ltd, 2005.

Spector, Ronald, *Eagle Against The Sun*, Vintage Books, 1985.

Tanaka, Toshiyuki, translated by John W. Dower, *Hidden Horrors: Japanese War Crimes in World War II*, Westview Press Inc., 1997.

Thompson, Peter & Macklin, Robert, *Kill the Tiger: Operation Rimau and the Battle for Southeast Asia*, Maverick House Publishers, 2007.

Wasserstein, Bernard, *Secret War in Shanghai: Treachery, Subversion and Collaboration in the Second World War*, Profile Books Ltd, 1998.

Williams, Peter & Wallace, David, *Unit 731: The Japanese Army's Secret of Secrets*, Hodder & Stoughton, 1989.

Zhou Mei, *Elizabeth Choy: More than a War Heroine: a Biography*, National Volunteer & Philanthropy Centre and Beaumont Publishers, 2004.

Newspapers and Journals
Beijing Bright Daily
Brisbane Times
Canyon County Zephyr
China Daily
Daily Mail
Life Magazine
New York Times
Saipan Tribune
The Straits Times
Time
Washington Post

Websites
Australian Broadcasting Corporation, http://www.abc.net.au.

A Prisoner of War Remembers by Colonel Richard T. King, Jr., http://www.powmiaff.org.

Australian War Memorial, http://www.awm.gov.au.

BBC Peoples War, http://www.bbc.co.uk/history.

Commonwealth Department of Veteran's Affairs, http://www.dva. gov.au.

Korea Web, http://www.koreaweb.ws.

YouTube, http://www.youtube.com.

Index